SALVATION
1944-1946

GENERAL DE GAULLE

WAR MEMOIRS

SALVATION

1944-1946

Translated from the French by Richard Howard

WEIDENFELD AND NICOLSON
20 NEW BOND STREET LONDON WI

PRINTED IN GREAT BRITAIN BY
THE SHENVAL PRESS
LONDON, HERTFORD AND HARLOW
SET IN 10-12 POINT BASKERVILLE
R.6913

Contents

I. LIBERATION

THE RHYTHM OF the Liberation was one of extreme rapidity. Six weeks after the Allies and the French had effected the breakthrough at Avranches and landed in the Midi, they reached Antwerp, were driving toward Lorraine and were penetrating into the Vosges. By the end of September, except for Alsace, the Alpine passes and the pockets on the Atlantic coast, all France was purged of the invaders. The German Army, broken by the mechanized might of the Allies, lacerated by the French resistance, was expelled from our territory in less time than it had taken, five years before, to appropriate it. Now that army only took its stand on the frontier of the Reich, where insurrection no longer paralysed its rear. Thus the tide, receding, suddenly revealed from one end to the other the convulsed body of France.

Consequently the innumerable and immediate problems raised by the guidance of a nation emerging from the abyss beset the Government most insistently at the very moment when their solution was most arduous.

First of all, for the central authority to function normally, it must be in a position to be kept informed, to transmit its orders, and to confirm their execution. Yet for many long weeks, the capital was to remain without regular means of communication with the provinces. Telephone and telegraph lines had been subject to countless breaks. Radio stations had been destroyed. There were no French liaison planes on the fields pitted with shellholes. The railways were virtually paralysed. Of our 12,000 locomotives, 2,800 were left. No train from Paris could reach Lyons, Marseilles, Toulouse, Bordeaux, Nantes, Lille or Nancy. None could cross the Loire between Nevers and the Atlantic, or the Seine between Nantes and the Channel, or the Rhône between Lyons and the Mediterranean. As for our roads,

3,000 bridges had been blown up; scarcely 300,000 vehicles, out of
the 3 million we once had, were in condition to travel; lastly, the
petrol shortage made a car trip something of an adventure. It would
take at least two months to establish any regular exchange of orders
and reports, without which the Government could function only by
fits and starts.

At the same time, the transport holdup disorganized all supply
services. Especially since the acknowledged stocks of food supplies,
raw materials, fuels and manufactured goods had altogether vanished. Though a 'six-month plan' based on a series of American
imports had been agreed on by Algiers and Washington, how could
it be put into effect when our ports were unusable? Dunkirk, Brest,
Lorient, St-Nazaire, La Rochelle, as well as the approach to Bordeaux, remained in enemy hands; and Calais, Boulogne, Dieppe,
Rouen, Le Havre, Cherbourg, Nantes, Marseilles and Toulon—
damaged by British and American bombings and then altogether
destroyed by the German garrisons before they laid down their arms
—offered nothing but ruined docks, flooded harbours, jammed flood-
gates and waterways choked with wrecks.

It is true that the Allies made every effort to furnish us with equipment in order to re-establish roads and railways along the strategic
routes: Rouen–Lille–Brussels and Marseilles–Lyons–Nancy; that
they immediately helped us restore our airports to the north, the
east, and around Paris; that they quickly laid a pipeline from
Cotentin to Lorraine; that, already holding the artificial ports of
Arromanches and St-Laurent-sur-Mer, they made haste to take
Brest and to clear Cherbourg, Le Havre, and Marseilles so that an
adequate tonnage could be unloaded on our shores. But the trains
and lorries in running order, the planes landing and the ships putting
in were chiefly intended for the forces already in operation. Moreover, at the urgent request of the military command, we were
obliged to furnish it a share of whatever coal was on hand at the
mines, to allow it to use a certain number of our factories in working
condition, and to place at its disposal an important fraction of our
remaining manpower. As we had expected, the Liberation was not
going to bring any immediate material relief to a generally drained
and dismembered nation.

But at least it would provide immediate moral emancipation. This
almost supernatural event, dreamed of for so long and so fervently,

had suddenly become a reality! At one blow, the people were released
from that psychology of silence into which the constraints of four
years' occupation had plunged them. Overnight, they could speak
out, meet anyone they chose, come and go as they liked! With
delighted astonishment, each man saw revealed perspectives he had
no longer dared to hope for. But just as the convalescent forgets the
crisis he has survived and imagines his health restored, so the French
people, savouring the joy of their freedom, were inclined to believe
that all their trials were at an end. In the immediate circumstances,
the widespread sense of euphoria was partly justified. At the same
time, many allowed themselves to indulge in illusions which were the
cause of as many more misunderstandings.

Thus many Frenchmen tended to identify the Liberation with the
end of the war. There was a temptation to see the battles still to be
waged, the losses to be sustained, the restrictions to be endured until
the enemy's defeat as empty—and therefore all the more burdensome
—formalities. Misunderstanding the extent of our debacle, the terrible penury we were up against, and the servitudes the prosecution
of the war imposed on us, our citizens supposed that production
would resume rapidly and on a large scale, that food supplies would
be immediately improved, that all the elements of renewal would
soon be co-ordinated. The Allies were thought of like story-book
heroes, as possessing inexhaustible resources and as being eager to
lavish them on a France they had fondly delivered and now wanted
to restore to all her former glory by their side. As for de Gaulle, that
almost legendary character who incarnated this prodigious Liberation in all eyes, it was naturally assumed that he would be able to
accomplish single-handed all the miracles expected of him.

Having reached poverty-stricken Paris at the end of a dramatic
summer, I myself laboured under no such illusions. I took account of
the food-stocks at famine prices, noticed the threadbare clothes, the
cold houses and dark windows; I passed by empty shops, shut-down
factories, forsaken railway stations; already I heard the complaints
of the people, the demands of factions, the rivalries of demagogues.
Certain that, though we could rely on sympathy from the people, the
iron-clad rule of states is to give nothing for nothing; convinced that
we would regain our status only if we paid for it; assessing the sacrifices to be made before we could seize our share of the victory and
consummate even a partial recovery, I could not delude myself with

fancies. Especially since I knew I was without any sort of talisman
that would enable the nation to achieve its goal painlessly. On the
other hand, I intended to apply the whole of the credit France had
granted me to lead her to salvation. To begin with, this meant establishing the Government; it meant inspiring the support of every
region, every cause; it meant uniting the troops from the Empire and
the Forces of the Interior into a single army; it meant enabling the
country to resume its life and work without yielding to paroxysms
which would only lead to further misfortunes.

Action would have to be taken at every level to put the Government in operation. Most of the Algiers 'commissioners', whether they
had been with me since the time of 'Free France' or had joined me
in North Africa, would remain ministers in Paris. But I was also
determined to invite others to join the Government—men, conse-
crated by the resistance, who had remained in Metropolitan France.
Yet the change could not be an immediate one, because the ministers
in office arrived from Algiers only turn and turn about. Four of them—
Diethelm, Jacquinot, d'Astier and Philip—had been visiting the
troops of the First Army and the southern departments. Massigli had
gone to London during the liberation of Paris to maintain our
foreign relations more easily. Pleven had been able to join me. But
the rest had been obliged to postpone their departure. As for those I
selected in Metropolitan France, several had only just emerged from
their clandestine lives and could not come to Paris at once. It was
only on September 9th, two weeks after my arrival in the Rue St-
Dominique, that the Government was able to be re-formed.

It included two Ministers of State, President Jeanneney and General Catroux. The former, whom we had summoned from Haute-
Saône where the enemy was still entrenched, was to elaborate
successive measures which would direct the powers of the Republic
toward its normal functions; the latter would remain Co-ordinator
of Moslem Affairs and Governor General of Algeria. François de
Menthon remained Minister of Justice, André Diethelm Minister of
War, Louis Jacquinot Minister of Marine, René Pleven Minister of
the Colonies, René Mayer Minister of Public Works and Transport,
René Capitant Minister of National Education, Paul Giacobbi
Minister of Food and Supply, Henri Frenay Minister of Prisoners,
Deportees and Refugees. The Ministry of National Economy became
the domain of Pierre Mendès-France, that of the Interior went to

Adrien Tixier, that of Public Health to François Billoux. Eight portfolios were entrusted to men who had just emerged from the struggle:
Foreign Affairs to Georges Bidault, Finance to André Lepercq, Air
to Charles Tillon, Production to Robert Lacoste, Agriculture to
François Tanguy-Prigent, Labour to Alexandre Parodi, Postal Services to Augustin Laurent, Information to Pierre-Henri Teitgen.

Eight national commissioners from Algiers were no longer Council
members: Henri Queuille asked to resign; René Massigli was to
represent us in London, where Pierre Vienot had died in July; Henri
Bonnet would take charge of our embassy in Washington, which had
finally been recognized as such by the United States; André Le
Troquer became president of the Municipal Council of Paris;
Emmanuel d'Astier, whom I should have preferred to divert from
purely political affairs, had declined the diplomatic post that had
been offered to him; André Philip, whose impetuous talents were
ill-adapted to the administrative framework, was not able to keep his
portfolio; nor was Fernand Grenier, induced by a manoeuvre of his
party during the battles of the Vercors Massif publicly to adopt an
attitude contrary to the Government's solidarity; and Jean Monnet,
whose mission as economic negotiator with the United States became
incompatible with a ministerial function once the department of
National Economy was created.

Around me, then, twenty-one ministers fell to their task with the
presentiment that there was no end to be seen. Because of this it was
even more necessary to specify our aims. Since June 1940, I had led
France towards liberation and the resistance had been her means.
Now a new stage was at hand which involved the effort of the entire
nation.

On September 12th a meeting at the Palais de Chaillot, attended
by 8,000 people—National Council of the Resistance, executive
committees of resistance movements and networks, municipal councils, state officials, civil servants, the University of Paris, representatives of management, trade unions, the press, the bar, etc—gave me
an opportunity of setting forth my policy. I did so all the more
sharply since, in an atmosphere where voices were already murmuring, I felt obliged to call things by their real names.

Having evoked 'the tide of joy, pride and hope' which had swept
the nation, having paid tribute to the resistance, the Allies, and the
French Army, I turned the spotlight on the obstacles still to be over-

come, the efforts to be made. No complacency, no slackening could be tolerated! No latitude accorded to any organization which claimed to interfere in legal affairs or the administration independently of the state. And I turned to the burning question of the 'militias'. 'We are at war!' I cried. 'In today's battle as in those to come, we intend to participate to the fullest extent. The same will be true, tomorrow, in the case of the occupation of Germany. . . . For this, we require large units adapted to manoeuvre, to give battle and to triumph, in which will be incorporated the ardent youth that constitutes our Forces of the Interior. . . . All France's soldiers are a part of the French Army, and the French Army, like France herself, must remain one and indivisible.'

Turning to foreign affairs, I emphasized the difficulties, disregarding the shock this gave those among us who preferred illusions to lucidity. 'We expect,' I said, 'that France's right to participate in the future settlement of the conflict will no longer be contested and that the official relegation inflicted upon her by her allies will give way to the same kind of relations which we have had the honour and the habit of maintaining with the other great nations for centuries . . . We believe it is in the higher interests of mankind that the arrangements which will tomorrow settle Germany's fate should not be discussed and adopted without consulting France . . . We believe any decision concerning Europe reached without consulting France to be a grave error . . . We believe any determination of the political, economic and moral conditions of the earth's inhabitants after the conflict to be a foolhardy one if that determination is reached without France . . . for, after all, one hundred million loyal men live under our flag, and any large-scale human edifice will be arbitrary and ephemeral if the seal of France is not affixed to it.'

To regain her status was not all. France must also be able to maintain it. This too, this especially, would not be accomplished without sacrifice, without severity. Having given an account of the ravages we had endured and the conditions hindering our recovery, I declared, 'We find ourselves in an extremely difficult period, one in which liberation allows us no relief, but calls instead for the maintenance of severe restrictions, a period which demands great efforts of organization as well as those of discipline.' I added that 'the Government intends, in this regard, to impose all necessary regulations'. Then I specified the objectives the Government had set itself:

'To raise the workers' standard of living as the rate of production rises; to requisition or sequestrate certain public services and enterprises for the direct use of the state; to appropriate for the nation the illegal profits made by those who collaborated with the enemy; to fix commodity prices and regulate commerce as long as what is produced and transportable is not equivalent to consumer demand. . .'

Certainly these were circumstantial measures. But they were in harmony with the principles of recovery which it had been the aims of the resistance to realize—'To subordinate private interest to public advantage; to exploit the natural resources of the nation and administer them to the general advantage; to abolish coalitions of interest once and for all; finally, to permit each of France's sons and daughters to live, to work and to raise their children in security and dignity.'

In conclusion, I appealed 'to the men and women of the resistance: and you, crusaders under the cross of Lorraine! You who are the yeast of the nation in her combat for honour and liberty, tomorrow it will be up to you to marshal France towards sacrifice and towards greatness. It is then, and only then, that the great victory of France will be won.'

At this time I spoke not of intentions formulated with an eye to the future, but of measures immediately engaging interests and individuals. Yesterday, in London or in Africa, it had been a question of what could be done. Now, in Paris, it was a matter of what we were doing. The mainspring of Free France had been a mystique which had necessarily dimmed in the schemes of the Algiers Committee. Now it was politics that dominated the Government's actions. But the same imperious and contradictory realities which now confronted our leaders were going to cleave ambition and interest into separate factions. Could the cohesion of feeling which the resistance had established be maintained once the hour of national danger had passed? The impression I got from the Chaillot meeting led me to doubt it.

It is true that as I entered the hall, took my place and made my speech after Georges Bidault's eloquent introduction, I was received with ringing cheers. Listening only to them, I might have imagined I was back in the unanimous assemblies of the Albert Hall and Brazzaville or among the sympathetic audiences of Algiers, Tunis, and Ajaccio. Yet some variation in the tone of the enthusiasm, a sort of self-consciousness in the applause, the signs and significant glances exchanged by the participants, the calculated and composed faces that acknowledged my remarks, reminded me that old or new 'politicians' had many nuances in their approval. It was apparent that their dealings would be complicated, as they proceeded, by an ever-greater number of reservations and conditions.

More than ever, then, I had to seek support from the French people rather than from the 'elite' groups which tended to come between us. My popularity was like capital with which I could pay off the disappointments that were inevitable among the ruins. To begin with, I would use it to establish the state's authority in the provinces as I had done in Paris.

The news that reached us from a vast majority of the departments showed them to be in tremendous confusion. No doubt the commissioners of the Republic and the prefects appointed in advance were fulfilling their functions. But they had the greatest difficulty restoring matters and men to theirs. Too much outrage, accumulated over four years, was fermenting under the lid to avoid an explosion in the chaos following the enemy's flight and the collapse of his accomplices. Many resistance units were proceeding with punishments and purges on their own. Armed groups, appearing out of the woods, yielded to the impulse to mete out justice against their persecutors without due process of law. In many places, public anger exploded into brutal actions. Naturally, political calculation, professional rivalry and personal reprisals took advantage of the circumstances, so that irregular arrests, arbitrary fines and summary executions added confusion to the chaos resulting from general destitution.

The local authorities found it the more difficult to master the situation because the forces at their command were desperately inadequate. Even if the *garde mobile* and the *gendarmerie* had been at full force and sure of themselves, they could not have coped with the responsibility. Reduced by the departure of a number of their units into the maquis and morally inhibited by the use Vichy had made of them they were all the more inadequate. Where the Army corps had passed—in Normandy, in Provence, in Paris, along the Rhône, the Saône, the Doubs—the presence of the troops prevented most untoward incidents. But in the areas where regular units had not penetrated, commissioners and prefects alike found themselves without means of keeping order. I could, of course, have provided those means by reassigning the forces from Africa to the interior of the territory. But that would have meant withholding the French Army from battle and thereby compromising our participation in the victory. I preferred to risk more or less violent explosions rather than make this disastrous renunciation.

Actually the risk would have been a limited one if the Communist party's policy had not been to exploit these disturbances in order to seize power in the provinces as it had tried to do in Paris. Though Government orders set up a single Committee of Liberation in each department composed of representatives of every movement, party and trade union and designed to give the prefect provisional assistance, in various localities, enterprises, public services and administrations a swarm of committees appeared which claimed to set the pace, control the mayors, employers and directors, and to hunt down the guilty and the suspect. The Communists, skilful and united in their aims, using various labels, and utilizing the sympathies and loyalties which many of them had won in various milieus during the conflict, were careful to provoke and sustain these splinter groups strengthened by arms. The 'Comac',* playing on the uncertainty as to the respective powers of the Government and the National Council of the Resistance, continued secretly to delegate emissaries, give orders and confer ranks. I decided to make immediate visits to the most sensitive areas to give the national governmental machine a start in the right direction. A two-months' series of trips was to put me in contact with the provinces, while in the intervals I directed the Government's work in Paris.

On September 14th, accompanied by André Diethelm, Minister of War, I landed at Bron airfield which was still littered with the scrap iron from its demolished hangars. Ten days before, the city of Lyons had been liberated by the French First Army and the Americans. It was now making every effort toward recovery, though the problem was arduous. All the city's bridges over the Saône and the Rhône had been destroyed save the Homme de la Roche and the Guillotière, and they could only be used by pedestrians. The Vaise, Brotteaux and Perrache stations and all the railways serving the city were out of commission. The industrial suburbs, particularly Villeurbanne, bared their gutted factories. But the enthusiasm of the populace made a vivid contrast to the ruins.

* Translator's note: the Communist 'Action Committee'.

The Commissioner of the Republic, Yves Farge, a resistance leader in a region distinguished for its action against the enemy, had his hands full. Imaginative and enthusiastic, he readily adapted himself to an unprecedented situation, but avoided taking extreme action. I ordered him to enforce the same policy elsewhere. In the streets every group cheered me, at the prefecture I received the officials and the *corps constitués* who were presented by Prefect Long-chambon, making contact at the *hôtel de ville*, with the 'temporary' mayor Justin Godard—'until Edouard Herriot returns', he told me —the municipal council, Cardinal Gerlier, representatives of industry, commerce, the trade unions, the liberal professions and the workers, I saw that most of the inhabitants of Lyons had no intention of overthrowing national life. Given certain changes, spectacular but ill-defined, and certain punishments, exemplary but vague, they hoped, instead, for order.

The next day I reviewed the Forces of the Interior. Colonel Descour, who had distinguished himself in the maquis battles and, more recently, in the recapture of Lyons, and who was now in command of the military district, presented a body of troops that were as moved by the occasion as I was. It was touching to see them attempting to look like regular units despite their disparities; the strongest military tradition impregnated this self-created force. I left Lyons convinced that the Government, provided it truly governed, would surmount all obstacles here, and that order would prevail since the state was reappearing at the nation's head.

At Marseilles, however, the atmosphere was ominous. I arrived on the morning of the fifteenth, accompanied by three ministers: Diethelm, Jacquinot, and Billoux. The destruction of the Old Harbour area by the Germans in 1943, then by Allied bombing and finally by the battle of the preceding August, had completely demolished large areas of the city, the piers and the harbour. In addition, the channel was full of mines and every means of unloading on to the ruined quays had been blown up by the enemy. Of course the public services, helped by the Americans, who wanted to use this base, were busy clearing the harbour. But the damage was such that it was doubtful if the port could be used for a long time to come. As for the populace, fed only at the cost of great effort, and extremely badly, it was combating destitution at every turn. Furthermore, an atmosphere of tension and almost of oppression floated over Marseilles, caused by a series of unwarranted actions. The Communists, taking advantage of old local dissensions and the persecutions inflicted by Vichy agents, had established an anonymous dictatorship in Marseilles which made arrests on its own account and even performed executions without the authorities opposing them decisively.

In this situation, the Commissioner of the Republic, Raymond Aubrac, who had distinguished himself in the resistance, found it difficult to adopt the psychology of high officialdom. He, the regional prefects and their colleagues gathered at the prefecture, and I told them firmly that the Government expected them to do their job. Henceforth the laws and decrees were to be applied, in a word they were to administer, and that it was they who were the responsible parties, to the exclusion of all others. The Forces of the Interior had helped General Monsabert's troops gallantly in taking Marseilles. I congratulated them upon this while they passed in review. It was easy to see which units—the majority—wanted to be sent into battle in Alsace and which, subject to a secret allegiance, wanted to remain where they were. I ordered General Chadebec de Lavalade, recalled from the Levant to command the military district, to give satisfaction as soon as possible to the former and to dissolve the latter; I instructed the Minister of War to send a regiment from Algeria to Marseilles at once to facilitate matters.

In this great city, chaotic and stricken as it was, I felt better than anywhere else that only the resistance movement could determine France's recovery, but that this supreme hope would certainly founder if liberation were confused with disorder. Besides, the very authorities which, in Marseilles, endorsed compromise showed themselves quite pleased with my own firmness. It must be said that the appearance of General de Gaulle speaking to the crowds gathered in the Place de Muy and the Rue St-Ferréol, or crossing the Canebière, or being received at the *hôtel de ville* by the mayor, Gaston Defferre, aroused a wave of popular enthusiasm which made every problem seem simpler. Probably they became so, in fact, as soon as they seemed so.

During the afternoon, a quick flight took me to Toulon. Nothing could surpass the scene of desolation of the arsenal, the Quai Cronstadt, the entirely demolished neighbouring districts and the hulls of ships scuttled in the roads. Yet, by comparison, nothing was more comforting than the sight of the naval squadron stationed out to sea for the review. Three divisions were presented to me, under the commands of Admiral Auboyneau, Admiral Jaujard and Captain Lancelot respectively. They included: the battleship *Lorraine*; the cruisers *Georges Leygues, Duguay-Trouin, Émile Bertin, Jeanne d'Arc, Montcalm, Gloire;* the light cruisers *Fantasque, Malin, Terrible;* and about thirty torpedo boats, submarines, escort ships and mine-sweepers. Accompanied by Louis Jacquinot, Minister of Marine, Admiral Lemonnier, Chief of the General Staff and Commander of the Naval Forces, and Admiral Lambert, the Maritime Prefect, I boarded the escort vessel *La Pique* and slowly passed down the line. Reviewing the forty vessels arranged in fighting trim, receiving salutes from their officers from the bridge of each, hearing the cheers of the crews lining the rails, I felt that our navy had swallowed its disappointments and recovered its hopes.

On September 16th, I went to Toulouse, a considerably disturbed city. Dissensions had always torn the southwest departments. Now Vichy's policies and the drama of the occupation had raised them to fever pitch. Besides, it happened that the numerous maquis groups in the area had waged a bitter battle so there were grave disturb-ances and many accounts to settle. Especially since enemy troops operating in Aquitaine had been guilty of particularly cruel brutali-ties, and odious complicity. Further, among the Forces of the In-terior, the best units were already rushing to Burgundy to join the First Army. Only the most heterogeneous groups remained on the spot. Finally, the immediate proximity of Spain increased the tension still further. Many Spaniards who had sought refuge since the Civil War in the Gers, Ariège and Haute-Garonne, had recently joined the maquis. Now they were leaving it, proposing to return to their own country under arms. Naturally the Communists, advantage-ously placed and well organized, stirred up these sparks in order to take matters in hand. They had partially succeeded.

I found the Commissioner of the Republic grappling with the encroachments of certain leaders of the Forces of the Interior. Pierre Bertaux, who directed an important resistance network, had been designated to occupy the position whose incumbent, Jean Cassou, had been seriously wounded during the riots that marked the Ger-man withdrawal. At present, Bertaux was trying to hold the reins of command; but Colonel Asher, alias Ravanel, leader of the Haute-

Garonne maquis, had assumed command of the military district and exercised an authority as vast as it was vague.

Around Ravanel, leaders of the armed units constituted something like a soviet. The members of this council claimed to carry out the necessary purges with their own men, while the *gendarmerie* and the *garde mobile* were confined to remote barracks. It was true that the Chief of the General Staff, Colonel Noetinger, an officer of wide experience, was attempting to divert these abuses into the administrative labyrinth but he did not always succeed. Furthermore, a Spanish 'division' was forming in the region with the loudly publicized purpose of marching on Barcelona. To top it all, an English general known as 'Colonel Hilary' and introduced into the Gers maquis by the British services, held several units under his command which took orders only from London.

On the morning of the seventeenth, with calculated formality, I passed all the military units in review. By making direct contact with the maquisards, I hoped to arouse in each man the soldier he wished to be. As I approached the ranks, a quiver of expectation made it clear that I was doing the right thing. Then Colonel Ravanel presented the entire corps. The parade was a picturesque one. At its head, bayonets crossed, marched a Russian battalion consisting of men from the 'Vlassov Army' who had deserted from the German side in time to join our own resistance. Then came the Spanish troops, led by their own generals. After these passed the French Forces of the Interior. The sight of their improvised flags and banners, their concern to organize themselves into regulation sections, companies and battalions, the efforts they had made to give their clothing a uniform appearance, and above all the attitude, the glances, the tears of the men passing before me, showed the high degree of virtue and effectiveness of military discipline. But there was also, with regard to me, the same kind of plebiscite which I recognized everywhere.

The day before, I had been given a similar testimonial at the prefecture and at the *hôtel de ville* where I received officers and distinguished citizens, first among them the valiant archbishop Monsignor Saliège. The crowd that shouted its joy in the Place du Capitole where it had gathered to hear me, or lined the streets in two cheering hedges, made the same point. Of course I was not at all sure that this adherence would compensate for all we lacked in maintaining public order. At least I hoped that it would enable us to prevent either the dictatorship of the few or general anarchy.

Before leaving Toulouse, I rescinded the order that kept the *gendarmerie* in barracks and restored these brave men to their normal duties. I decided to appoint General Collet, recalled from Morocco, to command the military sector. I informed the Spanish leaders that the French Government would not forget the services they and their men had rendered in our maquis, but that access to the Pyreneean frontier was forbidden them. Moreover, on my instructions, the First Army dispatched a good-sized unit to Tarbes and Perpignan in order to ensure the adequate patrolling of the Pyrenees passes. Lastly 'Colonel Hilary'. Within two hours he had been sent to Lyons, and from there immediately returned to England.

In Bordeaux, on September 17th, I found the atmosphere strained. The Germans had retreated but remained in the vicinity, entrenched at Royan and on the Graves peninsula, cutting access to the port and threatening to return. Under the command of Colonel Adeline, the Bordeaux Forces of the Interior and those of the surrounding area were brought into contact with the enemy on both shores of the Gironde, while Colonel Druille, commander of the military sector, attempted to reinforce their supply services and officer force. Actually, the German Admiral Meyer, while evacuating the Bordeaux region and occupying the coastal batteries, had led us to believe that he was about to surrender. He was still negotiating at the time of my arrival but it soon became apparent that this was only a ruse of the enemy's in order to withdraw with safety. Since the Germans had considerable stocks of material at their disposal and since our Forces of the Interior were neither well organized nor well enough armed to survive a pitched battle, Bordeaux tempered its joy at being free with its fear of ceasing to be so. Besides this, many grievances which had accumulated during the occupation of a city whose mayor, Marquet, was a notorious collaborator, were brought to light. In this troubled atmosphere various armed groups operated and refused to obey the official authorities.

Here, as elsewhere, I applied myself to reinforcing these authorities. Gaston Cusin, Commissioner of the Republic, a man full of common sense and presence of mind, presented to me as usual a parade of officials, officers and delegations at the prefecture. The archbishop, Monsignor Feltin, was first among the visitors. From the balcony where Gambetta had harangued the crowd in 1870, I addressed the Bordelais. Then I went to the *hôtel de ville* where the new mayor, Fernand Audeguil, was waiting for me, and drove through various sectors of the city. Finally, on the Intendance Parade Ground, I inspected the Forces of the Interior still under arms. Almost all expressed a co-operative attitude on which I complimented them. To some leaders who appeared recalcitrant, I offered the immediate choice of two alternatives: to submit to the orders of the Colonel in command of the sector, or to go to prison. All preferred the former. As I left Bordeaux, it seemed to me that the ground had grown firmer under our feet.

I headed for Saintes in order to make contact with Colonel Adeline's troops. The department, beneath the flags of liberation which fluttered from every window, was in a constant state of alarm. On the one hand the Germans were occupying Royan and the Ile d'Oléron, and on the other La Rochelle and the Ile de Ré. They had established themselves there under heavy fortification, and awaited the arrival of major Allied units. General Chevance-Bertin, appointed during the tumult of those first days to co-ordinate the actions of our southwestern Forces of the Interior, had impressed Admiral Schirlitz, commander of the La Rochelle pocket, to the point of determining him to evacuate Rochefort. But days passed without the Germans being menaced by anything other than our partisans, completely without heavy arms, artillery, armoured units, or planes. From one moment to the next, the enemy might return to the attack. Our own men, banded together as they had been in the maquis, infiltrated from the Gironde, Vienne, Dordogne, and both Charente departments, eager to fight but without the necessary equipment to open a military front. Besides, lacking services, supplies and transport, they were living off the countryside. This led to frequent confusion aggravated by the abuses of those leaders who thought that the hierarchy went no higher than themselves. Finally, the intervention of 'Comac' and its agents made its effects felt. Jean Schuhler, Commissioner of the Republic for the Poitiers region, Prefect Vaudreuil and the mayors of the region were faced with a number of problems.

Colonel Adeline applied himself to clearing up the confusion. In contact with the two German pockets of Royan and La Rochelle, he installed communications posts, formed units that were as regular as possible, and tried to organize their supply services. When this grouping received arms and assumed its consistency, an attack could be planned. In Saintes, I reviewed several thousand poorly equipped but eager men. The parade was impressive. I then summoned the heterogeneously trained officers, most of them wearing improvised insignia but all proud, and justifiably so, of being there voluntarily and thrilled to be gathered around de Gaulle who, beneath a composed serenity of expression, felt no less moved than they. I told them what I had to say, and then I left this force-in-the-making, resolved to end the struggle on the Atlantic coast by a French victory.

Orléans was the last stage of my journey. With a shudder at the sight of the ruins, I drove through the massacred city. The Commissioner of the Republic, André Mars, explained the problems he was patiently confronting. Sorely tried as it had been, this sector was not suffering from many outbreaks. In contrast to the inhabitants of the Garonne, the people of the Loire seemed quite temperate. Colonel Bertrand and Colonel Chomel, commanding the Forces of the Interior of La Beauce, Berri and Touraine, had organized them into regular battalions, then led them in brilliant engagements against the German troops withdrawing south of the Loire. This time, the maquisards, disciplined and self-assured, served as a guarantee of order. When I saw the splendid detachment which presented arms on the Bricy parade grounds, I thought sadly of the resistance forces we could have been had Vichy not prevented the military cadres from taking their places at the head of these young troops everywhere. I returned to the capital on the evening of September 18th.

On September 25th, after spending two days with the First Army, I went to Nancy, which General Patton's troops had just liberated. In Lorraine, the invader had never been anything but the enemy, so there was no political problem in the region. Law and order ran no risk of infringement; civil duties and rights seemed quite natural. The crowd cheered that day in the rues de Mirecourt, de Strasbourg, St-Didier, St-Georges and des Dominicans by which I crossed the departmental capital, and later in the Place Stanislas where I spoke from the balcony of the *hôtel de ville*. The addresses of the Commissioner of the Republic Chailley-Bert and Mayor Prouve, the speeches of the delegations, the attitude of the 2,000 maquisards whom their leader, Colonel Grandval, presented to me, bore witness to this ravaged region's faith in France, though part of it was still in German hands.

Back in Paris, I left again on September 30th, accompanied by my Ministers Tixier, Mayer and Laurent, this time for Flanders. We passed through Soissons and St-Quentin, where Pierre Pene, Commissioner of the Republic, guided us through the rubble of these demolished cities. In Lille, François Closon, his colleague for the Nord and Pas-de-Calais departments, was trying to furnish the means of getting back to work to the whole population which had lost them. No sooner on the scene than I was struck by the dramatic and urgent nature of the problem of workers' subsistence in the area. During the occupation the working classes had been forced to accept wages which the enemy's orders kept fixed at the lowest possible rate. Now many workers were out of work because factories were without coal, and workshops without fuel. Food supplies had fallen below the vital minimum. Crossing the city of my birth, cheered by the Lillois, I saw too many faces whose smiles effaced neither their pallor nor their emaciation.

Feeling and thought had already convinced me that the Liberation of the country must be accompanied by a profound social transformation. In Lille I saw its absolute necessity stamped on the faces of the people. Either there must be an official and rapid move to institute a marked change in the conditions of the working class, and profound limitations upon financial privilege, or the embittered and suffering mass of the workers would founder on disturbances which ran the risk of depriving France of what remained of her substance.

On Sunday October 1st, having attended Mass celebrated by Cardinal Lienart in the Eglise St-Michel, visited the *hôtel de ville*, where I was met by Mayor Cordonnier, reviewed the Forces of the Interior in the Place de la République, and received the authorities, committees and prominent citizens, I informed the crowd gathered before the prefecture of the steps that the Government was undertaking to establish the nation's economic recovery: 'state control of the nation's economic resources; . . . security and dignity for each worker'. The impassioned, swelling cheers that swept through the multitude on hearing these promises told me that my words had touched them to the quick.

On the way back to Paris, I visited the Lens mines. The damaged installations, the absence of half the miners, the disturbance of the staff, maintained the yield at a level well below average. Counting coal alone, barely a third of the pre-war output was produced. To re-establish production, it was obvious that a far-reaching reform was needed to improve morale and, further, large-scale operations involving credit which the national exchequer alone was in a position to provide. The only solution was to make that exchequer the owner of the coal mines. I headed for the capital by way of Arras, my mind made up.

A week later I was in Normandy, a province that surpassed all others in devastation. The ruins here seemed all the more tragic because this region had been famous for its prosperity in both ancient and modern times. Accompanied by Mendès-France and Tanguy-Prigent, conducted by Bourdeau de Fontenay, Commissioner of the Republic, and General Legentilhomme, commander of the military sector, I visited Le Havre, Rouen, Evreux, Lisieux and Caen, or more precisely their ruins. If, a few days before, my contacts with the inhabitants of the northern departments had confirmed me in my conviction that the national effort required great social changes, the extent of the damages endured by Normandy strengthened my intention to put the state back on its feet, a condition *sine qua non* of the country's recovery.

Besides, in contrast with the fallen cities, the countryside presented a heartening spectacle. In August, in the middle of battle, means had been found to get in the harvest. Although villages and farms had suffered heavily, and despite everything the farmers lacked in the way of equipment, there were cultivated fields and cared-for cattle everywhere. In Neubourg, the farmers I addressed seemed determined to keep their shirt sleeves rolled up. This persistence of the French farmers cast a favourable light on the prospects of national food supplies and constituted an essential element of recovery for the future.

On October 23rd, I got the same impression crossing Brie and Champagne. Once I left Boissy-St-Léger, the fields, stretching to the horizon, seemed eternally productive as usual. As before, a wilderness of haystacks heralded Brie-Comte-Robert. Provins was still surrounded by cultivation for wheat and sugar beet. There were as many regular furrows and no more fallow than before, in the plains of Romilly-sur-Seine. The rain falling on Troyes when I entered the city disappointed Marcel Grégoire, Commissioner of the Republic, and the townspeople who had gathered to express their joy in cheers, but as usual delighted the farmers. Sleek cattle still grazed in the pastures of Vendeuvre and Bar-sur-Aube. At Colombey-les-deux-Églises, I made a stop. The townspeople, gathered around Mayor Demarson, greeted me ecstatically. Thrilled by the Liberation, they were preparing to take every advantage of it to increase the productivity of their fields. As I reached Chaumont, where the official reception party of the Haute-Marne department was awaiting me, it was with a sense of solace that I watched night fall over this faithful and familiar countryside.

Having paid another visit to the First Army from here, I returned to Paris by way of Dijon. The great city had suffered only relatively light damage, but was still excited at having witnessed the invader's downfall. While the streets and squares resounded with cheers, the *corps constitués* were presented to me in the Ducal Palace by Commissioner of the Republic Jean Mairey—replacing Jean Bouhey, seriously wounded during the liberation of the city—and Canon Kir, the popular and truculent mayor. General Giraud, who had returned to his family in the Burgundian capital, was first among the citizens. 'How things have changed!' he said to me. 'True enough—for things', I thought. But as I looked at the noisy and excited crowd, I doubted if such was the case for the French.

On November 4th, 5th and 6th, I travelled through the Alpes departments. There had been fighting everywhere and there was fighting still on the approaches to the passes into Italy. Our mountains, with their passionately freedom-loving inhabitants, had supplied the resistance with many strongholds and many fighters. Now life was beginning to resume its normal course despite great difficulties of provisioning, the problems of action led by Moroccan troops and Alpine maquisards against the enemy, and incidents precipitated by clandestine fighters who wanted to mete out justice on their own. Accompanied by Ministers Diethelm and de Menthon, Commissioner of the Republic Farge, and Generals Juin and de Lattre, I went first to Ambérieu. Next came Annecy and Albertville where I reviewed the Dody division and the *tabors*. Chambéry, overflowing with enthusiasm, gave me the measure of Savoyard loyalty. Finally, I entered Grenoble.

The ardour that swept over the 'Allobroges' in the Place de la Bastille and along the Boulevard Gambetta, which I covered on foot, and in the Place Rivet, where the crowd gathered to hear the speeches, was indescribable. I presented Mayor LaFleur with the Cross of the Liberation on behalf of the city of Grenoble. Then the Twenty-Seventh Alpine Division passed in review. I saluted it with particular satisfaction, for, eager to assure France the mountain enclaves formerly in the possession of Italy and knowing that, as far as the Allies were concerned, we would get them only by taking them, I had plans for this growing force. On November 6th, I was back in Paris.

In several weeks, I had covered a great deal of the territory, been seen by ten million Frenchmen with the trappings of power and amidst demonstrations of national solidarity, I had delivered on the spot the urgent measures of authority, shown to those in office that the state had a head, revealed to the scattered elements of our forces that their only future lay in unity, their only duty in discipline. But how harsh the reality of the French situation appeared! What I had seen, beneath the speeches, the cheers and the flags, left me with the impression of enormous material damage and of a profound rift in the nation's political, administrative, social and moral structure. It was clear that in these conditions, the people, delighted though they were by their liberation, would still have to endure long and arduous trials which party demagoguery and Communist ambition would try to exploit for their own purposes.

In the provinces as in Paris I had also noticed the enthusiasm expressed towards me. Instinctively the nation saw that the confusion of the moment threatened it with anarchy and ultimate dictatorship unless I were there to serve as its focus and guide. Today it pledged itself to De Gaulle to escape subversion as yesterday it had counted on him to drive out the invader. By this token I considered myself reinvested by liberated Frenchmen with the same signal and unprecedented responsibility which I had assumed during the whole of their servitude. Such would be the case until the day when, all immediate danger past, facility and faction would once again sunder the French people.

Hailed by the voice of the people, recognized without reservation if not without murmurs by every political group, the legitimacy of this public trust was never contested for a moment. The administration, the magistracy and the educational authorities showed no more reticence with regard to my authority than the armies. The Council of State, now headed by President Cassin, was an example of this complete loyalty. The Audit Office followed suit. Wherever I made an appearance, the clergy promptly paid me official respect. On September 20th I received Cardinal Suhard and was assured of the episcopate's moral support. Through M. Georges Duhamel, its permanent secretary, the Académie Française sought my support. Even the representatives of previous regimes did not withhold signs of their adherence. The Count of Paris, inspired by national concern, wrote that he was sending me an authorized emissary. Prince Napoleon, an exemplary maquisard and a captain in the Chasseurs Alpins, came to offer me his support. General Giraud arrived from Algeria, where he had escaped a fanatic's bullet, and immediately offered his services. The former supporters of Vichy capitulated before the evidence. Pétain, in Germany, kept silence, and those officials, diplomats, military men and journalists who had assiduously served him now lavished obeisances and justifications on the Government. Finally, M. Albert Lebrun added the approval of the sad ghost of the Third Republic to the chorus.

I received him on October 13th. 'I have always been and I am still,' the President declared, 'in full agreement with what you are doing. Without you, all was lost. Thanks to you, all can be saved. Personally, I could not express myself in any other way than by this visit, which I ask you to publicize. It is true that I have not formally resigned. But to whom could I have sent a resignation, since there is no longer a National Assembly qualified to replace me? But I want you to be certain that you can count absolutely on my support.'

We spoke of the events of 1940. Albert Lebrun referred with disappointment to that June 16th on which he accepted M. Paul Reynaud's resignation and appointed the Marshal to form a new cabinet. With tears in his eyes, raising his arms to heaven, he admitted his mistake: 'What put me on the wrong track,' he said, 'along with most of the other ministers, was Weygand's attitude. He was so categoric in his insistence on an armistice! He declared so peremptorily that there was nothing else to be done! And yet I believed— like Reynaud, Jeanneney, Herriot, Mandel, and you yourself—that we should go to Africa, that we could continue the war with our army there, the forces we still had the means to send there, our undamaged fleet, our empire and our allies. But the Council yielded to Weygand's vehement arguments. What could we do? His reputa-

tion and his prestige were so immense! What a terrible thing it is
when, in times of extreme danger, it is the generals who refuse to
fight!'

President Lebrun took his leave. I shook his hand with compassion
and cordiality. As the leader of the state, he had lacked two essential
things: he was not a leader, and there was no state.

While the nation's passions crystallized, Allied military action
continued in the north and east. Eisenhower, using his main forces
on his left flank, meant to cross Belgium quickly, then cross the
Rhine near its mouth and to seize the Ruhr and with it victory. This
was the task entrusted to General Montgomery, at the end of August,
who was given maximum aviation support. In the centre, General
Bradley was to reach the Rhine between Dusseldorf and Mainz,
linking his movement with that of the armies in the north. The
French First Army and the American Seventh were told to combine
under General Devers' orders, and drive north from the Mediterranean to occupy the right wing of the Allied position and approach
the Rhine through Alsace. It was my wish, of course, that the advance
take place as soon as possible, that the Allied armies push on to the
heart of Germany, and that French forces play a major role in the
operations. This is what I wrote to Eisenhower on September 6th. I
urged him to accelerate the movement of our First Army, put the
2nd Armoured Division at his disposal, and informed him of the
French Government's desire to see its troops penetrate German
territory at the same time as the Americans and the British. But the
offensive, speedily conducted until the frontier was approached, was
stopped before it reached enemy territory.

As a matter of fact, in the Low Countries, the Ardennes, Lorraine,
and the Vosges, the adversary found means of re-establishing his line
of battle. Hitler himself, whose prestige as well as his health had
suffered from the preceding July's assassination attempt, now resumed the upper hand. Discounting the effect of the 'secret weapons'
—robot planes, V-2 rockets, new tanks, perhaps even atom bombs—
which the Reich was feverishly preparing, the Fuehrer planned to resume the offensive and obtained an overwhelming vote of confidence
from the German people. Moreover, the Allies, reduced to increasingly precarious supply services the farther they advanced, found
that the lack of fuel, shells and replacements greatly hampered their
operations.

This was particularly true in the case of the French First Army. The Allied command had expected difficult progress for the forces marching north from the Midi. It was believed that the fortified German strongholds of Toulon and Marseilles could be taken only after several weeks' fighting, that afterwards the necessity of covering themselves along the entire Italian frontier would force Patch and de Lattre to accept setbacks and delays, and lastly that the German Nineteenth and First Armies, totalling ten divisions, the former occupying Provence, the latter Aquitaine, Languedoc, and Limousin, would be in a position to obstruct the French and American forces for a long time against the Alpine foothills, in many points along the Rhône valley, and in the Massif Central. This is why plans for transporting troops and material from Africa, Corsica and Italy, as well as for subsequent supply services from the Mediterranean coast to the major units, involved prolonged delays. As it turned out, however, the forces of General de Lattre and General Patch advanced at a rate which invalidated all such plans. The other side of the coin, for our victorious troops, was a continual lack of petrol and munitions.

The French First Army, which had landed its first units in and around St-Tropez on August 15th, was, by the 28th, in complete possession of Toulon and by the 30th held all of Marseilles. It had captured 40,000 prisoners and mountains of weapons and material. Since it was his job to co-ordinate forces in the Midi, General Patch's initial intention had been to move the Americans directly north, while the French, once they held the two major Mediterranean ports, would act as a rearguard for their allies along the Alpine passes. But General de Lattre, still glowing from the victories won in Toulon and Marseilles, was not satisfied with the secondary role assigned to him. He intended to move up on the American Army's right and left flanks and then advance with them. I had, of course, supported this view. Patch himself, now full of admiration for the French First Army, adopted our suggestion with good grace.

Hence our II Corps, under Monsabert and consisting, at first, of du Vigier's and Brosset's divisions, crossed the Rhône at Avignon, then, operating on the eastern bank, drove the enemy out of Lyons on the 2nd and 3rd of September. Shortly afterward, in the Autun region, the left wing of this corps engaged the rear guard of the German First Army, which was retreating through the Massif Central in an attempt to clear itself a road to Burgundy. But the trap was sprung by du Vigier's division, so fast had the latter advanced. After four days of desperate fighting, the last enemy echelons, with our south-west Forces of the Interior on their heels as well as those of Berri, could find no way out and finally capitulated. However their leader, General Elster, his conscience stricken by the idea of sur-rendering to the French, had contacted the American officers posted at Orléans. On September 11th, he surrendered to them the 22,000 men still under his orders. On the same day, du Vigier liberated Dijon. The next day, the Brosset division, having become the left wing of de Lattre's army, joined up with Leclerc at Montbard. The latter had arrived from Paris on Bradley's right wing. On September 13th, Langres was taken by troops of the II Corps and the Haute-Marne maquis. After which, General de Monsabert's advance guard approached the upper Saône from Jussey and Port-sur-Saône.

During this time, the Americans had marched at the same speed along the Grenoble-Bourg-Besançon route, forcing a crossing of the Rhône between Lyons and Ambérieu. But this whole position had to be covered along the Alps, since Marshal Kesselring's troops were still entrenched in northern Italy, occupied the passes to France and were moving into the Hautes-Alpes, Savoie and Haute-Savoie de-partments, threatening our communications there. It was true that the local Forces of the Interior were relentlessly attacking the Ger-man detachments and the Italian Fascist units operating on the French border. But this flanking action had to be completed. To do so we employed one American division and Dody's Second Moroccan Division. The latter, aided by the Forces of the Interior and by the Moroccan Tabors, had taken Briançon, Modane and Bourg-St-Maurice.

On September 5th, General Bethouart assumed command of the First Army Corps and deployed it on the Americans' right wing on the Rhône between Ambérieu and the Swiss border. Initially having at his disposal Guillaume's 3rd North-African Division and Mag-nan's 9th Colonial Division, he pushed across the Jura and, on September 12th, reached the Doubs valley.

Thus ended the extraordinary pursuit in which the French and Americans had covered over 700 kilometres in three weeks. They would have moved more quickly still if the lack of fuel had not constantly delayed them. Petrol was laboriously unloaded in Marseilles, Nice and Toulon. Then it had to be delivered to the fighting lines. Since the railways on both banks of the Rhône had been destroyed, only convoys of trucks assured food provisions—for the French First Army this meant an average of 1,500 metric tons a day. Besides, the American services, having to divide supplies between Patch and de Lattre, were inclined, as was only human, to grant priority to their own troops. It can be imagined what fits of impatience, following hours of enthusiasm, the French troops, general-staffs, and commanding general suffered when they found themselves deprived of the success which they thought they could see before them. The same lack of fuel caused three major units, the 9th Colonial Division, the 4th Moroccan Division, and the 5th Armoured Division, as well as numerous reserve units, to lag behind the bulk of the First Army over long periods.

These setbacks must be taken into account in any fair reckoning of our progress from the Mediterranean to our entry into Alsace. On the other hand, our advance was greatly facilitated by the action of the maquisards. The hampering action the latter inflicted on the enemy, the fact that they had gradually made themselves masters of a large proportion of the routes to be covered, the support they furnished the regular units, had counted for a great deal in this overpowering result. On September 12th, at the end of this great pursuit, 120,000 Germans were in French captivity, as many taken by the First Army as by the Forces of the Interior and by the 2nd Armoured Division. This was a third of all the prisoners captured by all the Allied armies.

On September 13th, General John Lewis, assigned to me by Eisenhower, brought me a letter from the Supreme Commander. The latter informed me that the Allied position was now secure from Switzerland to the North Sea; the French First Army and the American Seventh constituting henceforth the Southern Army Group. Within this group, the Americans were to form the left wing and head for Saverne and later Strasbourg. The French were to regroup on the right wing around Vesoul, take Belfort and finally Colmar. Eisenhower asked my consent to this use of our forces. I gave it to him on September 21st, considering it suitable that the French should have their own zone of action, just as the British and the Americans had theirs, and regarding it as proper that this zone be Alsace. However, I informed the Supreme Commander that I reserved one condition in the case of the 1st Free French Division: the privilege of recalling it to Paris in case of necessity. Further, I invited Eisenhower to send one of four divisions to Bordeaux as soon as possible in order to take Royan and Graves. The great port would thereby be cleared and we could use it for provisioning all of France. Lastly, I indicated to the Supreme Commander that there was every reason to send a major French unit toward Strasbourg.

This was to be the Leclerc Division. After having kept it in Paris for several days, I had once again put it at the disposal of the Allied High Command on September 6th. Now, I wanted to see it operating with the American Seventh Army. As a matter of fact, the Alsatian capital was Patch's objective. For obvious national reasons, I wished it to be liberated by French troops, and I had no doubt that Leclerc, once he was in the proper place, would be able to find an opportunity to do so. The 2nd Armoured Division therefore continued to operate in the American sector.

But there was every indication that the capture of Strasbourg would not occur in the immediate future. The German Nineteenth Army had solidly entrenched itself on the slopes of the Vosges. Its leader General Wiese, whose troops had been withdrawn from Provence and reinforced by units from the interior, was in control of the whole area. Fierce fighting was to succeed the triumphant rout without transition. Such was to be the case along the entire Allied front. At the mouth of the Meuse, the offensive begun by Montgomery on September 20th ended in failure. In Lorraine and in Luxembourg, Bradley, too, had to call his offensive to a halt. It was clear that on the western front the breakthrough would be postponed for several months. There was no reason for thinking it would come any sooner in the east, for if the Russians had occupied Rumania and Bulgaria, thrown back the Germans from a large part of Poland and Yugoslavia, and established a foothold in Hungary and the Baltic States, they had still not penetrated the Reich itself at any point.

That the war was to continue was certainly tragic from the point of view of the losses, damage and expense which the French would still have to endure. But, from the viewpoint of France's higher interests—which is something quite different from the immediate advantage of the French population—I did not regret it. With the war dragging on, our help would be needed in the battle of the Rhine and of the Danube, as it had been in Africa and in Italy. Our position in the world and, still more, the opinion that our own people would have of themselves for many generations to come depended on this fact. Furthermore, the delays to come before the cessation of hostilities would enable us to value what was due at its true worth. Lastly, what an opportunity this supreme phase offered to national unity, for now every Frenchman would be subjected to the same trials, no longer divided, as they had been yesterday, into the free Empire and oppressed Metropolitan France, but henceforth living in identical conditions and governed by a single power! To begin with, we were able to resolve in time the problem of our military organization, burdened with political commitments as it was—in short, to weld our forces into a whole, whatever their origins.

In the First Army, fragmentary attempts had been made in this direction. One way or another, a certain pairing-off had been established between the African divisions and the maquisard groups. By September 20th, more than 50,000 men from the Forces of the Interior were already participating in General de Lattre's operations; 50,000 more were preparing to do so. Bracketed with the regular troops, therefore, were: thirteen Alpine battalions formed in the departments of Savoie, Isère, Ain, Drôme and Ardèche; the 'maquis' from Provence, Chambarrand, Haute-Marne, Morvan and the Ardennes; the 'groups' from Charolais, Lomont, Yonne and Franche-Comte; 'commandos' under various names; many minor groups, and a large number of individuals. Furthermore, considerable columns of maquisards from the central departments and from Aquitaine were also arriving.

At the end of August, I received General Chevance-Bertin, military delegate in the south-west, in Paris, and directed him to shift the greatest possible share of the Forces of the Interior in his region to the First Army. Chevance-Bertin had done this, entrusting to his subordinate Schneider the leadership of this huge and inchoate group. Schneider had managed to lead into Burgundy the 'Toulouse Light Division', including, in particular, the 'Corps Franc des Pyrénées', the 'Brigade Alsace-Lorraine' and contingents from the Tarn, Tarn-et-Garonne and Aveyron departments. He also brought 'brigades' from Languedoc, Lot-et-Garonne and Corrèze. Finally, he sent the 'brigades du Massif Central' and the 'Artillerie du Puy-de-Dôme', and the 'Gardes Mobiles de Vichy', forming together the 'Groupe d'Auvergne', to the same destination.

The arrival of these units, diverse as they were, obviously delighted the command of the First Army, the general staffs, and the services, but nevertheless caused them great difficulties. It is true that questions of subordination were soon resolved. General Cochet, whom I had put in charge of the Forces of the Interior south of the Loire, put an end to the outbursts of separatism shown by certain leaders and put all the units that reached his zone of action directly under General de Lattre's orders. But how organize these forces, how equip them, how employ them under normal military conditions? The decisions had to be made and the means furnished by the Government itself, according to the plan it had adopted for this final phase of the war.

Some demagogues were noisily urging us to mobilize all men old enough to bear arms. Mass conscription, a practice revived from the Revolutionary period, would, of course, have given us considerable manpower, despite the fact that two and a half million men were in enemy hands as prisoners of war, deported or at forced labour, and that 300,000 more had been killed or seriously wounded since the beginning of the conflict. But this was no longer a period when numbers counted more than anything else. What would we have done with this host of conscripts, when we had neither arms nor officers nor equipment to give them, and when it would have been both criminal and cretinous to send them as they were into open country to face the German Army's artillery, tanks, machine guns and planes? Taking advantage of circumstances wherever possible, but facing facts, I decided what my intentions were to be.

To organize for battle the eager and brave youth which had conducted the clandestine struggle and to add it to the troops from Africa—that was what seemed realizable from the military viewpoint and necessary from the national one. Given our state of extreme material impoverishment, this would be all we could do for the autumn and winter. If the war were going to last longer, we should know in plenty of time. In practice, I intended to incorporate as many maquisards into the First Army as it could absorb and with the remainder to form new major units.

As soon as we were able to sum up exactly the real position of the paramilitary units, that is to say, when I returned from my trip to the Rhône and the Midi, I explained my plan for this transformation to the Committee for National Defence. Four hundred thousand—

this was the approximate number of men in our Forces of the Interior. What an honour for France this new wave of combatants was! All voluntarily accepted the dangers of the maquis, despite the number of young men who were *hors de combat* and the fact that the official Vichy machine, until its last hour, had hunted down and condemned all who resisted the enemy. We first decreed, on September 23rd, that all men remaining under arms would be put under contract officially for the duration of the war. Thus the situation of the maquisards would be legalized. Forty thousand were transferred into the Navy and the Air Force. To help the Minister of the Interior to maintain public order, the *gendarmes* and *gardes mobiles* who had joined the maquis were to return to their original groups; besides, sixty 'Compagnies Républicaines de Sécurité' were formed; an innovation universally condemned at the time but still in force today. Finally, certain specialists of whom the nation's economy stood in the greatest need—miners, railwaymen, etc—were asked to return to their professions. Ultimately, the land army alone gained more than 300,000 soldiers who had spontaneously transferred to it from the Forces of the Interior.

From these, according to my plan, de Lattre would take some hundred thousand under his command at once. The others would form seven new divisions. The 27th Division under Valette d'Ozia in the Alpes department, the 10th Division under Billotte in Paris, the 19th Division under Borgnis-Desbordes in Brittany, were already in formation. The maquisards in contact with the German pockets in St-Nazaire, La Rochelle, Royan and the Graves peninsula were to form the 25th Division under Chomel and the 23rd under Anselme. At the beginning of Spring, the 1st Division under Caillies and the 14th under Salan would be sent on foot into Berri and Alsace respectively. Aside from these major units, the Minister of War would reconstitute regiments of all arms in order to allow of training in the rear areas and to replace losses at the front. In December, the class of 1943 was to be called to the colours. In April, it would be the turn of the classes of 1940, 1941 and 1942, in so far as the young men comprising them were not already conscripted. The military schools were immediately reopened.

This programme was realized. But the problem was not so much to create bodies of troops as to arm and equip them. The miscellaneous rifles, the rare machine guns and mortars, the few pathetic

cars and trucks which the maquisards possessed and had used in
skirmishes and ambushes were absurd for participating in pitched
battle. By regrouping these chance means, by sending to Africa for
the few available French arms still there, by collecting and repairing
the material captured from the enemy in France and even what had
lately been collected in Tunisia and Italy, we could give the new-
formed units an elementary supply service. But this was not enough
to equip them to meet the forces of the Wehrmacht. They needed
heavy arms. Yet there no longer existed in France a single establishment capable of manufacturing them. The installations and equipment of our specialized factories had been dismantled and removed
by the Germans; the remaining workshops had kept only what they
required for the accessory work carried out on behalf of the enemy.
Unless we were to wait until production began again—a matter of
many months—we were obliged to depend on the good will of the
United States.

Their good will was scanty. It must be admitted that our allies
were incontestably having difficulties in transporting the enormous
tonnage of equipment required in battle from America. They were
therefore not at all eager to furnish additional and unexpected con-
signments to be handed over to the French. Especially since they
were for use by units made up from the Forces of the Interior. To the
Anglo-Americans, these forces still seemed outrageous to the general
staffs and disquieting to the politicians. Certainly, during the battles
of the Liberation, supplies had been forthcoming for the 'troops of
rebellion'. But in Washington and London there was no question,
now, of providing them with heavy arms which would have to come
from America in additional convoys. Who could be certain that some
day these irregular forces would not use the powers they had acquired for subversive ends? Particularly since by furnishing General
de Gaulle's Government the means to equip eight or ten divisions,
it was apparent that by the end of the winter the French Army
would have doubled, that it would play a larger, perhaps decisive
role in the battle, and that therefore France would have to be
included in the armistice settlement. This Roosevelt wanted to avoid.
These motives brought the requests we made to the British and
American Governments to nothing. From the day of the landing in
Normandy to that of the German capitulation, our allies would not
give us supplies to equip a single additional major unit. During his

October visit to Paris, General Marshall left us under no illusion on
this point.

Would the Allies at least agree to equip the 100,000 men which
our First Army was trying to absorb into its divisions, its services, and
its reserves? Certainly not. Referring to the provisioning plans drawn
up in their offices, they still refused to take this increase into account.
As for food supplies and clothing, our own Commissariat supplied
the First Army with the supplements it needed. In other respects, we
had to fall back on makeshifts.

Winter in the Vosges threatened the health of our Negro troops,
so we sent the 20,000 soldiers from Central and West Africa serving
in the 1st Free French Division and the 9th Colonial Division to the
Midi. They were replaced by a similar number of maquisards who
were immediately equipped. Several North African regiments were
particularly exhausted by two years' fighting and returned to their
original garrisons, while troops drawn from the Forces of the Interior inherited their arms and their positions in the order of battle.
De Lattre, skilfully using the reserve equipment previously given to
his army, divided the contents among the new units. The ingenuity
displayed on every level, either in wheedling a little new material from
the American depots to replace outdated weapons, in repairing the
latter and then using them alongside the replacements, or in adopting all Allied armoured weapons, artillery and vehicles lying within
reach, gave us certain resources. Unfortunately, our poverty com-
pelled us to adopt any means of reviving our military strength which,
through the centuries, had often been superfluous, even squandered,
and now was so terribly reduced. Somehow the First Army was
furnished with the supplies necessary for its reinforcing manpower.

On September 23rd, I inspected this army. With Diethelm and
Juin, I landed at Tavaux, near Dole. First we visited general headquarters at Besançon and the next day examined the terrain. This
was the moment when the First Army was making contact with the
German positions. General de Lattre, still enthusiastic after his swift
advance from the Mediterranean, believed that he could drive his
left wing across the Vosges into Alsace. In this sector—that of the
II Corps—General de Monsabert was leading sharp action against
the foothills around Servance and Ronchamp. Optimistic and high
spirited, taking enormous risks, lavishing his unfailing enthusiasm,

his sharp eye, his sense of combat on every sector, de Monsabert used every man to the limit of his ability. Yet he was devoted to his men and completely disinterested where his own safety was concerned. At a time when it was my duty to bestow military honours, I often heard him speak of others' merits but never of his own.

The First Corps formed the right wing of the First Army from Lure to Lomont. I found it in the process of organizing its base in order to take the Belfort Gap. The undertaking would be an arduous one, given the narrowness of the terrain on which the enemy must be engaged and the power of the German opposition. But the general on whom this responsibility fell seemed made to lead the enterprise to a successful conclusion. General Bethouart left nothing to chance. His plans were methodically conceived and calmly executed. This earned him the trust of his subordinates and also, occasionally, the impatience of his superior.

Only complete success satisfied General de Lattre. Enthusiastic to the point of effervescence, as sensitive as he was brilliant, de Lattre was extremely anxious that nothing should fail and regarded each vicissitude as a personal matter. Those who served under him received many rebuffs and pinpricks, but his excellence was so obvious that their resentment was always short-lived.

On the occasion of my inspection, I saw a lot of General de Lattre in the exercise of his command. Despite the faults for which he was reproached and which were rather the excesses of his virtues, I always thought him highly qualified to lead operations. Without being unduly favourably prejudiced by my friendship for him, and although I occasionally interfered in his domain when reasons of national interest required it, I gave him my unfailing confidence in the task to which I had called him. In his relations with me for so long as I was in power, he never failed to show, not only his loyalty, but also his conviction of the predominant importance of the mission I was performing.

That day when I visited the troops and services in his company, everything was a pleasure to see. Of course, after their victorious pursuit, the men had good reason to be proud. They were literally beaming with good humour and technically speaking, they were second to none. It was readily apparent that, all things being equal, the French had achieved victories at least comparable to those won by the British and American troops. The Germans, of course, were well aware of this, for they sent a relatively high proportion of their forces against our men.

I also noticed that the amalgam of troops from Africa and of the Forces of the Interior could be brought to a high point of effectiveness. The reciprocal prejudices among the units of various origin had not altogether disappeared. The 'Free French' maintained a somewhat exclusive pride toward all others. The men of the secret army, long persecuted, feverish and destitute, would readily have claimed to represent all of the resistance forces. The regiments from Algeria, Morocco and Tunisia, although they had recently been divided among varying tendencies, seemed unanimously touchy about their *esprit de corps*. Whatever the complications to which fate had subjected every group, however, the satisfaction of finding themselves side by side and engaged in the same battle triumphed over other considerations in the minds of soldiers, officers and generals alike. In the cities and villages they passed through, their reception left no doubt as to their popularity with the population. Indeed the French Army, for all the unfortunately reduced proportions its reconstruction had made necessary, revealed a quality which it had never surpassed.

This was particularly so in the case of the 2nd Armoured Division. On September 25th, leaving General de Lattre's zone, I visited its positions at Moyen, Vathimenil, and Gerbeviller. During its brief sojourn in Paris, this division had recruited several thousand young volunteers. In addition, it attracted equipment as naturally as a magnet attracts iron. It had everything. On September 10th, this division had crossed the Marne north of Chaumont and then, during the succeeding days, fought its way to Andelot and Vittel, threw back the counter-attacks of many German tanks to Dompaire, and finally established a front along the Meurthe. Leclerc and his lieutenants were dissatisfied with this standstill, but I appealed to their good sense. Like genius, a brilliant feat of arms is a matter of patience. With Baccarat—still a captive city—before him, Leclerc now concentrated his ambitions upon it, in order to take it at the right moment.

A month later, paying a return visit to our troops, I found them ready for the general offensive which Eisenhower was shortly to inaugurate. At the end of October, in the French sector, the restiveness of officers and men alike was evident. Especially since emissaries

were continuously arriving either through Switzerland or across the
lines from the Vosges—from Belfort and Alsace urging our men to
push forward. I visited our aviation group, under Gerardot, confirm-
ing its mission, in accordance with the Allied command plans, to
support the French Army. On the front lines which I examined next,
the men were optimistic. 'At the time of the disaster,' de Lattre asked
me, 'did you imagine anything like this?'—'It is because I believed
in something like this,' I replied, 'that we are both here today.'

My movements throughout the country and my visits to the armies
produced the desired effect. But the effect would have been short-
lived unless it was followed by practical arrangements. Our plans
had been drawn up since Algiers. We could congratulate ourselves
on that. Despite the troubled conditions in which the Government
was established in Paris, the Councils which I called during an
overcrowded autumn were not wasted in tergiversations. In the
space of several weeks, the Government adopted a group of measures
which kept the nation from drifting from its course.

The greater the confusion, the greater the necessity of governing.
After enormous disorder, our first task was to restore the country's
labour force to its functions. But the first condition of such a restoration was that the workers be able to live. On July 16th, in Algiers,
the Government had decided 'that upon the Liberation there would
be occasion to proceed with an immediate and substantial wage
increase'. On August 28th, immediately after the liberation of Paris,
a conference of the secretaries-general of the ministries, presided over
by Le Troquer, Minister Delegate to the Liberated Territories, proposed that the increase be one of 40 per cent. It was this average
coefficient which the Council of Ministers adopted on September
13th. On October 17th, an additional decree provided for the reorganization of family allowances and increased them by 50 per cent.
This increase in wages and allowances, substantial as it might seem,
was nonetheless a modest one, since it raised the average level of
remuneration to 225 in relation to the October 1938 reading of 100,
whereas in the same period official prices had risen from 100 to 300
and some real prices to 1,000.

But what was the use of better wages if the value of the money paid
collapsed and the state went bankrupt? We walked on the brink of an
abyss. It was true that the levies—520 billion francs!—made by the
enemy on public funds had ceased. On the other hand, the war

effort had to be financed as well as the reconstruction of railways, ports, canals, electric plants and buildings, without which no recovery was imaginable. On the other side of the ledger from these crushing expenses stood the critically inadequate receipts. In the month of September, the nation's economic activity declined to about 40 per cent of the 1938 level. Further, bank note circulation and short-term liabilities reached 630 and 602 billion francs respectively; that is, three times higher than the pre-war level. This immense total of means of payment, completely disproportionate to an extremely reduced production, threatened an inflation which could become ruinous from one day to the next. To obtain funds from the treasury and at the same time control the inflation required a major public loan.

This was the 'Liberation Loan'. André Lepercq, Minister of Finance, set out its methods of payment and we adopted them: a permanent rate of 3 per cent and at par. The issue, open on November 6th, was closed on the twentieth. The operation claimed one victim, in the person of its director. André Lepercq, a man of faith and hope, was killed in an accident during a tour he was making in the northern departments to solicit subscriptions. On November 19th, thirty hours before the closing of the issue, I announced to the nation on the wireless that the figures reached already indicated success, but added: 'I ask you to make it a triumph!'

When the totals were finally calculated, the liberation loan produced 165 billion francs, which would be worth 1,200 billion today. Of that 127 billion were in 'hard cash', the rest in treasury bonds. A third of the total was subscribed during the last day. If we take into account the enormous economic distress into which the country was plunged at the time, severely limiting the resources of almost every Frenchman, and if we recall that since the first World War no credit operation had ever raised so much money and that none of those to follow even approached this result, we see that the liberation loan was a triumph of the confidence of Frenchmen in France. Circulation of bank notes was immediately reduced from 630 to 560 billion, and short-term liabilities from 601 to 555 billion. The catastrophe that would have been caused by an unchecked inflation was thereby avoided. Further, the funds furnished to the treasury by the loan, as well as by the confiscation of illicit profits, as decreed on October 18th, provided us with what we needed to finance the exceptional expenses of the war effort and the reconditioning of our communications and sources of energy. By taking into account the payment of taxes, the state had the wherewithal to pay what must be paid.

It would also have to be master in its own house. Among the various currents that had aroused passions to a pitch where the slightest concession would sweep away its authority, the state must discharge two imperative obligations: Justice must be done and public order guaranteed. This must be done vigorously and without delay, or it would never be done at all. The necessary measures were taken.

By September 13th, the Government had set up the special courts of justice provided for by the decree of June 24th. In each region there was to be a tribunal presided over by a magistrate and including a jury appointed by the president of the Court of Appeal. The list of citizens qualified to serve on this jury was drawn up by the Commissioner of the Republic. This tribunal was to judge cases of collaboration with the enemy under legal forms and guarantees: the right to a defence counsel, the possibility of taking a case to the Supreme Court of Appeal, recourse to the chief of state. As the courts of justice fulfilled their function, the local authorities were to dissolve the courts-martial set up during the conflict by the Forces of the Interior; arbitrary arrests became formally illegal; fines were to be regarded as pure extortion and summary executions no better than indictable crimes. Immediately the reprisals which threatened to dishonour the resistance ceased. There were still some sequestrations, pillaging or assassinations, but those guilty of such actions suffered the law's extreme rigour and the last outbursts were quite exceptional.

Of those Frenchmen who, by murder or delation, had caused the death of the resistance fighters, 10,842 were killed without due process of law, 6,675 during the maquis struggles before the Liberation, the rest afterward, during the course of reprisal actions. Seven hundred and seventy-nine more men were to be executed as the result of sentences pronounced by the courts of justice and the military tribunals. A total which, though painful in itself, is actually extremely limited in relation to the number of crimes committed and to their dreadful consequences, and far from the extravagant figures later advanced by the inconsolable lovers of defeat and collaboration; but it was saddening to realize that the behaviour of those executed was not always inspired by the lowest motives. Among the militia-men, officials, police and propagandists were some who had simply obeyed blindly. Some had let themselves be lured by the mirage of adventure. Some believed they were defending a cause sufficiently lofty to justify any means. If all were guilty, many among them were not cowards. Once again, in a national drama, French blood had flowed on both sides. The nation saw its finest sons perish in its defence. With honour and with love, it embraced them in its bereavement. Others, alas, had fallen into the enemy camp: the nation approved their punishment, but quietly mourned these fallen children too. Now time had done its work. One day, the tears would dry, the transgressions dim and the tombs disappear. But France would remain.

Once justice was functioning, there was no further excuse for maintaining irregular armed forces. Yet despite the Government's instructions, several organizations, particularly the 'National Front', insisted on keeping paramilitary units at their disposal. These 'patriotic militias' claimed to prevent 'an offensive return of fascism'. They were also prepared, obviously, to apply pressure which might constrain or even overthrow the Government as it stood. Under this camouflage, it was of course the 'Comac' that held the reins. This final ambiguity had to be stopped. Despite the objections of several ministers and the pleas of various committees, I induced the Government to decree the formal dissolution of the militias. On October 28th this measure was passed and published.

As I had expected, reactions were violent. On Sunday the 29th, the National Council of the Resistance asked for an audience. I received these comrades of yesterday's struggle at my residence with respect and friendship. But to their unanimous complaints pressing me to reconsider the decision I had taken, I could only answer by an absolute refusal. Was this the effect of intimidation by Communists or illusions common amongst reactionaries? The most ardent in their protests were those who represented moderate factions. On the other hand, the representatives of the 'party' maintained a reserved attitude at the interview, either because they saw that the outcome was already a foregone conclusion or because they intended to express their irritation in another way. On the 31st, detailed measures were adopted in the Council of Ministers. Any force which was not a part of the army or the police was to be dissolved at once, if need be by the authorities. It was forbidden, under penalty of severe punishment, to be in possession of arms without the warranted authorization of the prefects. Any arms in the possession of private citizens were to be turned in within a week to the police commissariats or the *gendarmerie* brigades. An invitation was issued—though rarely answered—'to those citizens who want to contribute to the defence of republican institutions and liberties', so that the authorities could call upon their help in case of need.

Whether by coincidence or through provocation, on the following day, November 1st, a munitions train was blown up in Vitry-sur-Seine. About thirty people were killed and over a hundred wounded. The disaster occurred on the morning that I was visiting Mont Valérien, the Ivry cemetery, and the Château de Vincennes to pay All Saints' Day homage to the resistance dead. The Communists immediately declared the disaster 'a crime by the fascist fifth column'. On November 2nd, the 'party's' political bureau issued a communique referring to the 'Vitry outrage' and vehemently attacking General de Gaulle for dissolving the militias. 'Once again,' the bureau declared, 'the President of the Government has assumed the responsibility of treating the French resistance as a negligible quantity.' Two days afterward, at the Vélodrome d'Hiver, a public meeting was held, organized by the National Front. The speakers shouted their protests. On November 25th, at the Château de la Timone, where a security company was billeted, a bomb exploded killing thirty-two men. The inquest did not manage to discover those responsible, but there was good evidence that it was the epilogue of the *affaire des milices*. The last illegally armed groups had disappeared. No further mysterious explosions occurred.

However, it was in the nation's interest that the men who had led the struggle against the invader should participate equally in the work of recovery. Apart from the Communist leaders, who aimed at a definite goal, the resistance fighters as a whole were somewhat disoriented. As the enemy withdrew and Vichy disappeared, they had been tempted, like Goethe's Faust, to say to the moment: 'Stay, you are so splendid!' The Liberation, in fact, deprived their activity of its principal point. Nostalgia came upon them. Especially since these brave and adventurous men had experienced the sombre attractions of the dangerous clandestine struggle, which they would not renounce. Those among them who were pre-eminently combatants were absorbed into the ranks of the Army. But the majority of the 'politicians', whether they had always been or recently become so, were eager to see the revival of public life. They aspired to an arena where they could make themselves heard and gain access to posts of command.

I myself wanted to put as representative an Assembly as possible in contact with the Cabinet. The measures determining the establishment of powers in Metropolitan France provided, moreover, that the Algiers Assembly should convene in Paris after being enlarged. Not that I gave such a body the capacity to act. I was well aware of the fact that Assemblies, despite their fine speeches, are ruled by the fear of action. Besides, I knew of the rivalries which already divided the men of the resistance; therefore I had no expectation that the representatives would effectively support a resolved policy. But I did hope they would support a mystique of recovery which would inspire the French people. In any case, I thought it wise to offer a sop to their seething spirits. And besides, how could I neglect the advice which such an Assembly would give the Government and the credit it would inspire abroad? On October 12th, a decree determined the composition of the new Consultative Assembly. *C. A.*

The latter consisted of 248 members: 176 representatives of resistance organizations, 60 members of parliament, 12 overseas councillors-general. In particular, the 18 members of the National Council of the Resistance participated in the Assembly, which met on November 7th. It convened at the Palais du Luxembourg, for, symbolically, I had insisted on reserving the Palais-Bourbon for the future National Assembly. Felix Gouin was elected president, as in Algiers. On November 9th, I inaugurated the first session.

From the tribune which I mounted in order to address the Government's greetings to the Assembly, I saw the amphitheatre filled with comrades delegated by all the national resistance movements and belonging to every political tendency. From one end of the span to the other, all did me the honour of applauding. Those present were, like myself, imbued with the feeling that this gathering commemorated a great French victory following upon an inordinate disaster. Here, in fact, was the end of France's oppression, but also the outcome of the dramatic shock of her liberation. Our actions had reopened the seas to the ship of state, though she had narrowly missed being scuttled at the outset.

Ten weeks had passed since Paris had been retaken. How much would depend on what had been done in this short space of time! Contact had been made between the people and its guide, and thereby all disputes about national authority had been silenced. The state was exercising its powers. The Government was at work. The Army, reunited, enlarged and more eager than ever, was fighting at the gates of Alsace, in the Alps and on the Atlantic coast, shoulder to shoulder with our allies. The administration was functioning. Justice was fulfilling its function. Public order was established. Tremendous reforms were being instituted, averting the threat of chaos and upheaval that hung over the nation. Bankruptcy had been avoided; the treasury was adequately filled; the value of currency temporarily assured. Above all, France was recovering a sense of her own value and looking toward the future.

The future? It was being forged in the trials which separated us from victory and eventual recovery. As long as the war lasted, I would answer for it. Afterward, everything would depend on the very men who, today, were gathered around me in the Palais du Luxembourg. Tomorrow the French people would transform them into elected and legal representatives. If they remained united for recovery as they were now for combat, all hopes were permissible. If they turned away from me and disputed the appearances of power among themselves, then decline would once again take its course.

But we were only in the present. France was at war again on her own territory. Now it was time for her to appear elsewhere.

II. STATUS

EVERY STATE TURNED its eyes upon liberated France. This nation, which had figured among the first for so many centuries, which yesterday had collapsed in an incredible disaster but for whose sake some of its sons had not stopped fighting, which today declared itself a sovereign and belligerent nation—in what condition would it reappear, what road was it about to take?

Many certainly believed that General de Gaulle, now established in Paris, would remain at the head of some executive body for a time. But over whom, and over what, would his authority be exercised? Would this leader whom no sovereign, no parliament, no referendum had installed in office, and who had at his disposal no political organization, properly speaking—would this leader be followed for long by the most mercurial and intractable nation in the world? On ravaged territory, with a population exhausted by privation, facing profoundly divided public opinion, would he meet such difficulties that he would find himself helpless against them? Finally, who could tell if the Communists, grown stronger in the resistance, with only the dregs of parties and the debris of police, justice and administration to deal with, would not seize power? Before adopting a specific attitude toward the Provisional Government, the chancelleries of the world waited to see which way France would turn.

They had to be made to admit that she had turned the right way: no civil war, no social upheaval, no military disorder, no economic collapse, no governmental anarchy. Just the opposite! A nation recovering its equilibrium despite its poverty, eager to rebuild, developing its war effort under the leadership of a virtually unopposed Government—here, despite the shadows, was the sight we offered the world. The Allies and the neutral powers could delay no longer giving a normal form to their relations with us.

Had they done so sooner, of course, those of the great powers who were fighting beside us could have provided significant moral support during the critical period from which we had just emerged. But the susceptibilities of the President of the United States and the grievances of the British Prime Minister had kept the decision in abeyance until the last possible moment. Now there was no further excuse for postponement! Moreover, Franklin Roosevelt himself was obliged to settle the matter, because of the American voters whose endorsement he was about to seek for a fourth term and who were impatient with his unjustifiable attitude toward their ally, France. The election was to be held on November 7th; it was on October 23rd that Washington, London and Moscow officially recognized the Provisional Government of the French Republic. To save face the White House and Downing Street stated that Eisenhower now thought it possible to transfer his authority on French territory to the De Gaulle Government, as if the Supreme Commander had ever exercised authority for a moment over anyone but his soldiers. Seeing that the 'great powers' bowed before the inevitable, the other states who had lagged behind now fell into line in turn. We naturally refrained from thanking any of them for this formality performed *in extremis*. At a press conference I held on October 25th, when I was asked 'my reactions to the recognition of the Government by the Allies', I confined myself to replying: 'The French Government is pleased that it is to be called by its name'.

Paris now saw all the great embassy doors reopen. They had been kept shut during the occupation and only ajar since. The diplomats who had been delegated to us in Algiers appeared before me to offer their credentials, but this time in unambiguous terms. Mr Jefferson Caffery, sent by Washington to replace Mr Edwin Wilson, was the only ambassador among the Allies whom we did not already know. As for the neutral states, the diplomatic corps they had set up in Vichy soon vanished, and the French Government good naturedly welcomed their new representatives. The only difficulty arose over the Papal Nuncio. The Vatican, apparently, wanted Monsignor Valerio Valeri to be accredited to General de Gaulle after having been Nuncio to Marshal Pétain. This, from our point of view, was impossible. After a number of fluctuations, the Holy See asked our approval of Monsignor Roncalli. We gave it at once, though I was careful to tell Monsignor Valerio Valeri, when the time came for his departure, that we had profound esteem for him personally.

For our part we had to supplement and rearrange our representation in the capitals of the world. René Massigli was assigned to London, Henri Bonnet to Washington, Jacques Maritain to the Vatican, General Pechkoff to Chungking. Among the Allies, our representatives were henceforth addressed by the traditional titles, while in Madrid, Ankara, Berne, Stockholm, Lisbon, etc., our ambassadors officially assumed their functions. The Quai d'Orsay, long the Sleeping Beauty's castle, now wakened into activity. The Foreign Minister Georges Bidault, seconded by the Secretary-General Raymond Brugère, dealt with a multiplicity of affairs suddenly confronting him all at once.

What would happen to Europe after the defeat of Germany, and what would be the latter's fate? These were the chief dilemmas posed by events from one day to the next and with which, of course, I was particularly concerned.

In one man's lifetime, France had survived three wars instigated by her neighbour across the Rhine. The first had ended in the mutilation of national territory and crushing humiliation. Victorious in the second, France had recovered Alsace and Lorraine, but at a cost of men and material that left her bloodless and ruined. Furthermore, the ill will of the Anglo-American powers, taking advantage of the inconsistency of our regime, led us, subsequently, to renounce the guarantees and reparations which had been granted us in exchange for control of the Reich and the Rhine frontier. The third war saw our army fall to pieces at the first encounter, the Government rush to capitulate, the nation endure occupation, organized pillage, forced labour and the imprisonment of two million men. By virtue of a kind of miracle, independence and sovereignty had been maintained in the remotest parts of the Empire. Gradually an army had been reconstituted, while resistance grew in Metropolitan France. France contributed to her own liberation with important military forces, a solid Government, a united public opinion. She had, henceforth, the assurance of being present at the victory. But it was all too obvious that she would then find herself reduced to such a weakened condition that her influence in world affairs, the adherence of her overseas territories, and the very sources of her life would be compromised for a long time. Unless by this very occasion—perhaps the last—she could reconstruct her power. This is what I wanted to effect.

To make France's recovery possible, the German collectivity must lose its capacity for aggression. In the dangerous world already looming before us, existence under the threat of war from a neighbouring state which had so often demonstrated its taste and its talent for conquest would be incompatible with France's economic recovery, her political stability, and the moral equilibrium without which all efforts would remain futile. It is true that the exhaustion of Germany, the Allied occupation, the annexation of her eastern territories, would prevent the worst for years to come. But afterwards? What would become of the German people, what changes would they undergo after their imminent defeat? Perhaps they would choose wisdom and peace? Perhaps this transformation would prove to be a lasting one? Obviously the conditions of our security would vary accordingly. But as long as we did not know the answer, we had to proceed as if Germany might remain a threat. What guarantees, what pledges would reassure us, while granting the great German people an opportunity to live, advance and co-operate with us and the rest of the world?

The abolition of a centralized Reich! This, in my opinion, was the first condition necessary to prevent Germany from returning to its bad ways. Each time a dominating and ambitious state had seized power in Germany, obliterating the Germans' diversity, imperialism had been the result. This had been only too evident under William II and under Hitler. Conversely, if each of the states within the German federation could exist by itself, govern itself in its own way and handle its own interests, there would be every likelihood that the federation as a whole would not try to subjugate its neighbours. This would be even more likely if the Ruhr, that arsenal of strategic material, were given a special status under international control. Further, the Rhineland would, of course, be occupied by French, British, Belgian and Dutch armies. But if its economy were also linked to a grouping of the Western powers—and with no opposition to other German units joining this alliance as well—and if the Rhine itself became an international freeway, then co-operation between complementary nations could be instituted forthwith. Lastly, there was every reason to suppose that the Saar, retaining its German character, would be transformed into a

separate state and united to France by trade agreements which
would settle the question of our reparations in terms of coal. Thus
the German federation, recovering its diversity and turning its
eyes toward the west, would lose the means of war but not those of
its own development. In addition, none of its fragments would be
annexed by the French, thus leaving the door to reconciliation open.

   This conception of tomorrow's Germany was closely related to
my image of Europe. After the terrible lacerations she had under-
gone in the last thirty years, and the vast changes which had occurred the world over, Europe could find equilibrium and peace
only by an association among Slavs, Germans, Gauls and Latins.
Obviously she must take into account what was momentarily
tyrannical and aggrandizing in the Russian regime. Using the procedures of totalitarian oppression and, on the other hand, invoking
the solidarity of the Central and Eastern European peoples against
the German peril, Communism was apparently trying to gain
control of the Vistula, the Danube and the Balkans. But once
Germany ceased to be a threat, this subjection, for lack of a *raison
d'être*, would sooner or later prove unacceptable to the vassal states,
while the Russians themselves would lose all desire to exceed their
own boundaries. If the Kremlin persisted in its desire for domination,
it would be against the will of the nations subject to its Government.
Yet in the long run there is no regime that can hold out against the will
of nations. I believed, moreover, that timely action by the western
Allies with regard to the masters of the Kremlin, on condition that
such action be concerted and categoric, would safeguard the independence of the Poles, the Czechs, the Hungarians and the Balkan
peoples. After which the unity of Europe could be established in the
form of an association including its peoples from Iceland to Istan-
bul, from Gibraltar to the Urals.

   This was the plan I had conceived, knowing perfectly well that
in such matters nothing turns out exactly as one has hoped. I
sounded the weaknesses in our policy of credit abroad and support
at home, yet I remained convinced that France could undertake
great actions, assume great proportions, and greatly serve her own
interest and that of the human race as well. But to begin with, we
would have to insinuate ourselves into the dissimulated and dis-
cordant arguments by which America, Russia and England were
settling issues without us.

To reach such a position, we were certainly starting off at a
great disadvantage. The Dumbarton Oaks conference of the preceding September, intended to prepare the future 'United Nations
Organization', had convoked representatives of the United States,
Great Britain, Russia and China, to the exclusion of France. Discussing the composition of the 'Security Council' which would
exercise control of the organization, the conference had determined
that this Council would consist only of the same four 'Great Powers'.
—'It is a splendid arrangement!' declared Mr Connally, head of
the Senate's Foreign Relations Committee, 'since the United States,
England, Russia and China are the four nations which have shed
their blood for the rest of the world, while France has only played
the role of a minor state in this war.'

In London the 'European Commission' had been sitting for over
a year, and delegates to it from the British, American and Soviet
Governments were studying questions concerning Europe and, in
particular, Germany, while we were excluded again. In September,
the President and the Prime Minister had met in Quebec to
determine their positions and did not invite us to attend. In
October, Churchill and Eden went to Moscow to reach an agreement with Stalin and Molotov without our being informed by
either party of the results. Everything occurred as if the Allies were
bent on excluding France even from the knowledge of their
arrangements.

We could not bring this relegation to a halt immediately, but we
could make it unendurable to those inflicting it upon us. For none
of their decisions concerning Europe, particularly Germany, could
be put into effect if France did not lend her voice. Soon we would be
on the Rhine and Danube with a strong army. Moreover, the war's
end would leave us in force on the continent, while America would
be back in her hemisphere and England on her island. Provided
that we knew what we wanted, we would then have the means to
break out of the circle of resigned acceptance and docile renunciation inside which our three partners intended to imprison us.
Already the liberation of our territory, the reinstatement of the
Government, the restoration of order throughout the country put us
in a position to deal with the situation. On October 30th we invited
Mr Churchill and Mr Eden to visit us in Paris. At the same time,
for form's sake, and with no illusions as to its acceptance, we sent

Mr Roosevelt and Mr Cordell Hull a similar invitation, which was declined.

Churchill and Eden arrived on November 10th. We gave them the best possible reception. Paris cheered them heartily. With Bidault and several other ministers, I met them at Orly and drove the Prime Minister to the Quai d'Orsay where he was to stay. The next day was the victory celebration. After a visit to the Tomb of the Unknown Soldier and a review of the troops, Churchill and I, in the same open car, moved down the triumphal avenue to a storm of cheers. The Prime Minister laid a bouquet at the foot of Clemenceau's statue while, on my orders, the band played 'Le Père de la Victoire'.—'For you!' I said to him in English. And it was only his due. Then I reminded him that at Chequers, on the evening of a black day, he had sung me our old song about Paulus word perfect. We visited Les Invalides and bowed before Foch's grave. After this, the distinguished Englishman bent for a long moment over Napoleon's tomb. 'In all the world,' he said to me, 'there is nothing greater!' The official luncheon at the Ministry of War, seat of the Presidency, ended with speeches in which friendship glowed on both sides.

After the meal, Winston Churchill told me he had been deeply touched by what he had seen and heard. 'Would you tell me,' I asked, 'what struck you most?'—'Yes,' he answered, 'your unanimity! After so many events during which you and I have been so fiercely attacked and reviled in France by so many pens in so many pages, I was astonished that only enthusiasm met us as we passed. This means that deep in its heart the French people is behind you, who have served it, and me, who have helped you to do so.' Churchill added that he was impressed by the orderliness of the ceremonies. He admitted that the British Cabinet had hesitated to approve his trip, so great had been its apprehension of upheaval in Paris. But everything he had seen had been normal and orderly, the crowds respecting the barricades and quite capable of bursting into cheers or keeping silent according to the demands of the situation, and the splendid troops—yesterday's French Forces of the Interior—parading in perfect marching order. 'I felt,' he declared, 'as if I were watching a resurrection.'

During the day, we had a meeting in my office in the Rue St-Dominique, at which we examined the possibility of a Franco-

British alliance for world-wide settlements. Churchill was seconded by Eden and Duff Cooper; Bidault and Massigli were with me. On this occasion we were no longer concerned with sentiment, but with business. We found our guests more reserved.

On the arming of French forces, they gave us no appreciable assistance and did not seem disposed to support our requests for co-operation from the United States. As for Germany, they agreed that France too should have her zone of occupation there, but remained evasive as to what that zone would be. They were even less willing to consider anything specific as to Germany's future regime, the fate of the Ruhr, the Rhine frontier, the Saar Basin, etc. On the other hand, they made no effort to conceal the fact that in Moscow, a few days before, they had sanctioned Stalin's proposal for the future Russo-Polish frontier; had brought from London to the Soviet capital three Polish ministers: Mr Mikolajczyk, Mr de Romer and Mr Grabski, urging them to come to an agreement with the 'Lublin Committee' as the Russians asked; and lastly, reached an informal agreement with the Kremlin on the division of the Balkans into two spheres of influence. 'In Rumania,' Churchill said, 'the Russians will have ninety per cent, the British ten per cent. In Bulgaria, they will have seventy-five per cent and we twenty-five per cent. But in Greece we will have ninety per cent, they ten per cent. And in Hungary and Yugoslavia, our influence will be equal.' The British ministers avoided all our attempts to discuss the problems of the Levant, and remained vague about Indochina and the Far East in general.

For all the well-mannered discretion of Churchill's and Eden's remarks, it was evident that they considered themselves players of a game to which we ourselves were not admitted and that they maintained a reserve imposed by the other players towards us. Nevertheless, they continued to express their faith in France and their confidence of seeing her resume her place among the great states. They proposed the immediate negotiation of a Franco-British treaty of alliance. They even brought us the joint invitation of England, the United States and Soviet Russia to take part with them in the London 'European Commission'.

This first step was not a negligible one, though it did not satisfy us. In any case, our remarks left Churchill in no doubt that the only situation we found acceptable was that of full partner. As his trip

continued, he realized, as he had already noticed on the Champs-
Elysées, that the French people deserved to settle its own affairs
without outside intervention.

On November 12th, he was received at the Paris Hôtel de Ville
and was met there, at his own request, not only by the Municipal
Council, but also by the National Council of the Resistance, the Paris
Committee of Liberation, and many combatants of the preceding
August. 'I am going there,' he had told me, 'to see the men behind
the insurrection!' Perhaps, too, he cherished the hope of finding
adversaries of de Gaulle among them. Upon his return, he described
his astonishment. 'I expected,' he told me, 'to find myself surrounded
by noisy and undisciplined insurgents. I was received by a procession of members of parliament, or men who looked like members of
parliament, saluted by the Garde Républicaine in full dress uniforms, taken into a hall filled with an enthusiastic but reasonable
crowd, addressed by two orators who were certainly preparing their
candidacy for the elections. Your revolutionaries look like Labour
Members! This is fine for law and order, but not very picturesque.'
That evening, after we had had another conference, including
Eden and Bidault, and a dinner at the British Embassy, I took
Churchill on a visit to the French First Army.

During the whole of November 13th, under ceaselessly falling
snow, Mr Churchill saw the renascent French Army, its major
units in position, its services functioning, its general-staff at work,
its generals confident; all were prepared for the offensive which was,
in fact, to be launched the next day. Churchill seemed to be deeply
impressed, and stated that he felt more justified than ever in placing
his confidence in France.

Churchill's confidence, however, was insufficient for him to
adopt, towards us, a policy of frank solidarity which might have re-
established Europe and maintained Western prestige in the Middle
East, in Asia and in Africa. The visit he paid us was perhaps the
last possible occasion to bring about a change of heart. I took every
opportunity to do so during the conversations we had together.
I repeated to Churchill: 'You see that France is making a recovery. But whatever my faith in her, I know that she will not regain
her former power all at once. You English, of course, will emerge
from this war covered with glory. Yet—unfair though it may be—
your relative power runs the risk of being diminished because of

your losses and expenses by the centrifugal forces at work within
the Commonwealth, and, particularly, the rise of America and Russia, not to mention China! Facing a new world, then, our two old
nations find themselves simultaneously weakened. If they remain
divided as well, how much influence will either of them wield?
On the other hand, should England and France act together on
tomorrow's peace settlements, they will weigh heavily enough in the
world's scales to prevent anything being done which they themselves have not consented to or determined. It is this mutual resolve
which should be the basis of the alliance you offer us. Otherwise
what is the good of signing a document which would be, at best,
ambiguous?'

'The equilibrium of Europe,' I added, 'the guarantee of peace
along the Rhine, the independence of the Vistula, Danube and
Balkan states, the creation of some form of association with the
peoples all over the world to whom we have opened the doors of
Western civilization, an organization of nations which will be
something more than an arena for disputes between America and
Russia, and lastly the primacy accorded in world politics to a certain
conception of man despite the progressive mechanization of society
—surely these are our great interests in tomorrow's world. Let us
come to an agreement in order to uphold these interests together. If
you are willing to do so, I am ready. Our two nations will follow us.
America and Russia, hobbled by their rivalry, will not raise any
objection. Moreover, we shall have the support of many states and
of world-wide public opinion, which instinctively shies away from
giants. Thus England and France will create peace together, as
twice in thirty years they have together confronted war.'

Winston Churchill answered: 'Certainly I do not envisage a
Franco-British schism. You are the witness and the proof of what I
have done to prevent such a thing when it was most likely. Even
today, I offer you an alliance in principle. But in politics as in
strategy, it is better to persuade the stronger than to pit yourself
against him. That is what I am trying to do. The Americans have
immense resources. They do not always use them to the best advantage. I am trying to enlighten them, without forgetting, of course,
to benefit my country. I have formed a close personal tie with
Roosevelt. With him, I proceed by suggestion in order to influence
matters in the right direction. At present Russia is a great beast

which has been starved for a long time. It is not possible to keep her from eating, especially since she now lies in the middle of the herd of her victims. The question is whether she can be kept from devouring all of them. I am trying to restrain Stalin, who has an enormous appetite, but also has a great deal of common sense. And after a meal comes the period of digestion. When it is time to digest, the surfeited Russians will have their difficult moments. Then, perhaps, Saint Nicholas can bring the poor children the ogre has put in the salting tub back to life. Meanwhile, I attend every meeting, yield nothing for nothing, and manage to secure a few dividends.'

'As for France,' Churchill repeated, 'Thanks to you, she is reappearing in the eyes of the world. Don't be impatient! Already, the doors are ajar. Soon they will be open to you. It will be only natural for you to sit at the table of the Administrative Council. Then nothing will keep us from working together. Until then, leave matters in my hands!'

The Prime Minister left on November 14th to inspect the British sector of the front. Eden had already returned to London. From the statements both had made, it was apparent that England favoured France's political reappearance, that she would continue to do so for reasons of equilibrium, tradition and security, that she desired a formal alliance with us, but would not consent to link her strategy with ours, believing herself in a position to function independently between Moscow and Washington, to limit their demands, but also to take advantage of them. The peace we French hoped to build in accordance with what we regarded as logic and justice, the British found expedient to approach with formulas of empiricism and compromise. Furthermore, they were pursuing certain precise goals which, in areas where the positions of states and the balance of power were not yet determined, offered British ambitions numerous possibilities of manipulation and aggrandizement.

This was especially true in the Mediterranean. Athens, Belgrade, Beirut, Damascus and Tripoli, under various London labels, would tomorrow supplement British influence previously dependent on Gibraltar, Malta, Cyprus, Cairo, Amman and Baghdad. Thus the concessions which Great Britain had not been able to avoid making to Russian voracity and American capitalist ideology found their counterpart. No ordeal changes the nature of man; no crisis that of states.

In short, we found occupying the comfortable chairs in the club of the great powers as many hallowed egotisms as there were charter members. On my visit to Washington, Roosevelt had disclosed American ambitions, which though draped in idealism were actually quite practical. The London leaders had just shown that they aimed at achieving specifically British goals. Now, the masters of the Kremlin were to show us that they served the interests of Soviet Russia alone.

Indeed, immediately after Mr Churchill's and Mr Eden's visit to France, Mr Bogomolov took every opportunity of urging me to visit Moscow. Since France was once again free and able to take an active part in the conflict, and since her Government was once again established in Paris, it was my intention to make direct contact with Stalin and his ministers. I therefore accepted their invitation, as well as the programme drawn up by Mr Molotov and our ambassador, Roger Garreau. It was agreed that, accompanied by Georges Bidault, I would spend a week in the Soviet capital. In this way we and the Russians could learn how each of us saw the future peace settlement. Perhaps it would be possible to renew old Franco-Russian solidarity which, though repeatedly betrayed and repudiated, remained no less a part of the natural order of things, as much in relation to the German menace as to the endeavours of Anglo-American hegemony. I even envisaged a pact by virtue of which France and Russia would commit themselves to act in common if Germany should ever become a threat again. This dangerous hypothesis would probably not be realized, at least not in the foreseeable future. But the signing of a Franco-Russian treaty could help us to participate at once in the elaboration of European settlements.

Before setting out for the Kremlin, I wanted to formulate France's conditions for future settlements in public. The Consultative Assembly were debating Foreign Affairs. As usual, the speeches revelled in generalities or quivered with idealism, but the discussion remained vague about practical objectives. All condemned Hitlerism, but failed to specify what should be done with Germany. They lavished their warmest tokens of admiration upon our allies, but asked them for nothing but friendship. They regarded it as essential that France recover her status, but avoided giving indications as to the route and the means. In my speech on November

22nd, therefore, I took particular pains to make our conditions explicit.

First of all I said that 'we were beginning to possess means of diplomatic action worthy of France'.—'Almost every foreign Government,' I said, 'has now recognized the Government of the Republic. As for Germany, our artillery, in Alsace and other places, is in the process of gaining recognition in the only suitable manner—that is, by victory. . . . Elsewhere, we are participating in the European Commission in London and in that on Italian Affairs. . . . We have just had a series of frank, extensive and friendly meetings with the British Prime Minister and Secretary of State for Foreign Affairs. We propose to have the same kind of meetings with the Soviet Government during our imminent visit to Moscow. . . . We intend to confer eventually, under similar conditions, with the President of the United States of America.' Thus I demonstrated that France was regaining the status she needed to play her role again.

This role was to be that of one of the greatest states. I emphasized the fact by referring to the future organization of the United Nations and to our wish to sit on the Security Council. 'We believe,' I said, 'that the powers which are in a position to act materially and morally in the various parts of the world should exercise in common the duty of encouragement and orientation. . . . In our eyes, France is, beyond all possible doubt, one of these powers.' I added, 'We are ready, once again, to bear our share of the responsibilities which preponderating powers imply. In return, we expect to be committed by no measure concerning Europe and by no major decision concerning other parts of the world in which we have not deliberated under the same conditions as those who adopted them.'

This was particularly important in regard to Germany. 'As for the occupation of German territory, the administrative system decided on for the occupied German peoples, their own future regime, the ultimate eastern, western, southern or northern German frontiers, the measures of economic, spiritual and military control to be imposed, or the fate of the populations which can be separated from the German State, France will be a party to such arrangements only if she has also been an adjudicator.' I further specified: 'We can countenance a settlement only if it guarantees us the elemental security which nature has defined by the Rhine, for us as for Bel-

gium, Holland and to a large degree, England.' But I declared that
by imposing upon Germany a fate that was obligatorily pacific,
France intended to lay the foundations for that valuable edifice:
the future unity of Europe. 'We believe in this unity!' I proclaimed,
'and we hope that it will be translated, to begin with, into specific
acts binding its three poles: Moscow, London and Paris.'

After indicating our intention of determining with Italy 'the
reparations for the injuries she had caused us' and our desire 'to
institute subsequently with the Italian Government and people,
relations which will establish a sincere reconciliation'. After men-
tioning events in the Pacific, our decision 'to play an increasingly
important role in the common war effort there', and our desire 'to
recover all that the enemy has snatched from us', I concluded:

'Perhaps France is now confronting one of those moments in
history when a people is offered a destiny great in proportion to the
gravity of its ordeal. But we cannot uphold our rights nor accomplish our duties if we forgo power itself. . . . Despite our losses
and our woes, despite human weariness, we must reinstate the power
of France! This, henceforth, is our great cause!'

The Assembly warmly applauded this speech. It unanimously
passed an order of the day approving the Government's action with
regard to foreign policy. In this sphere, however, there were profound differences of attitude between the 'politicians' and myself.
Not that the parliamentarians of yesterday or tomorrow had reservations about the concrete goals I indicated. But they hailed them
from afar and, in point of fact, committed themselves only vaguely.
Rather than the problems confronting states—frontiers, security,
the balance of forces—they were concerned with doctrinal attitudes
affecting public opinion. Hence their speeches were as nebulous as
they were moving.

As long as we celebrated, for instance, 'the coming victory of
justice and liberty by the defeat of fascism', or 'the revolutionary
mission of France,' or 'the solidarity of the democracies', or 'the
building of peace on the co-operation of peoples', the delegates were
in a receptive state of mind. But once explicit dealings with the Saar
Basin, the Rhine, the Ruhr, Silesia, Galicia, the Levant or Indochina were suggested; once someone said 'No!' ahead of time to what
our allies would decide without us; once it was stated that if we were
throwing in our lot with theirs it was not because England was a

parliamentary nation, America democratic, and Russia a soviet state, but because all three were fighting against our invaders— then the members of the audience, while seeming attentive and even approving, indicated by various signs that it found the light too bright. On the present occasion, however, the idea that I should go to Moscow and conclude a Franco-Russian pact received the Assembly's adherence. Its members were in favour of this action since most of them preferred to regard it solely as a friendly gesture toward an ally.

On November 24th, I flew to Russia, accompanied by Georges Bidault. With us were General Juin, M. Palewski, M. Dejean, etc.; Mr Bogomolov was to serve as our guide. Stopping in Cairo, I visited King Farouk. Prudent, well informed, quick-witted, the young sovereign made no attempt to conceal his anxiety about the situation in Egypt. Although his country was taking no direct part in the world conflict, the King was delighted by the approaching defeat of Hitler. But he was no less fearful that the Western victory would destroy an already precarious balance in the Middle Eastern Arab states. He feared that a Sudanese-Egyptian union would be checkmated by such a victory and, above all, that a Jewish state would be established in Palestine. The consequences of these events on the Arab world would be a wave of extremist nationalism, a serious crisis in foreign relations, and severe internal upheavals.

The sovereign, moreover, declared his and his people's sympathy for France. 'We have every confidence in your future,' he said, 'for we have great need of you.' When I pointed out that his Government had nevertheless censured us harshly about the conditions under which Syria and Lebanon were achieving independence, he declared, smiling 'That's only politics!' I knew that personally he was not in favour of Nahas Pasha, whom the English had appointed his Prime Minister. Finally, Farouk assured me of his esteem for the French colony which was vitally contributing to his country's progress.

Teheran was the next stop on our journey. The capital of Iran betrayed the strain of the triple occupation imposed on it. British, Russians and Americans jostled each other in the streets and watched each other amongst the poverty-stricken crowd, while the Persian elite sulkily withdrew. What a contrast to the favour with which educated circles regarded France! I had touching proofs of the latter when I received many distinguished Persians whom Ambassador Pierre Lafond invited to our legation.

During my visit to him, the Shah also showed himself to be extremely friendly. Sadly he explained the situation foisted upon his empire and himself by the presence and the demands of the three great powers whose rivalries threatened to dismember the state and national territory. The sovereign, obviously discouraged, asked my advice. 'You see,' he said, 'what we have come to. In your opinion, what should be my position? Having taken your country's destiny upon yourself at the most difficult moment, you are qualified to tell me.'

I replied to Mohammed Reza Pahlevi that if there had ever been a moment for Iran to have an emperor symbolizing the country's sovereignty and unity, that moment was now. Therefore he himself must not leave the throne under any pretext. 'As for the foreign powers,' I declared, 'in relation to them, Your Majesty must be independence personified. You may find yourself obliged to endure humiliation, but you must always repudiate them. If one or another of the three occupying powers attempts to obtain your co-operation to his advantage, let him find you inaccessible, even when this attitude involves considerable discomfort for yourself! Sovereignty can be nothing more than a spark in a woodpile: once it has been struck, it will sooner or later catch fire.' I assured the Shah that as France recovered her forces and her status, she would not fail to support Iran's efforts to bring about the departure of the Allied troops, as soon as the German threat was averted from the country. The emperor thanked me, adding that he had been comforted by the advice I had given him.

On November 26th, we landed in Baku. After a welcome by the Soviet authorities, I received a military salute and watched while a splendid detachment of troops—bayonets down, chests out, steps thundering—marched by. Here indeed was the eternal Russian Army. Afterward we were driven into the town at great speed, to a house where our hosts, Mr Bogomolov showing particular zeal among them, lavished attentions on us. While we should have preferred to continue our trip as soon as possible, the Soviets said that since our plane crew did not know either the route or the signals, it would have to be Russian planes that carried us; furthermore, since bad weather made flight too hazardous at the beginning of winter, a special train had been reserved for us and was soon due in Baku to take us to Moscow. In short, we had to spend two days visiting the half-deserted city, attending a performance at the municipal theatre, reading the Tass news dispatches, and eating meals of an incredible luxury and abundance.

The special train was called the 'Grand Duke' because Grand Duke Nicholas had used it during the first World War. In its well-furnished cars we made a trip that lasted for four days, due to the slow speed necessitated by the state of the roadbeds. Stepping outside at the station stops, we were invariably surrounded by a silent but obviously cordial crowd.

I had asked to visit Stalingrad, a gesture of respect to the Russian armies who had won the war's decisive victory here. We found the city completely demolished. Yet among the ruins, a large populace was working, while the authorities applied the watchword *reconstruction* in the most spectacular manner. After taking us on a tour of the battlefield, our guides drove us to a wrecked iron factory where, in a blast furnace only recently patched together, iron ore was again being smelted. But the great tank factory, which we visited next, had been completely rebuilt and re-equipped. As we entered the shops, the workers gathered around us to exchange friendly greetings. On our way back we met a column of men escorted by armed soldiers. These, it was explained, were Russian prisoners going to the yards. I must say that in relation to the 'free' workers, these condemned men seemed neither more nor less passive, neither better nor worse dressed. Having delivered the sword of honour I had brought from France for the city of Stalingrad to the municipality and attended a banquet, where the menu contrasted vividly with the poverty of the inhabitants, we returned to the 'Grand Duke'. We reached Moscow on Saturday, December 2nd.

Mr Molotov met us at the station. He was surrounded by People's Commissars, officials and generals. The entire diplomatic corps was present. Patriotic songs resounded. A battalion of 'cadets' paraded in splendid array. As we came out of the station, I saw that a considerable crowd had gathered, from which arose a hum of sympathetic voices. I then went to the French Embassy where I had decided to stay in order to remain apart from the comings and goings that negotiations inevitably provoked. Bidault, Juin and Dejean were installed in a house the Soviet Government had put at their disposal.

We stayed in Moscow for eight days. During this time, many ideas, inquiries, and suggestions were exchanged between the Russians and ourselves. Bidault and Dejean, accompanied by Garreau and Laloy—both of whom spoke Russian fluently—had various meetings with Molotov and his officials. Juin, accompanied by Petit, chief of our military mission, had a long conversation with the Russian general staff and its chief, General Antonov. But as was to be expected, it was Stalin and de Gaulle who said and did the most important things at these meetings. From Stalin's attitude to every subject we discussed, I got the impression that I was face to face with the astute and implacable champion of a Russia exhausted by suffering and tyranny but afire with national ambition.

Stalin was possessed by the will to power. After a lifetime of machinations he was used to disguising his features as well as his inmost soul, to dispensing with illusions, pity or sincerity and to see in each man an obstacle or a threat. He was all strategy, suspicion and stubbornness. The revolution, the party, the state and the war had given him the opportunity and the means of domination. He had seized them, using a thorough knowledge of the complexities of Marxist dialectic and totalitarian rigour, bringing to bear a super-human boldness and guile and by subjugating or liquidating all others.

Thenceforth, with all Russia in his hands alone, Stalin regarded his country as more mysterious, mightier and more durable than any theory or any regime. He loved it, in his way. Russia herself accepted him as a czar during a terrible epoch and tolerated Bolshevism to turn it to her own advantage, as a weapon. To unite the Slavs, to overcome the Germans, to expand in Asia, to gain access to ice-free seas—these were the dreams of Mother Russia, these were the despot's goals. Two conditions were essential to their realization: to make Russia into a great modern, that is to say industrial, power, and at the right moment to bring her into a world conflict. The first had been fulfilled, at the price of an unprecedented expenditure of human suffering and human loss. Stalin, when I saw him, was accomplishing the second in the midst of graves and rubble. It was his good luck to have found a people so vital and so patient that the worst slavery did not paralyse them, a soil full of such resources that the most terrible destruction and waste could not exhaust it, and allies without whom he would not have conquered his adversary but who would not have triumphed without him.

During the fifteen-odd hours which made up the sum of my interviews with Stalin, I saw the outlines of his ambitious and cryptic policy. As a Communist disguised as a Marshal, a dictator preferring the tactics of guile, a conqueror with an affable smile, he was a past master of deception. But so fierce was his passion that it often gleamed through this armour, and gave him a certain sinister charm.

Our first conversation took place in the Kremlin on the evening of December 2nd. A lift took us to the door of a long corridor punctuated by an imposing number of secret service men and off one end of which opened a large room furnished with a table and chairs. Molotov led us in and the 'Marshal' appeared. After an exchange of the usual compliments, we sat down around the table. Whether talking or silent, Stalin kept his eyes lowered and doodled with his pencil.

We broached the subject of Germany at once. None of those present doubted that the Reich must soon capitulate to the blows of the Allied armies; the Marshal emphasized the fact that the severest of these blows had been delivered by the Russians. We reached immediate agreement on the necessity of putting Germany in a position of harmlessness. But when I indicated to what degree the geographical separation of Russia and France had affected the outburst of German ambitions, the French capitulation, and consequently the invasion of Soviet territory, when I sketched the prospect of a direct *entente* between the Moscow and Paris Governments in order to establish a settlement which they would jointly propose to the other Allies, Stalin seemed reserved. He insisted, instead, on the necessity of studying each question with the United States and Great Britain, from which I inferred that he already had good reason to anticipate Roosevelt's and Churchill's agreement to what he wanted.

Nevertheless, he asked me what guarantees France hoped for in the West. But when I spoke to him of the Rhine, the Saar Basin and the Ruhr, he declared that the solutions of these problems could be studied only in four-way negotiation. On the other hand, he answered my question as to the German frontier in the east quite categorically: 'The former Polish territory of East Prussia, Pomerania

C

and Silesia must be restored to Poland.'—'In other words,' I asked, 'the Oder frontier?'—'The Oder and the Neisse,' he corrected. 'Besides, there are rectifications to be made in Czechoslovakia's favour too.'

I pointed out that we raised no objection in principle to these territorial changes which, furthermore, might enable the matter of Poland's eastern frontier to be settled in compensation. But I added: 'Permit me to remark that if, in your eyes, the question of the Rhine cannot be broached at present, that of the Oder has already been discussed.'

Stalin kept silent, still drawing his circles and stars. But soon, raising his head, he made the following proposal: 'Let us study a Franco-Russian pact together, in order that our two countries may take common measures against a new German aggression.'

'We are in favour of such a pact,' I answered, 'for the same reasons that led to the signing of the former Franco-Russian alliance and even,' I added, rather maliciously, 'of the 1935 treaty.' Stalin and Molotov, pierced to the quick, exclaimed that the 1935 pact, signed by them with Laval, had never been applied by the latter either in spirit or in letter. I then said that by referring to the 1935 treaty and the 1892 alliance I had intended to accentuate the fact that in dealing with the German menace, common action by Russia and France was in the nature of things. As for the way in which a new pact would eventually be applied, I believed that the painful experiences of the past could serve as lessons to the leaders of both countries. 'For my part,' I added, 'I am not Pierre Laval.' It was agreed that Bidault and Molotov should elaborate the text of a treaty.

On the days following, the two ministers met several times. They exchanged drafts which bore strong resemblances. At the same time, a series of receptions, visits and excursions were held in our honour. I remember particularly a dinner given at the Spiridonovka by Molotov, surrounded by Dekanozov, Litvinov and Lozovski, Deputy-ministers of Foreign Affairs. Stalin was present. At the dessert course, raising his glass, he toasted our imminent alliance. 'I mean,' he cried, 'an alliance that is real, not one *à la Laval*!'

We had a long conversation together. To my compliments upon the success of the Russian Army, whose central sector, under Tolbukhin, had just completed a successful offensive in Hungary, he replied: 'Pah! A few cities! We must drive on to Berlin and Vienna!' At times, he seemed relaxed, even playful. 'It must be very difficult,' he told me, 'to govern a country like France, where everyone is so restless!'

'Yes,' I answered. 'And I cannot imitate your example, for you are inimitable.'

He mentioned Thorez, whom the French Government had allowed to return to Paris. Met by an irritated silence, the Marshal said: 'Don't take offence at my indiscretion! Let me only say that I know Thorez and that in my opinion he is a good Frenchman. If I were in your place, I would not put him in prison.' He added, with a smile, 'At least, not right away!'

'The French Government,' I replied, 'treats the French according to the services it expects of them.'

On another occasion, our hosts took us to a splendid ballet performed at the Grand Theatre. They gave a gala reception in our honour at the Spiridonovka Palace, attended by many People's Commissars, high officials, generals, their wives and all the foreign diplomats and Allied officers in Moscow. They also escorted us to an impressive evening of songs and folk dancing at the Red Army Hall. During these ceremonies, Mr Molotov never left our side, his words were always precise, their object always circumspect. We had other guides, however, when we attended Mass in St-Louis-des-Français, the only Catholic church open in the capital, visited Sparrow Mountain where Napoleon had had his first view of Moscow, visited the military museum, examined the Moscow underground, and inspected several factories, a military hospital and a signal-corps school. Through the cold streets, across the snow, slipped silent and preoccupied citizens; those Russians we made contact with, whether among the people or in official circles, struck us as being eager to show their sympathy but hampered by orders which repressed their spontaneity.

We French, therefore, made greater efforts to express our friendly admiration of this great people, taking advantage of the various social festivities and diplomatic occasions. At the embassy, I gave a dinner for a throng of intellectuals and writers officially catalogued by the Soviet authorities as 'friends of France'. Chief among them were Victor Fink and Ilya Ehrenburg, both men of great talent though determined to use it only in the direction and tone

prescribed. General Ignatiev, who had been a count and the Czar's
military attache in Paris and a celebrated *émigré* for many years
afterwards, was among the guests, defying the years in a becoming
uniform and generous with his grand manner, though hampered by
his present role. Jean-Richard Bloch, 'seeking refuge' in Russia,
introduced them all to me with a certain stilted geniality. All,
mettlesome and touchy, reminded me of hobbled thoroughbreds.
One evening, we invited the whole of official Moscow to the embassy.
There was no flaw in the cordiality of the remarks exchanged. But
among those present could be felt the weight of vague anxiety. As
if by stereotype, each man's personality expressed itself in *grisaille*
which was the common refuge.

Nevertheless, the terms of the pact became increasingly complicated, though the minor divergences separating Bidault's text
from Molotov's could have been settled in a moment. But gradually
the Soviets revealed their bargaining intentions. They sought, first
of all, to gain an advantage over us by raising the question of ratification. 'Given the fact that your Government is a provisional one,
who amongst you is qualified to ratify such a treaty?', Mr Molotov
asked Dejean, then Bidault. Lastly the Soviet Minister of Foreign
Affairs turned to me. I put an end to his scruples. 'You have,' I
told him, 'signed a pact with Benes. Yet his Government, so far as
I know, is a provisional one. Moreover, it is established in London.'
After this, there were no further questions about ratification.

Then the real kernel of the discussion came to light. As we expected, it concerned Poland. Curious to know exactly what the
Russians intended to do in Warsaw when their troops entered the
city, I asked Stalin directly during a conference we were having in
the Kremlin on December 6th. Bidault, Garreau and Dejean were
with me; Molotov, Bogomolov and the excellent interpreter Podzerov were sitting with Stalin.

I remarked that France had always favoured and supported
Polish independence. After the first World War, we had significantly
contributed to its revival. Doubtless the policy subsequently adopted
by Warsaw, Beck's in particular, had displeased and ultimately endangered us, while it obliged the Soviet Union to differ with us.
Nevertheless, we regarded as essential the reappearance of a Poland
in control of her destiny, provided she was friendly to both France
and Russia. Whatever influence we might have over the Poles—I

specified 'over all the Poles'—we were resolved to wield in this direction. I added that the solution of the problem of the frontiers, as Stalin himself had explained it to us—that is, the 'Curzon line' in the east and the 'Oder-Neisse line' in the west—was acceptable to us. But I repeated that in our eyes Poland must be a truly independent state. It was therefore up to the Polish people to choose their future Government. They could do this only after the liberation, and by means of free elections. For the moment, the French Government maintained diplomatic relations with the Polish Government in London, which had never ceased to oppose the Germans. If France was eventually led to change this situation, she would do so only in agreement with her three allies.

Making his statement in turn, Marshal Stalin grew heated. Hearing his words, snarling, snapping and copious, it was apparent that the Polish question was the principal object of his passion and the centre of his policy. He declared that Russia had taken 'a major turn' with regard to this nation which for centuries had been its hereditary enemy and which it henceforth wished to regard as a friend. But there were conditions. 'Poland,' he said, 'has always served as a corridor for the Germans to attack Russia. This corridor must be closed off, and closed off by Poland herself.' To do this, the fact of placing her frontier on the Oder and the Neisse could be decisive, once the Polish state was strong and 'democratic'. For, the Marshal proclaimed, 'there is no strong state which is not democratic'.

Stalin then broached the question of the Government to be established in Warsaw. He did so harshly, his remarks full of hatred and scorn for the 'London Poles,' and praising the 'Lublin Committee' formed under the Soviet aegis and declaring that the latter was the only Government expected and desired in Poland. He gave for this choice, which he asserted was the one the Polish people themselves would make, reasons that demonstrated only his own bias. 'In the battle that is liberating their country,' he declared, 'the Poles do not see the purpose of the reactionary Government in London and the Anders army. On the contrary, they recognize the presence and the action of the "Committee of National Liberation" and the troops of General Berling. They know, moreover, that it was agents of the Government in London who were responsible for the failure of the Warsaw insurrection, which had been set off quite arbitrarily, without consulting the Soviet command and at a moment when the

Russian troops were not in a position to intervene. Furthermore, the
Polish Committee of National Liberation has begun to carry out an
agrarian reform on liberated territory which has won it the enthusiastic support of the people. The lands belonging to the reactionary *émigrés* have been distributed to the farmers. It is from this
that tomorrow's Poland will derive her strength, as Revolutionary
France derived hers from the sale of national assets.'

Then Stalin challenged me. 'You say France has some influence
over the Polish people. That is true! But why don't you use that
influence to recommend the essential solution? Why do you take the
same sterile position as America and England have hitherto adopted?
I should tell you that we expect you to act realistically and in the same
direction as we do.' He added, under his breath, 'Especially since
London and Washington haven't said their last word.'

'I do take account,' I replied, 'of your position. I see its vast
consequences. But I must repeat that the future Government of
Poland is the business of the Polish people and that the latter, we are
convinced, must be able to express themselves by universal suffrage.'

I had expected some violent reaction on the Marshal's part, but
he merely smiled and murmured softly, 'Bah! We'll understand each
other anyway.'

Eager to continue this exploration, I asked Stalin what fate he
envisaged for the Balkan States. He replied that Bulgaria, having
accepted the Allied armistice conditions, would keep her independence, but that 'she would receive the punishment she deserved'
and that she too must become 'democratic'. The same would apply
to Rumania. Hungary had been on the point of surrendering to the
Allies. But the Germans, having learned of this—'I don't know how,'
Stalin said—had arrested the regent, Horthy. 'If a democratic
Government is formed in Hungary,' the Marshal added, 'we will
help it turn against Germany.' There was no such problem in the
case of Yugoslavia, 'since the country has united and risen against
fascism.' Stalin spoke violently against Mikhailovitch, whom he
seemed to believe the British were concealing in Cairo. As for Greece,
'the Russians have not penetrated there, leaving it to the British
troops and ships. If you want to know what is happening in Greece,
you should ask the British.'

From this conference, it was evident that the Soviets were resolved
to deal just as they chose with the states and territories occupied or

about to be occupied by their forces. There was therefore every reason to expect terrible political oppression in Central and Balkan Europe. It appeared that in this regard Moscow did not believe in determined opposition from Washington and London. Finally, it was apparent that Stalin was going to try to sell us the pact in exchange for our public approbation of his Polish operation.

As in any well-constructed play, in which the plot remains unsolved while the threads mingle and multiply until the *dénouement*, the problem of the pact suddenly assumed an unexpected aspect. Mr Churchill showed his hand. 'I presume,' he telegraphed, in substance, to Marshal Stalin, 'that on the occasion of General de Gaulle's visit you are contemplating the signing of a security treaty including Russia, Great Britain and France. For my part, I am in favour of such a plan.' The Soviets informed us of the British proposal, which they apparently found satisfactory. This was not my opinion.

First of all, we could not accept the form Churchill employed. Why did he address himself exclusively to Stalin in a matter concerning France as much as London and Moscow? Above all, I considered that in regard to the German danger, Russia and France must make a private agreement, since they were the states most directly and immediately threatened. Events had proved as much, and at what cost! In case of a German threat, the chances were that British intervention would occur neither at the time nor on the scale required. Particularly since England could do nothing without the— problematical—consent of the other Commonwealth states. Must Paris and Moscow wait to act until London was ready to do so? Lastly, if I eventually wished to renew and sharpen the existing alliance between France and England, I wished to do so only after having settled certain fundamental questions with London: the fate of Germany, the Rhine, the Middle East, etc., so far there were no agreements. In short, we were not going to agree to the scheme of a tripartite pact. Furthermore, we considered that the moment had come to bring negotiations with the Russians to an end, whether they were successful or not. Accompanied by Bidault, Garreau and Dejean, I presented myself at the Kremlin on December 8th to have a last session of negotiation with Stalin, Molotov and Bogomolov.

I began by outlining how France envisaged the settlement of Germany's fate: no further sovereignty of the central German state on the left bank of the Rhine; the territories thus separated

retaining their German character but receiving their autonomy and
consistency, economically speaking, from the western zone; the
Ruhr placed under international control; the eastern German
frontier marked by the Oder and the Neisse. We regretted that
Russia was unwilling to conclude, with regard to these conditions,
an immediate agreement with France which would then be proposed
to England and the United States. But our position would not be
modified.

As for alliances, we considered that they must be constructed
'in three stages': first a Franco-Russian treaty providing for initial
security; the Anglo-Soviet pact and an agreement still to be made
between France and Great Britain constituting a second degree;
the future United Nations pact, in which America would play a
decisive role, crowning the entire edifice and serving as an ultimate
recourse. I repeated the reasons which determined us not to adopt
Churchill's proposal of a single Anglo-Franco-Russian pact.
Finally, I confirmed the fact that we would be leaving Moscow on
the morning of December 10th, as previously arranged.

Stalin challenged nothing that I said again regarding the German
frontiers. He emphasized the advantages which he believed a
tripartite pact would have. But suddenly, shifting the direction of his
interests, he exclaimed, 'After all, you're right! I don't see why the two
of us shouldn't make a pact. But you must understand that Russia has
a fundamental interest in Poland. We want Poland to be friendly to
the Allies and resolutely anti-German. This is not possible with the
Government in London, which represents as virulent an anti-Rus-
sian spirit as ever. On the contrary, we could come to an understanding with another Poland, a Poland great, strong and democratic. If
you share this view, recognize the Lublin Committee publicly and
make an official agreement with it. Then we can sign a pact with you.
Notice, furthermore, that we Russians have recognized the Polish
Committee of National Liberation, that this Committee is governing
and administrating Poland as the enemy is driven out by our troops,
and that consequently it is to Lublin that you should address yourself in anything that concerns your interests in the country, particularly the fate of prisoners and French deportees whom the retreating
Germans are leaving on the spot. As for Churchill, I shall telegraph
him that his proposal was not accepted. He will be offended, of
course. Once more. But he's offended me often enough.'

Henceforth, everything was clear. I declared openly to Stalin that France was ready to conclude a security pact with Russia; that she bore no ill will toward the Lublin Committee; but that she had no intention of recognizing it as the Government of Poland or dealing with it officially. The practical questions relating to the French prisoners could be settled, as they came up, by a delegate we would send to Lublin without his having diplomatic status. I added: 'France and Russia have a common interest in seeing an independent, united and genuine Poland on the scene, not an artificial Poland in which France, for her part, would have no confidence. In our eyes, the question of the future Polish Government can be settled only by the Poles themselves, after the nation's liberation and with the agreement of the four Allies.'

Stalin made no further observation on this statement. He merely said, good naturedly enough, that he was happy to be seeing us again the next day at the dinner he himself was giving in our honour.

The atmosphere was strained on December 9th. Molotov had confirmed to Bidault the condition set by Stalin for the pact's conclusion. Moreover, he had gone so far as to give him the draft of an agreement between the French Government and Lublin, by virtue of which Paris officially recognized the Polish Committee of Liberation. The Russians extended their good offices to the point of proposing to us, at the same time, the terms of a communiqué announcing the news to the world. The French Minister of Foreign Affairs, naturally, informed the Commissar of the Soviet People that his suggestion was unacceptable. As for me, I attributed our partners' attitude not only to their desire to see France associated with their Polish policy, but also to their estimation of our intentions. To proceed in this manner they must have imagined, despite what I said, that we were interested in signing the pact at any price, lest General de Gaulle find a difficult situation waiting for him in Paris. This was an error on their part, and I was determined to prove as much.

Nevertheless, the chief members of the Lublin Committee, arriving from Galicia a few days before, increased their requests to the French embassy to be received 'on matters of intelligence' by General de Gaulle. Two months before they had been received by Mr Churchill and Mr Eden during the British ministers' trip to Moscow. They had also met M. Mikolajczyk, head of the Polish

Government in London, and several of his ministers who had come to the Russian capital at the joint request of the British and the Soviets. I saw no reason to refuse their visit. Invited to the embassy, they were shown into my offices on the afternoon of the ninth.

Chief among them were Mr Bierut, their president, Mr Osubka-Morawski, in charge of 'Foreign Affairs', and General Rola-Zymierski, responsible for 'National Defence'. During the conversation, I was not greatly impressed by their group. When I expressed France's deep sympathy for their country, which despite its ordeal had never ceased to take part, everywhere in Europe, in the struggle against Germany; the French Government's desire to see Poland reappear independent and friendly to France and her allies; the fact that, without wishing to intrude in their own affairs, we hoped that the Poles would reach agreement among themselves in order to re-establish their Government, they replied in the most partisan tone, insistent upon their faction and their ambitions, subject to an obvious Communist allegiance and obliged to speak lines prepared for them in advance.

Mr Bierut said nothing of the war. He spoke of agrarian reform, explained what he expected from it politically and lavished bitter reproaches upon the *émigré* Government in London. Mr Osubka-Morawski resoundingly declared that Poland, traditionally friendly to France, was now more so than ever. Therefore he asked, in the same terms as Molotov and Stalin had used, for the signing of an agreement between the Polish Committee and the French Government, the exchange of diplomatic representatives, and the announcement of this fact by a mutual communiqué. General Rola-Zymierski declared that the Committee of Liberation had ten well-equipped divisions at its disposal and expressed his total confidence in the Soviet command. Despite my requests, he made no allusion to what the Polish Army had accomplished in Poland in 1939, in France in 1940, in Italy, France and the Low Countries in 1944, or to the battles fought by the national resistance. Between my interlocutors' hackneyed phrases and the way in which *Pravda* daily dealt with Polish affairs, there was too close a resemblance to incline me to recognize the Lublin Committee as an independent Poland.

I informed Mr Bierut, Mr Morawski and Mr Zymierski that the French Government was willing to delegate an officer, Captain Christian Fouchet, to territory in their control to settle practical

questions involving French nationals, particularly our prisoners. We
did not oppose the presence in Paris of a member of their organization to deal with parallel affairs, should there be any. But we remained on official terms, as did virtually all the Allies, with the
Polish Government in London and we contemplated neither agreement nor protocol nor exchange of diplomatic representatives with
the Committee of Liberation. I must say that Mr Osubka-Morawski
then declared, with some dignity, that under these conditions it
would be better to postpone the assignment to Lublin of Captain
Fouchet. 'As you wish!' I replied. My visitors took their leave.

Meanwhile, Mr Averell Harriman, United States ambassador to
Russia, and Mr John Balfour, England's chargé d'affaires, had come
to see me at my invitation. I was determined, as a matter of fact, to
keep them informed of our transactions with the Soviets and to let
them know that we were not going to agree to recognizing the Lublin
Committee. They seemed satisfied with this news. Harriman nevertheless told me, 'For our part, we Americans have decided to behave
to the Russians as if we trusted them.' Hearing this remark and
bearing in mind what Stalin suggested as to America's and England's
imminent reversal of attitude on the Polish problem, I requested the
two diplomats to inform Mr Roosevelt and Mr Churchill on my
behalf that if they were to modify their position, I expected them to
inform us of the fact with the same promptitude I had shown towards
them.

In this day devoted to diplomatic fencing, there was one affecting
hour, when I reviewed the pilots of the 'Normandie-Niémen' squadron. It had originally been agreed with the Russians that I would
inspect the squadron in the Insterburg region, where it was in
operation. But, as had occurred in regard to the Baku-Moscow
flight, our allies asked me to forgo a trip by air because of the bad
weather. Besides, the round trip by road or rail would have taken
three days and three nights. But Stalin, informed of this fact, had the
entire squadron brought to Moscow by train. I could thus salute this
magnificent unit—the only western force fighting on the Russian
front—and make contact with the individuals who were serving
France so valiantly. I took advantage of their presence to decorate, along with several of their number, those Russian generals and
officers who had come from the front for the occasion.

But when we attended the dinner given by Stalin, negotiations were still deadlocked. Until the last moment, the Russians had insisted on getting from us at least a communiqué which would proclaim the establishment of official relations between the French Government and the Lublin Committee, a communiqué which would be made public at the same time as the announcement of the Franco-Russian security pact. We had not agreed to this measure. I was determined not to commit France to an attempted subjection of the Polish nation; not that I had any illusions about what use this refusal might be from a practical point of view. Obviously we had no means of preventing the Soviets from executing their plans. Also, I foresaw that America and Great Britain would let them proceed as they wished. But however little weight France's attitude might have at the moment, it could later be important that she had adopted it at that particular moment. The future lasts a long time. All things are possible, even the fact that an action that accords with honour and honesty ultimately appears to be a prudent political investment.

Forty Russians: People's Commissars, diplomats, generals, high officials, almost all in brilliant uniforms, were gathered in the Kremlin *salon* when the French were shown in. The United States ambassador and the British chargé d'affaires were present. We were taken up the monumental staircase decorated with the same pictures as in the Czar's time. Terrifying subjects were represented in them: the furious battle of the Irtysh, Ivan the Terrible strangling his son, etc. The Marshal shook hands with us and led his guests to the dining room. The table sparkled with inconceivable luxury. We were served an overpowering banquet.

Stalin and I, sitting beside each other, chatted informally. Mr Podzerov and M. Laloy translated our remarks word by word, as we spoke. The operations under way, the life we led in our respective functions, the opinions we had of the chief enemy and Allied leaders, were the subjects of our talk. The pact was not mentioned. The nearest we came to it was when the Marshal asked me, in a detached tone of voice, my impression of the members of the Lublin Committee. To which I replied that they seemed to me a group capable of being turned to account, though they were certainly not 'independent Poland'. Stalin's remarks were direct and simple. He assumed the manners of a peasant of rudimentary culture, applying to the vastest problems the judgments of rough good sense. He ate heavily during each course and served himself copiously from a bottle of Crimean wine frequently replaced in front of him. But beneath these good-natured appearances the fighter engaged in a merciless struggle was apparent. Furthermore, the Russians around the table, watchful and constrained in manner, never took their eyes from him. On their part, manifest submission and apprehensiveness; on his, concentrated and vigilant authority—these were, as far as I could see, the relations of this political and military general staff with this sociably solitary leader.

Suddenly the picture changed. The time for toasts had come. Stalin began playing an extraordinary role.

He had, first of all, warm words for France and kind compliments for me. I made similar remarks on his behalf and on that of Russia. He toasted the United States and President Roosevelt, then England and Mr Churchill, and listened solemnly to Harriman's and Balfour's replies. He saluted Bidault, Juin and each of the other Frenchmen there, the French Army and the 'Normandie-Niémen' squadron. These formalities accomplished, he put on his big show.

Thirty times Stalin stood up to drink to the health of those Russians present. One after the other he designated them: The People's Commissars, Molotov, Beria, Bulganin, Voroshilov, Mikoyan, Kaganovitch, etc., received their master's tribute first. Then he moved on to the generals and officials. The Marshal solemnly described each man's task and his merit in fulfilling it. But he continually declared and exalted the power of Russia herself. He shouted, for instance, to the Marshal of Artillery: 'Voronov! To your health! You are the man in charge of deploying the system of our large- and small-bore guns on the battlefields. It is thanks to this system that the enemy has been overwhelmed all along the line. Go to it! Bravo for your artillery!' Then, addressing himself to the Chief of the Naval General Staff: 'Admiral Kuznetzov! Not enough is known about all that our fleet is doing! Be patient! A day will come when we shall rule the seas!' Calling on Yakovlev, the aeronautics engineer who had perfected the splendid *Yak* pursuit plane: 'I salute you! Your planes sweep the skies. But we need still more and better planes. It is up to you to make them!' Sometimes Stalin mingled threats with his praise. He attacked Novikov, Chief of the Air Force General Staff: 'You are the one who uses our planes. If you use them badly, you should know what's in store for you.' Pointing towards

one of the guests: 'There he is! That is the supply director. It is his job
to bring men and material to the front. He'd better do his best. Otherwise he'll be hanged for it—that's the custom in our country.' As he
finished each toast, Stalin shouted 'Come here!' to whoever he had
just named. The latter, leaving his place, ran forward to clink glasses
with the Marshal under the stares of the other stiff and silent
Russians.

This tragicomic scene could have no other purpose than to im-
press the French by displaying Soviet might and the domination of
the man at its head. Having witnessed it, I was still less inclined to
support the sacrifice of Poland. Therefore it was with marked un-
concern, in the *salon* after dinner, that I observed, sitting around
Stalin and myself, the obstinate chorus of diplomats: Molotov,
Dekanozov and Bogomolov on the one side; Bidault, Garreau and
Dejean on the other. The Russians tirelessly returned to the delibera-
tion on the recognition of the Lublin Committee. But since, for me,
the question was closed, and since I had announced as much, I
regarded this new discussion as futile. Knowing, furthermore, the
propensity of diplomacy's technicians to negotiate in every case, even
at the expense of political goals, and mistrusting the communicative
warmth of an extended encounter, I was apprehensive lest our team
of ministers be induced to make some distressing concessions with
regard to terms. Of course the issue would not be affected, for my
decision was made. But it would have been regrettable if the French
delegation appeared to lack unity.

I therefore pretended not to be interested in the council's arguments. Noticing this, Stalin bid even higher: 'Ah, these diplomats!'
he exclaimed. 'What chatterers! There's only one way to shut them
up: mow them all down with a machine gun! Someone get me one!'
Then, leaving the negotiators and followed by his other guests, he
led me into a neighbouring room to see a Soviet film made for
propaganda purposes in 1938. It was an extremely conformist and
quite naive affair; the Germans were shown treacherously invading
Russia, but the invaders were soon forced to retreat before the energy
of the Russian people, the courage of its army and the valour of its
generals. They were then invaded in their turn; revolution broke out
all over Germany, triumphing in Berlin where, on the ruins of
fascism and thanks to the help of the Soviets, an era of peace and
prosperity was prophesied. Stalin laughed and clapped his hands.

'I'm afraid Monsieur de Gaulle was not pleased by the end of the story.' Somewhat annoyed, I replied: 'In any case, your victory pleases me. Particularly since at the beginning of the actual war, relations between you and the Germans were not as we saw them in this film.'

Meanwhile, I had sent for Georges Bidault to ask whether the Soviets were ready to sign the pact. The Minister of Foreign Affairs answered that everything depended on our acceptance of a joint declaration by the French Government and the Polish Committee, a declaration which would be published at the same time as the communiqué about the Franco-Russian security pact. 'Under these conditions,' I told Bidault, 'it is useless and will become disadvantageous to continue the negotiations. I shall therefore bring it to an end.' At midnight, the film over and the lights on again, I stood up and said to Stalin: 'I am making my farewells. Soon the train will be taking me back to France. I cannot thank you enough for the way in which you yourself and the Soviet Government have received me in your gallant country. We have informed each other as to our respective points of view. We have marked our agreement on the essential point, which is that France and Russia shall continue the war together until complete victory. Au revoir, Monsieur le Maréchal!' At first Stalin seemed not to understand: 'Stay then,' he murmured. 'We're going to show another film.' But when I held out my hand, he shook it and let me leave. I reached the door, bowing to the other guests, who seemed paralysed with astonishment.

Mr Molotov rushed up. His face pale, he accompanied me to my car. To him, too, I expressed my delight with my visit. He stammered a few syllables without being able to conceal his confusion. There was no doubt that the Soviet minister was profoundly sorry to see the failure of a project he had pursued with such tenacity. There remained little time to shift positions before the French left the capital. Obviously the attempt to obtain recognition of the Lublin Committee by Paris had failed. But furthermore, as matters now stood, there was every danger that de Gaulle would return to France without having signed the pact. What effect would this have? Would it be Molotov that Stalin would blame for the failure? For my part, resolved to win the argument, I returned calmly to the French embassy. Learning that Bidault had not followed me, I sent someone to ask him to do so. We left Garreau and Dejean behind. They

would maintain contacts which might be useful but would not commit us.

Fundamentally, I had few doubts as to what would happen next.
As a matter of fact, toward two in the morning, Maurice Dejean
came to report a new development. After a long meeting between
Stalin and Molotov, the Russians had announced that they were
disposed to accept a profoundly adulterated text with regard to
relations between Paris and Lublin. Garreau and Dejean felt they
could suggest a version of this kind: 'By agreement between the
French Government and the Polish Committee of National Liberation, Captain Christian Fouchet has been sent to Lublin, M. . . . has
been sent to Paris.' Then Mr Molotov indicated that 'if General de
Gaulle accepted this solution of the Polish problem, the Franco-
Russian pact could be signed at once'.

Of course, I refused any mention of an 'agreement' with the
Lublin Committee. The only release which, for several days, could
accord with French policy and with the truth was simply: 'Captain
Fouchet has arrived in Lublin.' Dejean left to inform Molotov of
this, and the latter, after conferring again with Stalin, announced
that he was satisfied. A final condition, however, was that the date of
Fouchet's arrival in Lublin should be made public at the same time
as the announcement of the signing of the Franco-Russian security
pact, that is, within twenty-four hours. This was precisely the coincidence I wished to avoid, and I sent Dejean to say so formally. This
was on December 10th, which was to have been the date of the pact.
Fouchet's presence in Galicia would not be announced until the
28th, at the earliest. This condition was accepted.

Meanwhile, Bidault had returned to the Kremlin to draw up the
final text of the pact with our partners. This was presented to me and
I approved it as a whole: in it was stated the commitment of both
sides to continue the war until complete victory, not to conclude a
separate peace with Germany, and finally, to take in common all
measures designed to oppose a new German threat. Mention was
made of the participation of both countries in the United Nations
organization. The treaty was to be valid for a period of twenty years.

I was informed that the final negotiations had been concluded in
the Kremlin, in a room next to those where the evening's guests
continued to come and go. During these difficult hours, Stalin kept
himself continually informed of the negotiations and arbitrated, as

they went along, on Russia's behalf. But this did not keep him from going into the *salons* to chat and drink with one man or another. Colonel Pouyade, commander of the 'Normandie' Squadron, was the object of his particular attention. Finally, I was informed that everything was ready for the signing of the pact. This would take place in Mr Molotov's office, which I went to at four in the morning.

The ceremony became rather solemn. Russian photographers, silent and not making any requests for poses, took pictures. The two Ministers of Foreign Affairs, surrounded by the two delegations, signed the copies drawn up in French and in Russian. Stalin and I stood behind them. 'Thus,' I said to him, 'the treaty has been ratified. On this point, I imagine, your anxiety has been dispelled.' Then we shook hands. 'We must celebrate this!' the Marshal declared. In a second, tables were brought in and we sat down to supper.

Stalin was a good loser. In a low voice, he congratulated me: 'You played your hand well! Well done! I like dealing with someone who knows what he wants, even if he doesn't share my views.' In contrast with the fierce scene he had played a few hours before, drinking toasts to all his collaborators, he now spoke of everything in a detached way, as if he looked at other men, the war, history and himself from a pinnacle of serenity. 'After all,' he said, 'only death wins.' He pitied Hitler, 'a poor wretch who won't escape from this one'. To my invitation: 'Will you come and see us in Paris?' he answered, 'How can I? I'm an old man. I'm going to die soon.'

He raised his glass in honour of France 'who now had resolute, intractable leaders', and whom he wanted to see 'great and powerful because Russia needed a great and powerful ally'. Finally he drank to Poland, though there was no Pole present. It was as if he were insisting on underlining his intentions. 'The Czars,' he said, 'had a bad policy of trying to dominate the other Slav peoples. We have a new policy. Let Slavs everywhere be independent and free! Then they will be our friends. Long live a strong, independent and democratic Poland! Long live the friendship of France, Poland and Russia!' He looked at me. 'What does Monsieur de Gaulle think of that?' Listening to Stalin, I measured the abyss separating words from deed in the Soviet world. I replied, 'I am in complete agreement with what Monsieur Stalin said about Poland,' and emphasized: 'Yes, in agreement with what he said.'

The farewells, on his part, became effusive. 'You can count on me!' he declared. 'If you or France needs us, we will share what we have with you down to our last crumb!' Suddenly, calling over Podzerov, the Russian interpreter who had attended every meeting and translated every exchange, the Marshal said to him, his expression grim, his voice harsh: 'You know too much! I'd better send you to Siberia.' I left the room with my ministers. Turning back at the door, I saw Stalin sitting, alone, at the table. He had started eating again.

Our departure from Moscow took place that morning. The return trip, too, was made by way of Teheran. On the way, I wondered how French public opinion would view the Kremlin pact, given the avatars of the Franco-Russian alliance during the last thirty years and the propaganda battles which, because of the development of Communism, had for so long distorted the problem. On our way through Cairo, I had a first indication. Ambassador Lescuyer presented the French colony to me, this time united in its enthusiasm, whereas on the occasion of my earlier visits, in 1941 and 1942, the colony had been divided. Here as elsewhere it was apparent that of all influences, the strongest is that of success.

The visit to Tunis was distinguished by an impressive reception the Bey insisted on giving me at Palais du Bardo. Alongside this wise sovereign, meeting Tunisians of the highest quality, in this residence with echoes of history, I saw the elements necessary for the functioning of a state. The latter, prepared by our protectorate, seemed about ready to take to its own wings, with France's assistance. On December 16th we were in Paris.

The general reaction to the signing of the pact was indeed satisfactory. The public saw it as a sign of our return to the concert of great powers. The political parties appreciated it as a reassuring link in the chain that held the United Nations together. Certain professional critics—or fanatics—whispered that the treaty had been effected only by concessions to the French Communist party, its moderation in the political and social struggle and its participation in the nation's recovery. But on the whole, for various reasons, the response to the Moscow agreement was distinctly favourable. The Consultative Assembly, too, expressed its approval. Bidault opened the session on December 21st by discussing the stipulations the pact actually involved; I closed it by explaining 'what had been, what was, and what would be the philosophy behind the Franco-Russian alliance we have just concluded'.

Nevertheless the general euphoria did not distract my attention from the disturbing probabilities revealed by the Moscow discussions. We must expect Russia, America and England to conclude a series of bargains from which the rights of France, the liberty of peoples, and the equilibrium of Europe had everything to lose.

As a matter of fact, at the beginning of January, without any diplomatic communication having been made to us, the Anglo-American press announced that Mr Roosevelt, Marshal Stalin and Mr Churchill were to hold a conference. The 'Big Three' would decide what was to be done in Germany after the Reich's 'unconditional surrender'. They would determine their behaviour with regard to the peoples of Central and Balkan Europe. They would, finally, prepare the convocation of an assembly with a view to organizing the United Nations.

Naturally I was offended that we were not invited, but I was not at all surprised. Whatever progress we had made along the road that would lead France to her place, I knew the starting point too well to believe that we had reached our goal already. Moreover, there was every evidence that our present exclusion would provoke a demonstration greatly to our advantage. For matters had ripened so that we could not be kept out of what was to be done. Although Roosevelt, Stalin and Churchill could reach decisions regarding Germany and Italy, they would be obliged, in order to apply them, to ask for General de Gaulle's co-operation. As for the Vistula, the Danube and the Balkan States, America and England would doubtless abandon them to the discretion of the Soviets. In that case the world would discover that there was a correlation between France's absence and new lacerations for Europe. Finally, judging that the time was ripe to indicate that France did not approve of the way she was being treated, I decided to take this exceptional occasion to do so.

Actually, among the 'Big Three', only one state was opposed to our presence. To emphasize this fact, the British and Russians immediately had recourse to semi-official informants. Naturally I had no illusions that Marshal Stalin, who knew my position with regard to Poland, and Mr Churchill, who expected to obtain carte blanche in the Middle East from his partners, had stipulated that de Gaulle sit beside them ● the council table. But I could not doubt that the explicit refusal came from President Roosevelt. Moreover, he himself felt he must make his attitude explicit. For this purpose, he delegated his closest adviser and intimate friend, Harry Hopkins, as his 'special envoy' to Paris.

Hopkins arrived several days before the Yalta Conference began. I received him on January 27th. Accompanied by Ambassador Caffery, Harry Hopkins was supposed to 'sugar-coat' the pill. But since he was a high-minded as well as a skilful man, he approached the matter from its most significant aspect and asked to discuss the fundamental question of Franco-American relations. It was in this way, certainly, that matters could best be illuminated. Hopkins expressed himself with great frankness. 'There is,' he said, 'a discomfort in the relations between Paris and Washington. Yet the war's end is approaching. To a certain extent the world's future will depend on the concerted action of the United States and France. How can we bring their relations out of the impasse in which they are lodged?'

I asked Hopkins what, in American eyes, was the cause of the unfortunate state of relations between the two nations. 'The cause,' he replied, 'is above all the stupefying disappointment we suffered when we saw France collapse and surrender in the disaster of 1940. Our traditional concept of her value and her energy was overthrown in an instant. Add to this the fact that those French military or political leaders in whom we successively placed our trust because they seemed to symbolize the France we had believed in did not show themselves—and this is the least that can be said—worthy of our hopes. Do not seek elsewhere for the true source of the attitude we have adopted towards your country. Judging that France was no longer what she had been, we could not trust her to play one of the leading roles.

'It is true that you yourself, General de Gaulle, appeared on the scene; that a French resistance movement formed around you; that French forces have returned to the fight; that today all France cheers you and recognizes your Government. Since at first we had no motive for believing in this prodigy, since you then became the living proof of our mistake, since you yourself, finally, have not dealt sparingly with us, we have not favoured you up to the present. But we acknowledge what you have accomplished and are delighted to see France reappear among the Allies. Yet how could we forget what we have lived through on her account? Furthermore, knowing the

political inconsistency that riddles your country, what reason have
we to suppose General de Gaulle will be in a position to lead her for
long? Are we not then justified in being circumspect as to the share
we expect France to bear of the burden of tomorrow's peace?'

Listening to Harry Hopkins, I felt I was hearing again what
President Roosevelt had said to me about France in Washington,
six months before. But at that time the Liberation had not yet taken
place. I and my Government were still established in Algeria: there
was still some excuse for American doubts as to the mind of Metropolitan France. At present, everything was decided. It was known
that our people wanted to take part in the victory. It was apparent
that our reviving army was worthwhile. It was recognized that I had
been installed in Paris at the head of a Government surrounded and
supported by national enthusiasm. Yet the United States was no
more convinced that France was capable of becoming a great power
once again. Did it truly want to help her? These were the questions
which, from the French point of view, dominated the present and
future of our relations with the United States.

I declared as much to the President's special envoy. 'You have
told me why, from your side, our relations are flawed. I am going to
show you what, on our side, contributes to the same result. Let us
pass over the episodic and secondary frictions provoked by the ab-
normal conditions under which our alliance is operating. For us,
this is the crux of the matter. In the mortal dangers we French have
survived since the beginning of the century, the United States does
not give the impression that it regards its own destiny as linked with
that of France, that it wishes France to be great and strong, that it is
doing all it can to help her to remain so or become so once again.
Perhaps, in fact, we are not worth the trouble. In that case, you are
right. But perhaps we shall rise again. Then you will have been
wrong. In either case, your behaviour tends to alienate us.'

I reminded him that the disaster of 1940 was the result of the
excessive ordeals the French had endured. Yet during the first
World War the United States intervened only after three years of
fighting in which we had exhausted ourselves repulsing German
aggression. America, moreover, had entered the conflict solely because of the damage to her commerce by German submarines and
after attempting to make a compromise peace according to the terms
of which France would not even have recovered Alsace and Lorraine.

Once the Reich was conquered, America had refused France the
security pledges formally promised her, had exercised a stubborn
pressure upon her to renounce the guarantees and the reparations
due to her, and lastly had given Germany all the help she needed for
a return to power. 'The result,' I said, 'was Hitler.'

I recalled the immobility of the United States when the Third
Reich attempted to dominate Europe; the neutrality she clung to
while France suffered the disaster of 1940; the rejection by Franklin
Roosevelt of Paul Reynaud's appeal, when a mere promise of help,
even secret and long-term, would have been enough to persuade our
Government to continue the war; the support granted for so long by
Washington to those French leaders who had subscribed to capitulation and the rebuffs continually offered to those who had continued
the war. 'It is true,' I added, 'that you were obliged to enter the war
when the Japanese, as Germany's allies, attacked Pearl Harbor.
The colossal war effort you have since mustered is about to make
victory a certainty. Rest assured that France is thoroughly aware of
the fact. She will never forget that without you her Liberation
would not have been possible. Still, while she is slowly recovering, it
cannot escape her notice that America is counting on her only as a
subordinate, as is proved by the fact that Washington is furnishing
only a limited supply of arms for the French Army, as well as by what
you yourself have just told me.'

'You have explained the past,' remarked Mr Harry Hopkins, 'in
an incisive but accurate manner. Now America and France face the
future. Once again, how shall we behave so that henceforth they
may act in agreement and in full mutual confidence?'

'If this is really America's intention,' I replied, 'I cannot understand how she can undertake to settle Europe's future in France's
absence. Especially since after pretending to ignore her in the
imminent "Big Three" discussions, she must ask Paris to agree to
whatever has been decided.'

Mr Hopkins and Mr Caffery agreed. They declared that their
Government now attached the highest importance to France's participation in the London 'European Commission', on an equal
footing with America, Russia and Great Britain. They even added
that so far as the Rhine was concerned, the United States was more
disposed than our two other great allies to settle the question in
conformity with our wishes. As for this last point, the question of the

Rhine would not be settled by America any more than by Russia or Great Britain. The solution, if there was one, could eventually be found only by France or by Germany. Both had long sought for it, one contending against the other. Tomorrow, they would perhaps discover it in association.

To conclude the meeting, I said to the two ambassadors: 'You have come on behalf of the President of the United States to discuss the profound problems of Franco-American relations. I think that we have done so. The French have the impression that you no longer consider the greatness of France necessary to the world and to yourself. This is responsible for the coolness you feel in our country and even in this office. If you want relations between our countries established on a different footing, it is up to you to do what must be done. Until you reach a decision, I send President Roosevelt a salute of friendship on the eve of the conference that will bring him to Europe.'

While the 'Big Three' were conferring at Yalta, I felt I must publicly call France to their attention, if indeed they had forgotten her. On February 5th, speaking on the wireless, I gave this warning: 'As for the future peace settlement, we have informed our allies that France will of course be committed to absolutely nothing she has not been in a position to discuss and approve in the same way as the others . . . I specify that the presence of French forces from one end of the Rhine to the other, the separation of the territories on the left bank of the Rhine and of the Ruhr Basin from what will be the German state, the independence of the Polish, Czech, Austrian and Balkan nations are conditions which France judges to be essential . . . We are not distressed, moreover, by the likelihood that it will be up to us to bring some of them to realization, for we are 106 million men, united under the French flag, in immediate proximity to what concerns us most directly.'

On February 12th, the 'Big Three,' concluding the conference, published a communiqué which proclaimed the principles on which they had agreed. They declared that the war would be continued until the Reich surrendered unconditionally; that the three great powers would occupy its territory, each in a different area; that the control and administration of Germany would be exercised by a military commission formed of the commanders in chief, with head-quarters in Berlin. But in the terms of the communiqué, France was invited to join America, England and Russia in occupying a zone of German territory and in being the fourth member of the German Government. Further, the communiqué declared the intention of the 'Big Three' to dissolve all German armed forces, to destroy for ever the German general staff, to punish the war criminals, and lastly to make Germany pay reparations, to whatever degree possible, for the damages she had caused.

To maintain peace and security throughout the world, a 'General International Organization' was to be set up. For this purpose, a conference of all the states which had signed the Atlantic Charter would be held in San Francisco on April 25th and would take as the basis of the 'Organization' the principles defined at the Dumbarton Oaks Conference. Although France had not taken part in this, it was specified that she would be consulted immediately by the three great powers in order to discuss final arrangements with them. This obviously meant that she would sit with them on the 'Security Council'.

The communiqué also included a 'Declaration Regarding Liberated Europe'. This actually concerned Hungary, Rumania and Bulgaria, who had fought with Germany and were now occupied by Russia. The declaration proclaimed the right of all peoples to settle for themselves the re-establishment of democracy, the freedom of elections which would create their Governments, but remained vague as to the practical measures to be applied. In practice it meant leaving the Soviets to their own devices. The three great powers expressed their hope that 'the Government of the French Republic would associate itself with them in regard to the proposed procedure'.

Lastly the 'Big Three' announced that they had 'come to an agreement' regarding the Polish question. They decided that Poland would be bounded, on the east, by the Curzon line and would receive, in the north and west, 'a substantial increase of territory'. As for the political regime, no allusion was made to free elections. A Government, referred to as one of 'national unity', was to be formed 'starting with the provisional Government already functioning in the country', that is, the Polish Committee of Liberation, known as the 'Lublin Committee'. No doubt, it was indicated, the latter would be enlarged 'to include democratic leaders residing in Poland and abroad'. But since there was no reference to the London Government-in-exile,

since the composition of the new Government remained quite unspecified, since no control on the part of the western powers was
provided for, there could be no doubts as to the kind of Government
Poland would receive. Nor as to the authority that would be established in Yugoslavia. Although in regard to this country the Yalta
communiqué referred to the ratification by a future 'National
Assembly', as a matter of fact Tito's dictatorship was recognized
unconditionally. Thus Stalin was given all he asked for in Warsaw
and Belgrade. To this, and this only, France was not—and for good
reasons—invited to accede.

In the course of the same day that the American, British and
Russian leaders published their communiqué, Ambassador Jefferson
Caffery brought me two 'communications' from them. The first was
a formal invitation to France to join the three allies at the council
table to discuss Germany. The second, imputing to 'circumstances'
the fact that France had not been able to discuss the terms of the
'Declaration Regarding Liberated Europe', expressed the hope that
the French Government would nevertheless agree to assume in
common with the other three powers the eventual obligations which
this declaration implied. At the same time, Mr Caffery handed me a
memorandum from the President of the United States in the name
of the 'Big Three'. The President asked France to be a 'sponsoring
power', along with America, Great Britain, Russia and China, at the
next United Nations conference and to participate in the deliberations which the Moscow, Washington, London and Chungking
Governments were going to institute in order to further the organization established at Dumbarton Oaks.

In other words, if it remained inadmissible, from our point of view,
that our three allies should have held their Crimean conference
without us, the steps they were now taking on our behalf were in no
way offensive. Certainly several of their conclusions were irritating
to us, and the proposals by which they sought to attract us would
have to be studied carefully before we accepted them. But on certain
essential points, their communications gave us important satisfac-
tions. This is what I decided after examining the documents brought
by Mr Caffery on February 12th.

During the course of the afternoon, the ambassador asked for
another audience. He brought me a personal message from President
Roosevelt. The latter informed me of his wish to confer with me. He

himself fixed the site of our meeting, which was to take place in
Algiers. If I agreed to go there, he would also set the date.

Roosevelt's invitation seemed to me inopportune. To Mr Harry
Hopkins, who had referred to its likelihood during his visit to Paris,
Georges Bidault had made it clear that it would be better not to
extend it at all. To meet the President immediately after a conference
at which he had opposed my presence was scarcely a suitable move
on my part. The less so since my visit would offer no practical advantage, the Yalta decisions being made, though on the other hand it
might lead others to believe that I agreed to everything that had
been settled there. As a matter of fact, we did not approve the fate
arbitrarily imposed not only upon Hungary, Rumania and Bulgaria,
who had joined the German cause, but also upon Poland and Yugoslavia, who were our allies. Further I suspected that on certain questions—Syria, the Lebanon and Indochina—of direct interest to
France, the 'Big Three' had reached some agreements amongst
themselves which were incompatible with our interests. If Roosevelt
wanted to see de Gaulle for good reasons, why had he not allowed
him to come to the Crimea?

Then again, why should the American President invite the French
President to visit him in France? Early in November I myself had
invited him to meet me in Paris. Although he had not come, he could
either do so now or ask me to choose another site. But how could I agree
to be summoned to a point on the national territory by a foreign chief
of state? Perhaps for Franklin Roosevelt Algiers was not France, but
all the more reason to remind him of the fact. Furthermore, the
President was beginning his journey home through the Middle
Eastern Arab states. On board his cruiser passing through their
waters, he summoned their kings and chiefs of state, including the
Presidents of the Syrian and Lebanese republics placed under French
mandate. What he was offering was to receive General de Gaulle on
the same ship and under the same conditions. I regarded such treatment as an affront, whatever the present relationship of forces. The
sovereignty, the dignity of a great nation must be inviolable. I was
responsible for those of France.

Having consulted my ministers on February 13th, I asked Mr
Jefferson Caffery to inform the President of the United States 'that
it was impossible for me to come to Algiers at this time and without
warning and that, consequently, I could not, to my regret, receive

him there. The French Government had invited him, last November, to come to Paris and greatly regretted that he could not do so at that time, but would be happy to welcome him in the capital should he wish to make a visit at any time whatsoever. If he wished, during his trip, to make Algiers a port of call in spite of this, would he be so kind as to inform us of the fact, in order that we might give the necessary instructions to the Governor General of Algeria for everything to be done in accordance with his wishes.'

This incident provoked a considerable reaction in public opinion the world over. Personally, I should have preferred to avoid such outbreaks. But the American newspapers, obviously trimming their sails to catch the prevailing wind, took pains to present the episode as an insult General de Gaulle had deliberately inflicted on the American President. The latter, moreover, felt no need to conceal his mortification. Upon his return to Washington, he published a communiqué betraying his acrimony about the meeting which had not taken place. In the speech he made to Congress on March 2nd to reveal the results of the Yalta Conference, he made a transparent reference to de Gaulle, as a certain 'prima donna' whose whim had prevented a valuable discussion. For my part, I was content to provide the press with a note explaining the facts.

Roosevelt's bitter remarks offended me, of course. But I was persuaded that they indicated ill humour rather than any profound feeling he entertained in my regard. Had he lived longer, and had we had an opportunity, once the war was won, to discuss matters at leisure, I believe he would have understood and appreciated the reasons that determined my actions as chief of state. No incident could ever have brought me to ignore the range of his mind, his talents or his courage. When death tore him from his gigantic task, at the very moment when he was about to see its victorious conclusion, it was with all my heart that I saluted his memory with regret and admiration.

In France, however, a large proportion of the elements organized to understand one another disapproved of the way in which I had received the President's 'invitation' to come to Algiers. A number of 'politicians' professing to see in Roosevelt the infallible champion of democracy and inhabiting a universe quite unrelated to the motives of superior interest and national dignity which I served, took offence at my attitude. The Communists condemned it because it charac-

terized my reserve towards the excessive concessions Roosevelt had
made to the Soviets. Many businessmen were distressed because my
gesture affected their hopes of American assistance. Prominent citizens are generally inclined to favour the foreigner, provided he is
rich and strong, and to criticize any French action which seems to
indicate a policy. Furthermore, and despite formal precautions, all
these groups had begun to withdraw their support from me as they
foresaw the possibilities of returning to the pleasant tactics of illusion
and denigration.

I was therefore forced to recognize that the notion I had formed of
France's status and rights was shared by few of those who shaped
public opinion. To support my policy, that of national ambition, I
could count less and less on their voices, their pens and their influence. I must confess that I was profoundly affected by this initial
dissension, which with increasing effect compromised all my future
efforts.

But what was won was won securely. No foreign opposition, no
internal discord could henceforth keep France from resuming her
proper status. After all, the Yalta Conference itself had just demonstrated the fact: if we were invited to become, at once, a member of
the council formed by the great powers to settle the fate of our
enemies and organize the peace, it was because we were regarded as
one of the chief belligerent—and shortly to be victorious—powers.
In world politics, soon nothing would remain of the conquered-
nation status which France had appeared to stoop to, nor of Vichy's
legitimacy which had inspired a pretence of support. The success of
the undertaking begun on June 18th, 1940 was assured in the international sphere as it had been in the domain of arms and in the soul
of the French people. The goal would be achieved because the action
had been inspired by a France which would remain France for its
sons and for the world. In spite of the misfortunes endured and the
renunciations paraded, this was the truth of the matter. There is no
success which does not start from the truth.

III. ORDER

IF THE SOURCES of style, as Buffon says, are order and movement, the same is true of politics. Now the (winds of change) were sweeping over liberated France, but order had to be enforced or all would be lost. Yet so serious were the wounds our country had endured, so painful the living conditions in which the war's damages and continuation had kept us, so great the upheaval of established values—within the state, social hierarchies, families and tradition—that we were plunged into a general crisis affecting the life of every citizen at some point. The joy the French took in their Liberation may have momentarily concealed the true state of affairs from them. Now, the realities appeared all the harder to bear. For myself, when I looked into the distance I could see blue sky on the horizon. But close at hand, seeing the terrible elements of chaos seething in the crucible of public affairs, I was reminded of Macbeth before the witches' cauldron.

First of all, we lacked food to satisfy the barest needs of existence. Twelve hundred calories a day was all the official rations allowed for each individual's sustenance. The essential extras could be procured only by recourse to the black market which was both ruinous and demoralizing. Since there was no wool, no cotton and scarcely any leather, many citizens were wearing threadbare clothes and walking on wooden shoes. There was no heat in the cities, for the small amount of coal being mined was reserved for the armies, railways, power plants, basic industries and hospitals. Nothing filtered through to private citizens. Yet the first winter of the Liberation happened to be one of the severest ever known. At home, at work, in offices and in schools, everyone shivered with cold. Save for an occasional hour, gas pressure was low and electricity subject to interruptions. Since trains were rare, buses out of commission and petrol unheard of, city dwellers prolonged their workday by hours of walking or at best of bicycling, while rural citizens stayed close to their villages. The resumption of normal life was further retarded by the absence of four million young men—either mobilized or prisoners deported to Germany—and by the uprooting of a quarter of the population —displaced persons or refugees camping in the ruins or in shanties.

Many Frenchmen were astonished and irritated by so much hardship and privation, particularly since they had supposed it would vanish as if by magic with the coming of the Liberation. Nevertheless, the moment was at hand when these aggravations would begin to diminish. It was expected that hostilities would end in a few months, imports resume immediately afterwards, the men deported to Germany and many of those under mobilization return to work, communications gradually be re-established, and production develop again. Of course, it would take years before we returned to pre-war living standards. Yet in spite of everything, the end of the tunnel was in sight. Considering what we had survived, the remaining ordeals could not be so harrowing or protracted as to put the future in doubt. But what made the situation a serious one was that they contributed to the profound social, spiritual, moral and political upheaval from which the country was suffering.

This national crisis filled my life from day to day. Not that I let myself be absorbed by details, advice, condolences or criticisms which flowed in upon me from all sides. Though as sensitive as anyone else to the daily trials of the French people, though making every effort to restore public services, I knew that our dilemma was not remediable at once. The present was still suffering from the aftereffects of disaster but the future was ours to build. To do so, we must have a policy. I attempted to make mine equal to the demands and the dimensions of the subject: to revise social conditions so that work could begin again and subversion miscarry; to prepare for the moment when the people would have the power to speak, without allowing anything to breach my authority until then; to restore justice, so that crimes were punished quickly, repression was taken out of partisan hands, and, once sentences were passed, nothing stood in the way of rehabilitation; to restore freedom to the press, while liquidating papers which had served the enemy; to guide the country towards economic and financial equilibrium, encourage its activity and avert excessive upheavals; to govern by bold and arduous efforts, and despite all disadvantages. This was my programme.

As I saw it, what was at stake in the conflict was not only the fate of nations and states, but the fate of humanity as well. This was only to be expected, for war in its technical aspect is always a movement of societies. The passions that animate it and the stratagem it invokes invariably cover a dispute over the material or spiritual destiny of men. Alexander's victories were those of a civilization. It was the barbarian's passionate hunger which caused the fall of the Roman Empire. There would have been no Arab invasion without the Koran and no crusades without the Gospels. The *ancien régime* in Europe rose against France when the Assembly announced that 'Men are born free and equal by law'.

Like everyone else, I noticed that in our time technology dominated the universe. This was the source of the century's great debate: would the working classes be victims or beneficiaries from technical progress? This was the source of those recently formed mass movements—socialism, communism, fascism—which dominated several great peoples and divided all the rest. This was the reason why various banners—Liberal, Marxist, Hitlerian—now floated over the battlefields and why so many men and women, swept on by the cataclysm, were haunted by fears of what would become of them and of their children. There was unquestionable evidence that the flood of passions, hopes and griefs that broke over the belligerent powers, the enormous human mass to which they found themselves subject and the effort needed for reconstruction, placed social questions first amongst those the Government had to resolve. I was convinced that without profound and rapid changes in this sphere, there would be no lasting order.

How true this was for France! The war had come to her at the height of a class struggle that was all the more intense because our economy was desperately out of date and refused to change while our political regime was lacking in vigour and faith and could not impose these changes. There were undoubtedly unavoidable causes for such stagnation. Unlike other nations, we were not lucky enough to own sufficiently abundant sources of coal and petrol to develop our heavy industries. Before the first World War, the armed peace had obliged us to devote a large part of our resources to military needs; after it, since we got no reparations, we had been overwhelmed by the burden of reconstruction. Lastly, before the renascent German threat, we had had to make renewed armament efforts. Under such conditions, productive enterprises were too often neglected, the manufacture of equipment was rarely converted to civilian needs, wealth remained inert while national budgets were balanced with difficulty and currency lost its value. So many delays and hardships, so many sacrosanct routines and egotisms, had a bad effect on the economy and also on the powers willing to undertake the reforms which might have given the workers their share. It is true that in 1936 popular pressure imposed a few concessions, but the impulse was soon sucked under by parliamentary quicksands. When France entered the war, an ominous social unrest divided her citizens.

During the catastrophe, beneath the burden of defeat, a great change occurred in men's minds. To many, the disaster of 1940 seemed the failure of the ruling class and system in every realm. There was therefore a tendency to seek their replacement. Particularly since the collaboration of certain business circles with the occupiers and the contrast between the almost universal penury and the immense prosperity of a small group exasperated the mass of the French people. Then too, a war in which Hitler was simultaneously opposing democrats and Soviets threw the whole working class on the side of the resistance. The nation saw its workers reappear as patriots and revolutionaries too, which had been the case during the Revolution, in 1830, in 1848, and under the Commune. But this time, it was against the enemy that French workers were striking or joining the maquis, and the idea that they might again withdraw from the national community was distasteful to the country at large. In short, to renew the economy so that it served the collectivity before furnishing profits to private interests, and, at the same time, to raise the condition of the labouring classes—that is what was on the nation's mind.

The Vichy regime had attempted to accomplish these goals. Its technocrats in the financial and economic realm had shown incontestable skill despite all setbacks. It was also true that the social doctrines of 'national revolution'—corporate organization, a labour charter and family allowances—embodied ideas which were not without attraction. But the fact that this enterprise was identified with the capitulation influenced the masses toward an entirely different mystique.

That of Communism offered itself to their enthusiasm and their hopes. Their aversion for the structure of the past was exacerbated by poverty, concentrated by the resistance and exalted by the Liberation. Here, then, was an extraordinary opportunity for the 'party'. Deliberately confusing resistance with the class struggle and posing as the champions of both varieties of revolt, the Communist party had every chance of seizing control of the country, even if it could not do so by means of the Council of the Resistance, the committees or the militia. Unless de Gaulle took the initiative, carried out a number of reforms by which he could regroup alliances, get support from the workers and ensure economic recovery on a new basis.

This was the immediate task on which I set the Government to work. The programme had long since been determined. For I had prepared the realization of my original intentions at the start, while the resistance fighters, of whatever tendency, were unanimous in their intentions. The various movements had taken up their positions. The study committees working clandestinely in France or openly in London and in Africa, had prepared drafts. The delegates, particularly those sitting in the Consultative Assembly in Algiers, had approved the main outlines of these drafts. An essential characteristic of French resistance was its desire for social reform, but this desire had to be translated into acts. By virtue of my powers and the support public opinion had given me, I had the means to do so. In the course of one year, decrees and laws passed on my responsibility involved changes of enormous significance for the structure of French economy and the condition of the workers, changes which pre-war Governments had discussed fruitlessly for more than half a century. The new edifice was apparently a solid one, since nothing was subsequently either added or taken away.

Thus the principal sources of energy were put in the state's hands. In 1944 the National Coal Group of the Nord and Pas-de-Calais departments was set up and the Loire group was added soon afterwards. A short while later, the Government determined to put the production and distribution of electricity and gas under its control. This decision was carried out as soon as the terms could be specified. In 1945 the 'Petroleum Bureau' was created, its object being to encourage, regulate and co-ordinate all matters relating to the fuel and oil industry. At the end of the year, the High Commission on

D

Atomic Energy was created. The country's activity depended on coal, electricity, gas and petroleum, and would eventually depend on atomic fission and in order to bring France's economy to the level that progress demanded these resources must be developed on the largest possible scale. Expenditure and efforts were necessary, therefore, which only the state was in a position to realize and nationalization was a necessity.

Proceeding on the same principles, credit regulation was also arrogated to the state. As a matter of fact, once the state had assumed responsibility for financing these large-scale projects itself, it would need to receive the means directly. This would be accomplished by the nationalization of the Bank of France and the major credit establishments. Since the development of the territories within the French Union had become one of France's chief and perhaps supreme opportunities, the old *Caisse centrale de la France Libre* was converted into the *Caisse centrale de la France d'outre-mer*, concentrating the state's participation in the development of these new countries. Similar motives inspired the decision to group the air lines operated on state subsidies before the war into a single network: Air-France. By the end of 1945, our transport planes were flying to all the continents of the world. The Renault works was turned into a national trust not on principle but as a sanction, and this pilot factory *par excellence* was placed under state control. Finally, to encourage the new economy to invest, that is to levy on the present in order to build up the future, the 'High Commission on Plans for Equipment and Modernization' was created during this same year.

But true progress can be made only if those who create it with their own hands find their reward within it. The Government of the Liberation intended to bring this about, not only by wage increases, but more particularly by institutions which profoundly modified working conditions. During 1945 the social security programme was entirely recast and extended to many areas it had not previously covered. Every wage earner was obligatorily covered. The fear, as old as the human race, that sickness, accident, old age or unemployment would fall with crushing weight upon the workers, vanished. 'The poor are always with us,' but not the wretched, the starving or the hopeless. Further, a complete system of family allowances was implemented. The nation supported its families in proportion to the number of their children, the support lasting from

the day of the child's birth until the day he became capable of
earning his own living. This provision was to revive the French
birth rate, once so high it had nourished the spirit of enterprise and
the greatness of our nation, but which, in a hundred years, had
declined until France was no more than a static and sparsely
populated country. At the same time, tenant-farming status was
entirely revised; henceforth, a man working a rented farm was
assured he could stay on the land as long as he wished, provided
that he fulfilled the conditions of his lease. Furthermore, he had right
of pre-emption, if the land should be offered for sale. In this way a
remedy was provided for one virulent cause of farm agitation and
the flight from the countryside.

The programme I had drawn up proceeded far beyond these
material reforms. It aimed at granting the workers in the national
economy responsibilities which raised them far above the role of
instruments to which they had hitherto been confined. That they
should be associated with the progress of industry, or their labour
enjoy the same rights as those accorded to capital, or their remuneration be linked, like the revenue of stockholders, to the results
of the industry's developments was the goal I proposed to realize.
In order to prepare this promotion of labour, the Committees of
Enterprise were created in February 1956. Each committee included the director of the establishment, the workers' representatives,
the employers and the executives. It was kept informed of all
forms of activity. It formulated advice in all matters concerning
production. It administered its own funds which were devoted, over
and above wages and salaries, to the material and social life of the
personnel. By uniting all who, in whatever capacity, participated in
the same concern more closely, by encouraging them to study together the functioning, progress and inadequacies of their enterprise,
by inspiring consciousness and organizing the basis of solidarity, I
intended to take a major step toward the association of capital,
labour and technology. In this I saw the human structure of
tomorrow's economy.

These metamorphoses, extensive as they were, were carried out
without serious upheavals. Of course those in privileged positions
received them sullenly enough. Some nursed their grievances in
secret, planning to air them later. But at the moment, all recognized the force of the current and resigned themselves to it at once,

particularly since they had feared much worse. The Communists naturally preferred to regard what was being done as inadequate and to allege that the Government was prevented from going any further by its reactionary connections. Nevertheless there was no opposition to our measures. As for the 'politicians', they lost no time, in accordance with the rules of their art, in formulating reservations in one direction or another, though on the whole they approved the work being done and granted it overwhelming majorities in the Assembly. Many of them favoured these measures because they corresponded, generally, to old and familiar demands. Others accepted them as a concession to social harmony. All intended to take credit for them tomorrow, before the electorate. Once again I remarked that if the goal was perhaps the same for them as for myself, the motives guiding them were not identical with my own. They adjusted their attitude to the prejudices of their respective parties but such considerations did not affect me. On the other hand, I saw that they were scarcely aware of the motive inspiring me, which was the power of France.

Today, as ever, it was incumbent upon the state to create the national power, which henceforth would depend on the economy. The latter must therefore be directed, particularly since it was deficient, since it must be renovated, and since it would not be renovated unless the state determined to do so. This was, in my eyes, the chief motive of the nationalization, control and modernization measures adopted by my Government. But this conception of a Government armed to act powerfully in the economic domain was directly linked to my conception of the state itself. I regarded the state not as it was yesterday and as the parties wished it to become once more, a juxtaposition of private interests which could never produce anything but weak compromise, but instead an institution of decision, action and ambition, expressing and serving the national interest alone. In order to make decisions and determine measures, it must have a qualified arbitrator at its head. In order to execute them, it must have servants recruited and trained so as to constitute a valid and homogeneous corps in all public functions. Of these two conditions, the first was fulfilled today, and I was ready to make certain it would be so tomorrow as well; the second led me to establish the National Administrative School in August 1945. If the structure thus outlined became definitive, the new levers in the

hands of the state would give it sufficient control over French activity for it to be able to make the nation stronger and happier.

Independently of the spirit of justice and opportunity, it was this
same motive that led me to promote our workers to the rank of
responsible associates. The unity of France demanded that her
workers morally reintegrate the national community, from which,
either out of direct opposition or out of discouragement, many had
tended to withdraw. If, further, the working class applied itself of
its own accord to the development of its capacities, what resources
would be added to the nation's productive activity and thereby to
the power of France!

But it would take time to enable the new structure to produce
effects. Meanwhile, it was a question of survival. Yet the resumption
of work in factories and mines, the reconstruction of bridges, ports,
railways, power plants and canals, the reconditioning of trains,
trucks and ships, required everyone's participation. Things being as
they were, I intended to use on behalf of public welfare everyone
capable of furthering it. Of course, the Communists could not be
excluded in this period when the very substance of France would be
seriously compromised if the whole people were not brought to the
task, all the more if social upheaval lacerated the nation. Not that I
had any illusions as to the 'party's' loyalty. I knew it aimed at
seizing total power and that, if I yielded even once it would immediately rise to the attack. But its participation in the resistance,
the influence it wielded over the workers, the desire of public
opinion, which I myself shared, to see it return to the nation,
determined me to give the 'party' its place in the task of recovery.
Plunging, biting, rearing, but strongly harnessed between the shafts
and submitting to bit and bridle it was to help draw the heavy
wagon. It was my job to hold the reins. I had the strength to do so
because of the confidence of the French people.

This policy of unity had led me, since Algiers, to invite Communists to become members of my Government. I had done the same
thing in Paris. In addition, one Commissioner of the Republic, three
prefects and several high officials belonging to the 'party' were
part of the experiment. In the composition of the Consultative
Assembly, I had given the Communists representation corresponding to their importance. And now, in November 1944, I approved
the proposal of the Minister of Justice to grant M. Maurice Thorez,

condemned for desertion five years before, the benefit of amnesty. The latter was pronounced by the Council of Ministers. The 'party's' secretary general could now leave Moscow and return to his country. For some time past, my indulgence had been sought on his behalf from the most disparate quarters. Thorez himself had sent me many requests. I felt it wise to adopt this measure of clemency precisely at this moment and it was performed quite deliberately. Taking former circumstances into account, the events occurring subsequently, and today's necessities, I considered that the return of Maurice Thorez to the head of the Communist party would involve more advantages than drawbacks at the present moment.

This was, in fact, to be the case, so long as I myself was at the head of the state and the nation. Of course, day after day, the Communists multiplied their intrigues and their invective, though they attempted no insurrectional movement. Better still, so long as I was in office not a single strike occurred. It is true that the 'party' would spare no effort to control the political, trade union and electoral contingencies and to dominate the other groups, exploiting their secret hopes of inducing de Gaulle to withdraw and the inferiority complex inspired by their own inconsistency. But once the Communists adopted preponderance in a parliamentary regime instead of revolution as their goal, society ran far fewer risks. It is true that they greatly multiplied the obstacles in my path and conducted a backstage campaign of denigration. Yet until my withdrawal they were always careful not to override my authority to or insult me personally. Everywhere I appeared, their representatives were present to pay their respects, and even their militant members in the crowd shouted *Vive de Gaulle!* with the other Frenchmen.

Thorez, while making every effort to advance the interests of Communism, was to serve the public interest on several occasions. On the day after his return to France, he brought an end to the last vestiges of the 'patriotic militias' which certain of his people insisted on maintaining in a new clandestine situation. So far as his party's harsh and secretive rigidity allowed, he opposed the attempted provocations of the Committees of Liberation and the acts of violence their gangs tried to commit. To those—and they were numerous—of the workers, particularly the miners, who listened to his speeches, he continually urged maximum efforts at work and production at any cost as the national watchwords. Was this out of

patriotism or political opportunism? It was not my job to unravel
his motives. It sufficed that France was served.

The leaders of the 'party', provisionally renouncing domination,
were basically interested in preparing for what would come after the
victory. The same was true of the other political factions, of course.
As the electoral prospects grew clearer, each group focused increasingly on its own concerns, organized itself and drew up a
separate platform. We had seen, first of all, the Committees of
Liberation gathering in various regions to demand 'the *Etats-
Généraux* of the French resistance'. But the attempt failed because of
the opposition immediately apparent between those elements which
were Communist-inspired and those which were not. Subsequently,
the Assembly was lacerated by the various parties. In November the
Socialists had staged their shake-up. In January, it was the turn of
the 'Movement of National Liberation', then that of the 'National
Front'. In February the delegates of the 'Republican Federation'
convened, soon imitated by the old 'French Socialist party', while
the 'Popular Republican Movement' was being constituted. During
the same month, Socialists and Communists decided to function in
co-operation and formed a 'committee of unity' to direct their
mutual action. In April the 'Communist Youth Movement' held a
session. During this time, the officers of the Radical party began to
reorganize. In short, every sort of political organ, all of which had
for years performed only *en sourdine*, now tried out its tone and timbre.

Naturally I did not mix directly with the activity of any group.
But I watched this gestation of political forces most carefully. In
immediate circumstances, it was true, the conventions and their
notions were only of limited importance, since de Gaulle was governing and would continue to do so until he returned his power to the
nation. But he would do so soon. What happened then would depend to a large extent on what was being elaborated at this very
moment. I must say that I considered the ferments at work to be
quite disappointing.

What particularly struck me about the regrouping parties was
their passionate desire to give themselves all the powers of the
Republic in full and at the earliest opportunity, and their incapacity,
which they revealed in advance, to wield them effectively. In this
respect, nothing promised any sort of improvement in regard to the
futile manoeuvring associated with the regime's activity before the

war and which had led the country to such fearful disaster. The
politicians jealously emulated each other in denying such practices
in their speeches. 'Revolution!' was the watchword that echoed
most loudly. But no one defined just what this meant, what effective
changes were to be made in the previous structure and particularly
what authority, and endowed with what powers, would be in a
position to carry them out. As for the Communists, they knew what
they wanted, but were careful not to say what it was. The groups
which for all their bold phraseology were fundamentally moderate
cloaked their circumspection beneath Georges Bidault's formula:
'Revolution by law!' As for the groups and men of the Left, or laying
claim to be such, they appeared rigorous in criticism and repudia-
tion, but vague and querulous on every constructive issue. Receiving
delegations, reading newspapers, listening to speeches, I was inclined to think that for the renascent parties the revolution was not
an undertaking with definite goals implying action and risk, but
rather an attitude of constant dissatisfaction toward every policy,
even those they had advocated themselves.

I did not conceal the apprehension these signs inspired in me.
When Governmental confusion and impotence had been the direct
causes of our social and moral chaos, of our diplomatic weakness, of
our strategic collapse, and lastly of the national renunciation, which
had cast us into the abyss, what evil genius, what mad hallucination
was leading us towards the same quicksands? Given the tremendous
problems confronting France, how could anyone think they could
be solved except under the aegis of a state which was both impartial
and strong? I was forced to recognize that my ideas were rarely
shared.

In my own view the separation of powers, the authority of a
genuine chief of state, recourse to the people by means of referendum
whenever its destiny or its institutions were in question, were the
necessary bases of democracy in a country like ours. Yet it was only
too clear that everything that counted or was going to count in the
political realm was tending in the opposite direction. Future Governmental personnel conceived their future powers as organically
identified with the discretion of parties, the chief of state—if such
an institution existed at all—was to be a figurehead mandated by
parliamentary groups, and universal suffrage was exclusively destined to elect deputies. As far as I myself was concerned, while

everyone conceded my primacy in the provisional system, admitted my popularity and the services I had rendered France, exhibited spectacular loyalty to me on appropriate occasions no one concealed the impatience which such so-called 'personal' power inspired. Though there was no direct opposition to my action yet, I saw the clouds gathering on the horizon and henceforth advanced in an atmosphere heavy with criticisms and objections.

This way of regarding de Gaulle both favourably and disapprovingly was made quite clear in the Consultative Assembly. I appeared there often, eager to receive ideas from them and to mount the platform in order to explain my actions and my motives to all. I was naturally attracted by the parliamentary body's element of profound yet thwarted life, of ardent yet evasive humanity, of constrained yet violent passions which sometimes subsided as if to belie themselves and sometimes burst into noisy explosions. For reasons of protocol, my arrival and my departure were marked by a certain formality. But during the whole time I participated in the Assembly's tasks, I was careful not to offend its procedures in any way, respecting its agenda, sitting on one of its benches, speaking at the same tribunal as its members and chatting with them in the corridors. The sessions, I must admit, were frequently dull, the majority of the speakers read off monotonous texts whose generalities aroused scant attention. Still, from time to time, the talent of certain individuals— whether ministers or not—like Auriol, Bastid, Bidault, Boncour, Cot, Denais, Duclos, Hervé, Laniel, Marin, Mendès-France, Philip, Pleven, Schumann and Teitgen, gave a measure of distinction to the sessions. Sometimes, on a subject of burning interest, feelings ran high and a warm collective emotion hovered over the benches. Then the eloquent sentences, melting in the strained atmosphere, provoked sudden outrage or enthusiasm.

Many times over, I addressed the Consultative Assembly, sometimes in order to explain major subjects. For example on November 22nd the Government's general plans, on December 21st the Franco-Russian pact which had just been signed, on March 2nd the home policies adopted, on March 20th Indochina, where the Japanese had just opened an offensive, on May 15th the lessons to be drawn from the war after victory. In other cases, I intervened informally during the discussion. On each of these occasions, there occurred among the members a fusing of minds which momentarily expressed an imposing manifestation of unity. The importance of the subjects under discussion, the effect of the words, the human contact with de Gaulle himself reminded the delegates of the solidarity which linked us all together and deepened the attraction of the national community. For a moment, we felt ourselves closer—that is, better—men.

But if all agreed that de Gaulle should be applauded, no one hesitated to criticize his Government. The bitterness of the general remarks was notable, and sometimes it overflowed in formal attacks against one or other of the ministers. One day, Jules Jeanneney, Minister of State, was assailed with insults about some deferential words he had spoken in July 1940 regarding Marshal Pétain. Yet since then he had unceasingly supported and served the resistance. During the first months of 1945, when the budget was submitted for the Consultative Assembly's approval, there was a stormy session. When the appropriations for the Ministry of Justice were under discussion, the subject of the purges was broached. The Minister, François de Menthon, had to endure a running fire of implacable indictments. A huge majority attempted to punish his criminal weakness by refusing him a vote of confidence, a platonic manifestation, certainly, but one which showed the extent of the general agitation. Shortly after Pierre-Henri Teitgen, Minister of Information, served as a target in his turn. The difficulties into which the paper shortage had plunged the press was imputed to him in extravagant terms: 'Pornographer, protector of German agents, representative of the trusts, scorner of the Rights of Man, persecutor of the resistance press, cause of France's absence at Yalta—these are the names which I am called,' Teitgen said in answer to his accusers. When the budget for prisoners was examined, Minister Henri Frenay was the object of furious reproaches from all sides, though since at this date the prisoners were still in enemy hands, no one could yet judge the value of the measures taken for their return.

Such acrimony and agitation actually concealed precise demands. The Assembly was not able to resign itself to being merely Consultative. It would have preferred to take the power into its own hands, and this preference was soon confirmed. On March 19th I received a delegation from all the parties. 'We are here,' the representatives said, 'to inform you that the Assembly is extremely distressed because of the limited role to which it is confined and because the Government acts without considering itself bound by our opinion or votes.

We ask that henceforth the executive power take no decisions
contrary to the positions adopted by the Assembly.'

To yield to this reprimand would obviously have meant to lapse into
confusion. 'Only the people are sovereign,' I replied to the delegates.
'Until the French people are in a position to express their will, I have
taken the responsibility of leading them. You have been willing to
help me do so by responding to my call to honour. This has been
your role and it will be your glory. But my responsibility remains no
less complete. Even the action you are taking at this moment proves
that the Government's entire power is in my charge, since it is from
me that you ask to receive a share of the power. However, France's
situation does not allow of such dispersion.'

'All the same,' exclaimed the delegates, 'we represent the resistance! It is the responsibility of the resistance to express the will of the
people in the absence of the legal powers.'

'You are mandated,' I said, 'by the resistance movements and
parties. This gives you, of course, the right to make yourselves heard.
That is indeed why I set up the Consultative Assembly and designated you to participate in it. All Governmental issues are submitted
to you there. I myself and my ministers participate in your sessions.
You are associated in the Government's actions by the questions you
ask, the explanations the Government gives you, and the opinions
you express. But I will not go beyond that. Furthermore, consider
the fact that the French resistance was more inclusive than these
movements, and that France is greater than the resistance. It is in the
name of France as a whole, not of any fragment or fraction, however valuable, that I am carrying out my mission. Until the future
general elections, I am responsible for the nation's fate to the nation
and only to the nation.'

The delegates retired without concealing their discontent. After
their visit, however, there was a relaxation in the Assembly's tone.
Accommodating themselves to what was so clearly defined, its
members returned to their tasks. As a whole, its functions were very
helpful. The study by commissions and the discussion in public
session of programmes of economic and social reforms, justice, administration, education and overseas territories, brought to the Cabinet
not only the support of the majority of votes, but also of many good
suggestions. The attention and respect paid to the action of the
armies by men who were themselves familiar with many trials

encouraged leaders and men alike. Abroad, the spectacle of a
parliamentary prefiguration in the Luxembourg amphitheatre, the
ideas expressed there without restraint, and the fact that the Government's policy was generally approved, reinforced the hearing France
obtained throughout the world. Lastly, the impression in the public
mind that the principal measures adopted by the Government were
openly discussed, that there was a channel of expression for requests
and criticisms, that we were thus making progress toward a state of
affairs where the people would be restored to its rights, certainly
contributed to re-establishing that free côurse of ideas and feelings
which is an essential condition of order.

Another is the demonstration that justice is being rendered. Yet
in this respect, we were faced with an outbreak of vindictive demands.
After what had occurred, this reaction was only too understandable.
Collaboration under various forms of political decisions, police and
occasionally military action, of administrative measures, and of
propaganda publications and speeches, had espoused not only the
character of national abasement, but even the persecution of a huge
number of French citizens. With the co-operation of a considerable
number of officials and a mass of informers, 60,000 persons had been
executed and more than 200,000 deported of whom a bare 50,000
survived. Further, 35,000 men and women had been condemned
by Vichy tribunals; 70,000 'suspects' interned; 35,000 officials
cashiered; 15,000 officers degraded under suspicion of being in the
resistance. Now resentment was beyond control. The Government's
duty was to keep a cool head, but to pass the sponge over so many
crimes and abuses would have meant leaving a monstrous abscess
to infect the country for ever. Justice must be done.

And it was. During the winter the courts that had been formed to
judge evidence of collaboration actively performed their task. Of
course the severity of the sentences was variable, depending on the
composition of the juries. Local atmosphere made itself felt. Sometimes the sessions were disturbed by mob interventions. In several
regions there were even riots to snatch the prisoners from the courts.
This was the case, for instance, in Nîmes, Maubeuge, Bourges,
Annecy, Alès and Rodez. In fact, about twenty unfortunate prisoners were lynched throughout the country. On several occasions
the Government had to repress these outbreaks. I had to urge the
Ministers of the Interior and of Justice to vigilance and firmness,

to inflict punishments on officials guilty of laxity in the maintenance of order, to insist on the inculpation of those who had infringed it. Nevertheless, justice was meted out as impartially as was humanly possible, considering the passions awakened. Those judgments which later proved to be ill-founded were extremely rare.

Two thousand and seventy-one death sentences were passed by the courts, not including those sentenced *in absentia*. The files were subsequently submitted to me, after examination by the Commission of Mercy and the warranted estimation of the Minister of Justice. I studied them all, directly assisted by President Patin, director of criminal cases and reprieves at the Chancellery, and receiving the lawyers whenever they requested it. Nothing ever seemed more painful than this procession of murders, tortures, delations and appeals to treason that passed in review before me. Conscientiously, I attested that with the exception of about one hundred cases, all those condemned had deserved their execution. Yet I granted pardons to 1,303 among them, commuting, in particular, the death sentences of all women, of almost all minors, and, among the men, of the majority of those who had acted upon formal orders and at the risk of their own lives. I was obliged to reject 768 appeals from condemned men whose personal and spontaneous action had caused the death of other Frenchmen or directly aided the enemy.

As for the 39,900 prison sentences which the courts of justice handed down, they were, on the whole, equitable and moderate. There were 55,000 such sentences in Belgium at the same time, and more than 50,000 in Holland. Again, by remission of penalties, the Government mitigated the effect of a large number of decisions, particularly in the case of the unfortunate young men who had been lured into the 'Militia', the 'Legion of French Volunteers' or the 'African Phalanx', and who were given the alternative of joining the Indochinese Expeditionary Corps. It should be added that the examining magistrates decided that there were no grounds for prosecution in 18,000 cases. By the middle of 1945, among the 60,000 guilty or suspected men arrested at the time of the Liberation, there was not one individual still held unless he had been formally and legally sentenced. Considering the mass of collaboration evidence and the number of atrocities committed against the resistance fighters, and recalling the torrent of rage which spread in all directions once the enemy began to withdraw, it can be said that the judgements of the courts of justice were given with as much indulgence as possible.

The same was true in the realm of public office. Here, however, resentment was particularly sharp, for Vichy had cashiered more than 50,000 people and, furthermore, in the case of certain officials had displayed odious zeal in the service of the invader. The Provisional Government decided to consult the adminstrations themselves to determine what sanctions to take. Recourse to the Council of State remained open, of course. As a matter of fact, the immense majority of officials had behaved honourably. Many of them, in fact, had actually helped in the struggle against the enemy and his accomplices in the exercise of their functions. Out of a staff of more than 800,000, only about 20,000 cases needed investigation, as a result of which 14,000 sanctions were pronounced, of which scarcely 5,000 resulted in dismissals. I was on firm ground, therefore, when I declared on the wireless, on January 18th, 'Those who have the honour to serve the state do so, I am convinced, with enthusiasm and discipline and deserve to be encouraged by the respect of their fellow citizens.'

The High Court, established to judge acts of collusion with the enemy and interference with the security of the state committed in the highest positions, opened its doors in March. It was directed by the First President of the Supreme Court of Appeal, M. Mongibeaux, assisted by the President of the Criminal Chamber, M. Donat-Guigne, and by the First President of the Paris Court of Appeal, M. Picard. The jury, drawn by lot from two lists of fifty names established by the Consultative Assembly, consisted of twenty-four members, of whom twelve were deputies or senators in 1940. President Mornet was the Public Prosecutor. The preliminary investigations for the trial were made by an 'Investigations Committee' consisting of five magistrates and six members of the Assembly.

I thought it necessary that the men who had taken responsibility, in the highest office, for the acts of the Vichy regime should appear before a jurisdiction established for this purpose. Neither the ordinary tribunals, the courts of justice, nor the councils of war, were in a position to deal with such cases. Since the persons concerned, either as ministers, high commissioners, residents-general, or secretaries-general, had played a political role, the courts which judged them must be politically qualified to do so. This condition was established for all cases of the same kind, at all times, and in all sectors. It was to observe it myself that I instituted the High Court by decree on November 18th, 1944.

This installation took place under exceptional legal conditions. Naturally, I arranged later for authority to be established by formal legal measures. But France's internal order and the world situation demanded that the 1940 capitulation, the breaking of alliances and the deliberate collaboration with the enemy be judged without delay in the persons of the leaders who had made themselves responsible. Otherwise, how and in whose name punish the guilty? How and in whose name claim for France the status of a major belligerent and victorious power? In this matter, as in so many others, I took it upon myself to do what had to be done. It would subsequently be the responsibility of the new National Assembly to ratify the procedure. This it did. Of course, once the High Court was created, I was particularly careful not to influence the prosecution, the investigation and the judgements, abstained from making statements and received no legal commissions of inquiry. Since I wanted the discussions to be undisturbed by manifestations or disturbances from those present, I refused to let the High Court sit in the hall of the Palais Bourbon—as many wanted. Instead I installed it in the Palais de Justice and gave it a considerable police guard.

The first trial to come before the High Court was that of Admiral Esteva, Resident General in Tunisia at the time of the Allied landing in North Africa. Following Pétain's orders, the unfortunate man had allowed the Germans to disembark, had ordered the roads to be opened to them, and had forbidden the French forces in the country to join those fighting the enemy. But the occupation of Tunisian territory, particularly of Bizerta, by Axis troops forced the Americans, French and British to engage in an extended battle. Furthermore, the presence of the Germans and the Italians in the Kingdom of Tunis gave agitators many opportunities to turn the citizens against France which resulted in serious political consequences.

Admiral Esteva was sentenced to solitary confinement. At the close of a career which had hitherto been exemplary, this old seaman, misled by false discipline, had become the accomplice and ultimately the victim of an ill-fated enterprise.

General Dentz succeeded him on the stand. As High Commissioner in the Levant, he had in the spring of 1941 allowed German squadrons to land on Syrian territory in accordance with Vichy's orders, had established the points where the Wehrmacht was to disembark and had used the forces under his command against the Free French and the British. After an initial resistance which might have passed for an attempt to salvage his honour, Dentz had asked for an armistice. These conditions, determined by myself in agreement with the British command, involved the transmission of the Vichy's High Commission to that of Free France, and the opportunity for all French soldiers and officials to join my forces. I informed Dentz that if he accepted our terms, no legal prosecution would be taken against the High Commissioner or his subordinates.

Instead of agreeing to the terms, General Dentz had ordered bitter resistance, which could only benefit the enemy. The unfortunate man went so far as to ask for direct support from the German Air Force. Obliged to lay down his arms after heavy losses had been suffered on both sides, he had concluded a cease-fire with the British which had suited England, of course, but not France. As a matter of fact, it was to the British and not to Free France that the Vichy High Commissioner abandoned the fate of the states under French mandate. At the same time, the troops and officers under his command were withdrawn from contact with the 'Gaullistes' and immediately returned to Metropolitan France on ships sent by Vichy, acting with the Germans. There was no further justification for the immunity I had once been able to offer General Dentz.

General Dentz was sentenced to death. Because of the loyal and excellent services he had rendered on other occasions, and touched by the tragedy of this ruined soldier, I remitted his sentence immediately.

The prosecution of Vichy's servants soon determined the High Court to institute proceedings against its master. On March 17th, that court decided that Marshal Pétain would be judged in absentia. This was a lamentable but inevitable issue, I considered it necessary, both from an international and a national points of view, that French justice give a formal verdict, but I also hoped that some accident would spare the soil of France an accused man of eighty-nine, a leader once distinguished by the most exceptional powers, an old soldier in whom at the time of the catastrophe many Frenchmen had put their trust and for whom, in spite of everything, many still felt respect or pity. General de Lattre asked me what action he should take if his troops, approaching Sigmaringen, happened to find Pétain and his former ministers. I replied that all must be arrested, but that so far as the Marshal himself was concerned I hoped that no such encounter would take place.

On April 23rd, Pétain reached Switzerland. He had persuaded the Germans to take him there and the Swiss to receive him. When Mr Karl Burckhardt, Ambassador of the Confederation, came to announce the fact to me, I told him that the French Government was not at all eager to have Pétain extradited. A few hours later, Karl Burckhardt reappeared. 'The Marshal,' he declared, 'wants to return to France. My Government cannot oppose his wish. Philippe Pétain will therefore be conducted to your border.' The die was cast. The old Marshal, of course, did not doubt that he would be condemned. But he intended to appear in person before the French courts and receive the punishment, whatever it was, to which he would be sentenced. His decision was a courageous one. General Koenig took Pétain in charge at Vallorbe. Travelling by special train and protected by a strong escort against acts of violence which some wished to commit against his person, the Marshal was interned in the fortress at Montrouge.

While justice was doing its duty, I wanted public opinion to be kept informed of the motives for its decisions. Of course excessive publicity given to the trials would have been scandalous, but in questions which laid every passion bare, an objective report would set the public mind at rest. Unfortunately, the courts were functioning at a time when the newspapers, reduced to skeletal formats, could devote only extremely summary accounts to the sessions. It was the same indigence which kept the public from being adequately informed of military operations, diplomatic transactions, the state of the economy and the reactions of opinion in Allied countries. The essential episodes of this period by and large escaped the notice or the knowledge of the average French citizen. Many believed that censorship was withholding news. But many others, relying on their imagination for a notion of the problems involved and the proceedings under way, and unaware of the steps taken to control the latter and resolve the former, mournfully concluded that France could do nothing about either.

A terrible paper shortage, as a matter of fact, was strangling the French press. Our paper industry was almost completely without raw materials, and so long as we lacked currency, we could purchase only meagre supplies abroad; besides, the Allied convoys were fulfilling entirely different commitments. We therefore had to ration the newspapers most severely, which limited them to absurd dimensions. Since, furthermore, almost all expressed revolutionary tendencies, their propaganda seized on whatever it could to the detriment of the facts. How remote was this reality from the projects cherished during the days of the resistance!

To create a great press had been the dream of the clandestine fighters. They wanted it to be honest and sincere, free from financial pressures, particularly since the indignation provoked by the occupation journals had added to the bad memory left by the pre-war papers with regard to independence and veracity. Further, the majority of the resistance movements and parties had been created in the shadow of the old dailies and weeklies. They now felt entitled to appear in broad daylight, and with priority.

In Algiers, the Government had prepared in advance for the situation of the press at the time of the Liberation. According to the decree of May 6th, 1944, the newspapers published in either zone under enemy rule could no longer appear. Their funds would be confiscated and the resistance organs receive the option of renting their buildings. Since there was no question of creating a monopoly, other newspapers, new or old, were allowed to appear or reappear. Furthermore, the decree intended to safeguard the independence of the press with regard to financial groups. Therefore both press and advertising societies were closely regulated. It was also established that the selling price of the publications should be high enough to allow of survival and that accounts should be published by law.

It was on this basis that the French press had gradually reappeared. Not, of course, without upheavals. In Paris and in the departmental capitals, a usually inexperienced staff turned out enthusiastic leaflets in the buildings where familiar organs of the press had once been produced. Yet so gratified were the French to recover freedom of ideas and information that the newspapers and reviews sold widely. There was an extraordinary burgeoning of publications. Each was—and with reason—tiny in size, but appeared in many numbers. Moreover, the papers reflected the whole gamut of opinion.

Taking advantage of the arrangements of the decree, the resistance

papers had leaped to prominence. Naturally the Communists had
not lagged behind. Under their aegis, two Paris dailies, *L'Humanité*
and *Ce Soir*, seventy weeklies, including *Action*, *L'Avant-Garde*, *La
Terre*, *Les Lettres françaises*, *Le Canard enchaîné*, and fifty provincial
papers, claimed to uproot fascism and its works everywhere and
supported every grievance advanced against it. The Communists
also played a large role in the editorial policy of the *Front national*,
of *Franc-Tireur*, *Libération*, and so on. The Socialists, limiting themselves, in Paris, to *Le Populaire*, but with numerous local papers in
various departments where they had supporters—*Libération-Nord*,
Le Provençal and *La République du Sud-Ouest*, for instance—applied
themselves to what for them was the major concern, the reconstitu-
tion of their party. The Christian Socialists felt the wind blowing
across their bows and revelled in the influence of *L'Aube*, the wide
circulation of *Ouest-France*, and the development of *Temps présent* and
Témoignage chrétien. As for the eclectic and varied papers resulting
from the resistance movements themselves—*Combat*, *Le Parisien
libéré*, *Résistance*, *Défence de la France* and *France libre*—they prospered,
as did local papers with the same origins, *La Voix du Nord*, *L'Espoir*,
La Montage, etc.

New publications attempted to follow in the wake of the formerly
clandestine papers. They required authorization to do so. I intervened on their behalf whenever the journal in question had sufficient
means to be able to take its chances. *Le Figaro*, which had been
'scuttled' during the occupation of the Southern Zone, had resumed
publication two days before the capital was liberated, though its
owner had had no right to do so. I made it possible for him to print
the paper nonetheless. *L'Aurore*, *L'Epoque* and *L'Ordre*, which had
also put an end to their existence in order not to submit to enemy
control, received permission to reappear, and, thereby, their share of
paper. I also pronounced the *nihil obstat* in the case of *La Croix*,
which had somewhat extended its survival in the Southern Zone after
the German arrival, but many of whose editors participated in the
resistance. To several new papers—*Le Monde*, *Paris-Presse*, *Les
Nouvelles du matin*, *La Dépèche de Paris*, etc.—I gave the right to enter
the market place, for I regarded it as desirable that the French press
be accessible to new and various formulas and styles.

The same cyclone with which events had swept over the press
worked havoc in literary and artistic circles as well. Writers in

particular, concerned by the very nature of their calling with exploring and expressing men's ideas, had found themselves enlisted in this war in which so many doctrines and passions confronted each other. It must be said that the majority—and frequently the greatest among them—had taken France's side, sometimes in a magnificent manner. Others, alas, had ranged themselves in the opposite camp with all the power of their ideas and their style. Against the latter now arose a great tide of indignation. Particularly since it was all too well known towards what crimes and what punishments their eloquent agitations had impelled so many wretched, credulous men. The courts of justice condemned several notorious writers to death. When they had not directly and wilfully served the enemy, I commuted their punishment, on principle; but in contrary cases I did not feel I had the right to reprieve them. For in literature as in everything talent involves responsibility. Most often, the courts gave verdicts that were less severe. But apart from actual crimes, which were punished, certain frivolous or inconsequential acts were noisily censured in a number of writers whose very success had brought them to public attention. Naturally rivalries inspired rumours and occasionally errors. The whole world of literature, the arts and the theatre was living under a turbulent sky.

Even the *Académie Française* was concerned, for it was the object of harsh attacks and its dissolution was the theme of a campaign which found echoes on all sides. Naturally the culpable behaviour of several of its members and the hearing they had found among their colleagues until the very end was widely criticized. I was urged to use my powers to 'renovate' the Academy; in other words, to suppress it. The whole body was profoundly disturbed and distressed.

Its permanent secretary, the illustrious and courageous Georges Duhamel, came to discuss the elements of the situation with me. He described the difficulties which he himself had had to surmount, with the aid of several other members, in order to keep the Academy from adopting an unfortunate attitude during the occupation, when the strongest pressure was exerted to induce it to do so. To resume its normal course, the body now faced severe obstacles. Should it exclude or at least suspend those of its members who had been condemned or were threatened with collaboration sentences? Painful discussions loomed ahead! Furthermore, a dozen academicians had died since 1939, and had not been replaced. Of course, elections could now be held; but how reach a quorum, given the fact that certain members were not at all eager to appear? It was particularly to be feared that the institution was henceforth so shaken and divided that it would have the greatest difficulty in making a recovery. But how could it remain the incomparable representation of French thought, language and literature which it was intended to be and which had so powerfully contributed to our nation's brilliance for three centuries? 'Everything would be much easier,' my eminent visitor added, 'if you yourself would agree to join the Academy.'

After careful consideration, I set aside this possibility. 'The chief of state,' I replied to Georges Duhamel, 'is the protector of the Academy. How could he become a member? And then, as you know, de Gaulle cannot belong to any category, nor receive any distinction. Admittedly it is in the highest French interest that the Academy resume the role which it fulfils. My intention is not to change the constitution Richelieu provided and, except for certain sentences under way against certain members, to guarantee the entire body independence and security. Nevertheless, I think it would be to the Academy's advantage to profit by the extraordinary circumstances to start afresh. Since many of its chairs are empty, why should we not institute exceptional proceedings and provisionally suspend the rule of candidacy? Why should the Academy not invite among its number several writers known to be worthy of the honour and, as they have shown during the recent ordeal, champions of freedom and of France as well? The Academy's prestige and popularity, I am convinced, would have everything to gain.'

However, a few days later when I met all the academicians in a position to appear, I discovered that my comforting promise had been favourably received but my suggested reforms had been less so. In the end, the Academy, reassured by the law and order it saw everywhere, returned to its traditional procedure. For my part, I was delighted to see this precious institution revive, though I regretted that it had not been able, as a body, to give adequate homage to the Liberation of France.

By the joint effect of social reforms enacted, of liberty recovered, of justice rendered, of authority restored, the nation was regaining its spirits. After all the lacerations inflicted by the war, this was the beginning of convalescence. The latter, however, would be precarious if the ravaged country failed to recover its physical equilibrium. If, at the very moment when fortune was beginning to smile on us once more, our finances collapsed and our economy fell apart, there would certainly be no further hope of status, order or future for France. If on the other hand, despite the terrible conditions we were struggling against, the Government managed to get a solid basis of recovery for national activity, everything else could gradually be restored into the bargain. There was certainly no question of a talisman or a magic wand. Only stern measures would have any effect.

The budget drawn up for 1945 by the Government cast a cold light on our finances, as they appeared after five years of war and four years of occupation. 390 billion francs of expenditure was provided for, of which 175 billion was for military needs. On the other side of the ledger, 176 billion francs of normal receipts; a deficit of 55 per cent. The public debt rose to 1,800 billion francs—in other words, four times higher than before the war. Of this amount, short-term liabilities accounted for 800 billion francs whose creditors could demand repayment at any moment. Since a quarter of the expenses had been settled by advances from the Bank of France since 1939, bank note circulation had quadrupled.

This enormous inflation of expenditures, of the national debt and of the means of payment was supported by a terribly deficient economy. At the beginning of 1945, the rate of production did not exceed half that of 1938, and foreign trade was non-existent. The liberation loan, drawing on liquid assets, had averted the catastrophe which the sudden afflux of this floating mass would have provoked in markets more than three-quarters empty. Further, the treasury had in the loan the substance enabling it to deal with the immediate situation. But salutary though the expedient had been, something more was now required—a long term policy.

Doctrines and experts contradicted each other. Apart from the Communist system of compulsory production and controlled consumption and the extreme liberalism which left matters to arrange themselves, we found ourselves with two theories to choose from.

The first said: 'Confronted with inflation, let us take the bull by the horns. Let us perform a radical puncture in the liquid assets by immediately decreeing that the existing bank notes are no longer valid, that the bearers must immediately exchange them at the public banks, that they will receive in return only a quarter of their

funds in new currency and that the balance will be credited to the
owners but without being usable. At the same time, let us block
accounts and allow each depositor to withdraw only an extremely
limited sum. In this way, we shall reduce the possibilities of purchase and, at the same time, the extent of the black market. Let us
freeze prices too, and at a level low enough for consumers, with their
means of payment controlled, still to pay for what they need. Only
the prices of luxury products may be raised at will. We must allow
for the fact that the treasury's resources will be seriously affected by
such a contraction. There is only one way to guard against this:
to levy a major tax on capital. Such measures are harsh. But
provided General de Gaulle gives them his authority, they will
enable us to overcome the crisis.'

Thus reasoned the champions of the 'tough' method. In support of
their thesis they cited the example of the Brussels Government, where
M. Camille Gutt, Minister of Finance, had effectively stabilized
the Belgian franc thanks to the simultaneous freezing of bank notes,
bank accounts, prices, salaries and wages.

Others said: 'Inflation is not so much the cause as the effect of
disequilibrium. The latter is inevitable. In a time of total war, nothing can keep production of commodities and consumer goods at
normal levels, since many raw materials, tools and workers are employed to other purposes. Nothing, moreover, can keep the Government from distributing vast remunerations to a large number of
social categories. In every belligerent state, we therefore see the
public furnished with nominal resources which are superior to what
they were, consumer goods are inadequate to demand, prices are
rising and money stocks are depleted. The situation is more serious
in France than elsewhere because the country has for years been cut
off from the outside world, because the occupiers have made
exorbitant demands upon our resources, because their presence has
provoked the stoppage or the slowing down of many branches of
industry, and because the present lack of raw materials and equipment, the absence of imports, the necessity of using a large share of
our remaining means in urgent reconstruction programmes, retard
the resumption of production. Yet everything depends on this resumption. Severe artificial devices would add to our difficulties by
depriving the producers of the initiative and the means of setting to
work and by ruining the state's credit as well as that of its currency.

On the contrary, let us encourage the economy to function and to expand. The excess of liquid assets should be eliminated by treasury bonds which favour the spirit of thrift and foster the feeling that every man controls what is his own. Let us also avoid a systematic tax on capital. Let us merely pursue the confiscation of illegal profits. This method is not miraculous, but thanks to the nation's confidence in de Gaulle, it will lead to recovery.'

Ultimately, the decision was up to me. Therefore I was a party to the dispute through every kind of administrative report, through the advice of interested groups, through arguments in the press. At the beginning of March in the Consultative Assembly, André Philip, general budget liaison officer, Jules Moch, and other delegates, made themselves eloquent apostles of levies on monetary notes, bank accounts and capital, while René Pleven set forth an altogether different plan. The Government was divided over this question. Each of the theses had a protagonist as ardent as he was qualified. Pierre Mendès-France, Minister of National Economy, identified himself with the first. Pleven, Minister of Finance, warmly advocated the second. Since both were men of merit and ambition, since they were entrusted with equal responsibility, the former for prices and trade, the latter for currency and the budget, I thought it futile and inappropriate that they should be rivals in a dispute which concerned a problem affecting the fate of the French people. Therefore, after long consideration of the matter both with them and with myself, I decided on the progressive plan and rejected the freeze.

I was not convinced by theoretical arguments. In economy as in politics or strategy, I do not believe that there can be absolute truth, but only circumstances. It was my conception of the latter which dictated my decision. The country was sick and hurt. I therefore felt it was preferable not to press its subsistence and its activity at this moment particularly since the months to come would inevitably improve its condition. If there had been no other means of recovery than to play all or nothing, I would certainly not have hesitated. But why throw the nation into dangerous convulsions, if it would recover its health sooner or later in any case?

As for the experiment which the Brussels Government had conducted so successfully, I did not believe it would work in France. For material and moral conditions were profoundly different for the Belgians and for us. Belgium suffered less than France from the

occupation. The demands made upon her resources had remained
rather limited. By virtue of a manoeuvre of German propaganda, her
prisoners had long since been returned. At present, the share the
Belgians were taking in the war cost them little. Besides, they had
not had a regime like Vichy; the Communists were not powerful in
the country; the national upheaval did not reach such dimensions as
in France. In this country of small size and simple structure, whose
communications were re-established by the Allied armies themselves,
the administration's control could be imposed without difficulties.
But above all, M. Camille Gutt was in a position to keep the freezing
of prices and currency from cutting off supplies. The Brussels Government had a huge reserve of currency at its disposal in America, the
result of ore sales—particularly uranium ore—made to the United
States by the Congo throughout the war; the port of Antwerp was
the destination of the majority of the Allied convoys; the British
and American authorities, for reasons that were both political and
strategic, wanted to facilitate matters for the Belgian authorities,
therefore the Pierlot-Gutt-Spaak Government could import large
quantities of American and Canadian commodities. Thus, immediately after the freeze, when Belgian producers suspended all
deliveries, the Government supplied the markets with food and goods
bought in the New World and sold at regulated low prices. This is
why, after many upheavals, equilibrium was re-established without
hunger and chaos having appeared in Belgium.

But we had no credits. Abroad, we had only debts. The agreements recently concluded with Washington and Ottawa for 'imports within six months' had only begun to be acted upon by the
spring of 1945. Aside from the political motives which determined
our allies to make us dance to their tune, they were not interested in
overloading their ships and sending them to our ports, which were
far from the battlefields. In no respect, therefore, did the Belgian
experiment decide me to adopt the system of price and wage freezing and deductions. Let the liberated nation produce as much as
possible! Let the state help and encourage it to do so! In exchange,
let it furnish the state, under the form of normal taxes and savings
investments, the means to cover the expenditures the latter was
making for the public welfare! This was the decision I took in
March 1945.

My decision was not to be changed. Until the end, it guided the

Provisional Government's financial and economic policy. However, in addition to our regular burdens, we had to furnish money against the enormous deficit occasioned in the 1945 budget by war and reconstruction expenditure, by the return and relocation of prisoners and deported men, by the repatriation of refugees, by the reestablishment of demobilized men in their homes, and by the transport of troops to Indochina. Supplementary receipts, the confiscation of illicit profits, the conversion into 3 per cent income of the 4 per cent securities of 1917 and 1918, the $4\frac{1}{2}$ per cent securities of 1932, and particularly the treasury bonds to which the public continued to subscribe, provided us with the means for dealing with everything. Indeed we had recourse in June to the exchange of bank notes, which rendered null and void, to the profit of the state, old currency that was not presented. But the operation was undertaken franc for franc. Indeed we continued, between January and December, to adjust both prices and salaries, but the Government remained in control and at maximum the increases did not exceed 50 per cent. At the same time, production continued to rise, particularly since, following a series of agreements made in February and March with Belgium, Switzerland, Great Britain and the United States, imports were resumed. All in all, by the end of 1945 economic activity had doubled its level at the time of the Liberation, and bank note circulation had not risen above the level it had attained at the time of my arrival in Paris. At a period and in a sphere where there was no possibility of satisfying everyone, I did not expect this result to provoke enthusiasm. I myself considered it satisfactory, however, for after having staggered along on a path bordering one abyss after another, the nation, by the year's end, had set off upon the road to new prosperity.

As was to be expected, Pierre Mendès-France resigned from the Government, at his own request, during the month of April. He did so with dignity, and I kept all my admiration for a colleague of such exceptional merit. Furthermore, if I did not adopt the policy he advocated, neither did I adopt an attitude preventing me from doing so eventually, should circumstances change. For Mendès-France to be in a position to apply it eventually, however, he must remain faithful to his doctrine. For this reason his resignation was really a service to the state. I united Finance and Economy into a single ministry of which Pleven was put in charge. A long-standing col-

league of broad and brilliant mind, though invariably modest, an
economist equal to the complex tasks which his flexible intellect
readily encompassed, Pleven acquitted himself of his functions without our poor means allowing him spectacular successes. He did so
in such a way that the nation advanced with regard to both
resources and credit. Although occasionally I thought his complications superfluous and his flexibility excessive, I gave him my entire
confidence and unceasingly supported him.

I did as much for all the ministers. I was obliged to maintain the
singular position which my function as arbitrator required, but I was
convinced of their merit and appreciative of their friendship. Today,
after many years and many reversals in attitudes, it is not without
emotion that I recall the loyalty of this body and the support its
members gave me in our historic task. However various my twenty
collaborators may have been, the fact is that we had one and the
same policy until the day of victory. Of course these men were, for
the most part, attached to various parties, but the sufferings of
France were too recent, and my powers too widely recognized, for
any of them to expect to function individually, or even to contemplate the prospect of doing so. As a Cabinet member each man was
responsible to General de Gaulle and to him alone. The result, in
Government action, was a unity which itself encouraged the restoration of order in the state and the nation.

I frequently consulted Jules Jeanneney, the austere and reserved
senior member of our Government. One of Clemenceau's ministers
during the first World War, he had subsequently refused to hold such
a post under anyone else. He agreed to do so in my Government.
Utterly devoted to public welfare, Jeanneney brought us a juridical
capacity and a political experience which led me to entrust him with
the preparation of plans for political institutions. No one was more
convinced than the former President of the Senate that the old
regime must be transformed from top to bottom. I had constant
dealings with the three 'military' ministers: André Diethelm, than
whom I cannot imagine a more faithful companion nor a statesman
of higher conscience, organized, staffed and equipped an Army
whose morale was low, whose units were heterogeneous, whose means
were insolvent, yet which was to be the Army of victory. Louis
Jacquinot skilfully applied himself, despite guns fired in the wrong
direction, ships destroyed or scuttled and the wreckage of arsenals,

to reviving the Navy. Charles Tillon, firm yet sensitive, devoted himself no less effectively to the resurrection of the aircraft factories. I worked daily with Georges Bidault, Minister for Foreign Affairs. Long experienced in the history and criticism of the subjects confronting him but coming only lately to the practice of affairs, impatient already to try his own wings but still concerned to keep to the line I had drawn, tempted to consecrate himself to his ministerial task but at the same time heedful of the nascent political movement whose leadership he intended to assume, Bidault surmounted these contradictions by dint of intelligent finesse. On many occasions, Adrien Tixier talked to me about public order. No vicissitude altered the intellectual tranquillity of the Minister of the Interior, though he had only inadequate forces at his disposal and was unceasingly harassed by the protests of the vengeful or the exhortations of certain groups eager to have the authorities learn nothing and forget everything. Yet Adrien Tixier, wounded in the war, suffered continual pain and died within a year.

At intervals, resentment was expressed against the other ministers. This was the experience of François de Menthon, Minister of Justice, one of whose responsibilities, and a heavy one, was to constitute the courts, the civil chambers, the High Court, and to assure their independence. De Menthon did so with distinction. The young, idealistic, eloquent Pierre-Henri Teitgen was also criticized often, since he was in charge of the Ministry of Information and regulated all press affairs. Those who attacked him found that they had met their match. Nothing could mar the robust lucidity of Robert Lacoste, Minister of Production. His task, however, was an ungrateful one—whether it concerned power, equipment or raw materials, whether it was mines, metallurgy or the textile and paper industries that were involved, his programme always consisted of deficits, impasses and bottlenecks. Yet, without advertising the fact, Lacoste accomplished an enormous amount of work and was never swamped by problems. At the Ministry of Labour, Alexandre Parodi patiently and uncomfortably spun out the Penelope's web that constituted the French wage scale. The return of the prisoners of war was prepared by Henri Frenay. As the parties outbid each other in advance over the claims to be made in the name of these two million electors, a storm rumbled round the minister. But of all the members of my Government, the man harnessed to the most arduous task, and the man most certain of being able to satisfy no one, the man least spared by critics and caricatures, was Paul Ramadier, Minister of Food and Supply. I had appointed him to the post in November; gallantly and methodically, he applied himself to its problems and succeeded in uniting and distributing the few rations available at the time, opposing his rocklike solidity to the flood of gibes and lampoons, but sensitive to their injustice.

A few ministers were somewhat more sheltered from the censure of public opinion. This was true of Paul Giacobbi, a skilful mind and an ardent heart, who replaced Pleven as Minister of the Colonies and was responsible for Indochinese affairs; of François Billoux, who headed Public Health without conflicts but not without success; of François Tanguy-Prigent, minister and servant of French Agriculture, who made every effort to organize and confederate his charge; of the astute Augustin Laurent, who reorganized the postal services and the telegraph and telephone systems ravaged by the battle. It was also in a relatively calm atmosphere that René Capitant, René Mayer and Raoul Dautry directed the ministries they ran. With audacity and success Capitant undertook to renovate the structure and methods of National Education. Mayer, responsible for Transport, found means of resolving the immediate problems of the demolition of the railways, ports, bridges, roads, canals and naval yards. Dautry, fertile in ideas and familiar with every technique, set in operation the Ministry of Reconstruction which I had created in December. At Dautry's request, I joined the Bureau of Urbanism to his ministry, so that cities would be restored according to a general plan. On the whole, seeing how all my colleagues handled their tasks in their respective spheres, I was certain that the resistance offered the country great political and administrative capacities, provided that there was a captain on board the ship of state.

Since we had many tasks of the most difficult kind to accomplish, the Government functioned according to fixed rules. Except in secret matters concerning military operations, or when it was a question of a diplomatic emergency, all important decisions were adopted in Council. The latter met, on an average, twice a week. This was not too often, given the wealth of subjects and the fact that the Government had to make decisions for the legislative as well as the executive branches. The sessions were prepared with the greatest possible care. The constitution of the reports, liaison between the

Presidency, the ministers and the Council of State were arranged by
a general secretariat, directed by Louis Joxe. Speaking little and low,
always standing in the wings, Joxe assured the smooth functioning of
the mechanism upon which everything else depended.

The Council met in the Hotel Matignon. In the barewalled hall,
the atmosphere was one of objectivity. The session, however important or affecting, proceeded according to an agenda established once
and for all. On each of the points dealt with, the minister concerned
presented his report as he saw it. Members who felt they should
formulate objections or suggestions were always heard. It was my
task to clarify the debates by asking questions. If a serious problem
was under discussion, I consulted each of the members. It happened, moreover, as I had consistently noticed for over five years, that
the principles of our policy rarely gave rise to discussion. The action
of the armies, the aims of the war, the attitude towards the Allies, the
transformation of the Empire into the French Union, the duty to
give justice to the 'collaborators', the obligation to maintain order
against all dangers, the necessity to accomplish far-reaching social
reforms—all this provoked no protests or challenges. On these matters,
everyone agreed to take the direction de Gaulle himself had pointed
out. But once we approached the measures to be taken—that is, the
interests involved—the sessions immediately became heated. This
was particularly true in the case of plans of an economic and social
kind, financial arrangements, production, food supplies and the terms
of suffrage and eligibility. In questions concerning individuals, the
controversy reached its maximum pitch.

During the discussion I insisted that opinions be expressed un-
reservedly. Ultimately I made my own point of view known.
Frequently a kind of general agreement was established among the
members. I would say as much, and the matter was settled. In other
cases, I formulated the decision I felt to be the right one, and it
thereby became the decision of the Council. I attempted, in every
case, to make our procedure clear and swift, for once the cause was
heard, nothing would cost dearer than the Government's uncertainty.

How short the hours, and how few! I had to prepare these Government Councils, and many other matters. National defence, economy,
finance, population, Indochina, North Africa were first examined by
sub-committees, over which I presided, consisting of the ministers
responsible with their chief assistants. I also had to deal with one or

other of the members of the Government separately, frequently consulting experts, asking the advice of René Cassin, Vice President of the Council of State, drawing up the agenda with Louis Joxe, and signing the ordinances, decrees and decisions which resulted.

What happened from day to day was brought to me by my immediate staff; Palewski brought me telegrams, letters and reports about policy and diplomacy, the French and foreign press and radio analyses and messages arriving from all points of France and the world. Juin kept me informed of military events and brought me reports and requests from our armies. I then wrote my own letters, dispatches and directives and signed the correspondence prepared by the Cabinet.

The audiences I gave were limited to the essential, which meant they were many. Aside from conferences with members of Allied Governments who came to negotiate in Paris—like Mr Churchill and Mr Eden in November, Mr Hopkins in January, M. Spaak in February, Mr van Kleffens and later Sir John Anderson in March, Mr Ford and Dr Evatt in April—I received ambassadors. Duff Cooper, Bogomolov and Caffery were assiduous visitors. But Monsignor Roncalli, Mr Morawski, Baron Guillaume, General Vanier, Mr Cerny, Mr Burckhardt and others, frequently visited my office as well. The chief Allied or French military leaders had permanent access to me. Periodically the Commissioners of the Republic were summoned to Paris and I met them on each occasion to hear their reports and give them general instructions. Our representatives abroad, when they passed through France, came to report on their missions. Occasionally I received the director of the Bank of France, the Secretary General of the Quai d'Orsay, the Prefect of Police, the director of the intelligence service. It was my duty to make contact with various eminent men in other countries, as well as with French notables—presidents of associations, academicians, prelates, leaders of the economy, trade union chiefs, etc. In addition, the members of the 'Consultative Assembly', the presidents of parties and certain delegates were received when they asked for an audience.

Up to the day of victory, I went to the Assembly thirty times. On twenty of these occasions I spoke there. During the same period I frequently broadcast to the nation. Speeches, addresses and press conferences allowed me to keep the country informed of its affairs, of what I expected of it, and also to carry the voice of France abroad.

In certain cases I was obliged to improvise my remarks. Then, allowing myself to be caught up in deliberate emotion, I showered my hearers with the ideas and phrases uppermost in my mind. But often I wrote the text in advance and then spoke it by heart. No doubt this was the result of my love of exactitude and of a certain oratorical vanity, but it was also a heavy burden, for, although my memory serves me well, my pen is not a facile one. My journeys were numerous—eleven visits to the armies, tours in all the provinces, a trip to Russia by way of the Near East and returning by way of North Africa. In eight months, I was away from the capital for seventy days. Each time I returned I was greeted by the mountains of work that had accumulated in my offices.

It was in the Rue St-Dominique that the latter were installed. The former Hotel Brienne is central and symbolic. From morning to evening I worked and held my audiences there. Here, too, took place the presidential receptions—presentation of credentials, acknowledgment of delegations, official dinners, etc. Here convened the interministerial committees and, occasionally, the Council of Ministers. I refused to establish the Palais de l'Élysée as my residence, thereby showing that I would prejudice neither tomorrow's institutions nor the place I would take in them. Moreover, the style of life which the Élysée would impose on General de Gaulle and cost the state was inappropriate at a time of national austerity. For the same reason, I did not stay at the Château de Rambouillet. I rented a private house on the outskirts of the Bois de Boulogne, on the Route de Bagatelle, where my wife and I lived with our two daughters. Our son was at the front. On spring and winter evenings, agreeable French and foreign guests occasionally dined with us. After they left, my evenings were filled with the study of reports, the writing of speeches and the conscientious examination of the appeals of condemned war criminals. On Sundays I was driven to a wood outside Paris where I took walks for several hours.

From the position I occupied, nothing that was part of France was unknown or concealed from me. Now, in reports, audiences, inspections, ceremonies, a thousand signs revealed that the country was making a recovery, and in the direct contacts I made with the people, I sensed that order was triumphing over an agitation in which the nation certainly risked dismemberment.

This was the impression I received at Nantes, where I went on

January 14th, accompanied by Ministers Dautry and Tanguy-
Prigent, to bestow the Cross of the Liberation upon Mayor Clovis
Constant. Angers, which I visited next, sounded the same note of
confidence and peace that I had heard in Nantes. Presiding at the
opening of the University in Paris, I was struck by the vitality of the
atmosphere in the Sorbonne. On January 27th and 28th I drove
through the Parisian suburbs. The cities of Boulogne-Billancourt,
Montrouge, Sceaux, Ivry, St-Maur, Nogent, Neuilly, Asnières,
St-Denis, Aubervilliers, Montreuil and Vincennes saw me pass
through their vibrant and flag-decked streets on foot, and received
me in their municipal buildings. The bitter cold made the enthusiasm of the people and the homage of the municipalities all the more
moving, whether they were Communist or not. Meanwhile, I had
several times paid the respects of France to Alsace. On February
11th, I was in Metz. The cheers of the people, the fanfares, the speeches
of Prefect Rebourset, Governor Dody, Mayor Hocquard and the
Bishop Monsignor Heintz made it apparent that it was here, as
always, that French victories were most warmly welcomed. On
March 4th, accompanied by Tixier and Lacoste, I went to Limoges.
Our reception was magnificent. Though serious disturbances had
shaken the Limousin, order now prevailed. Commissioner of the
Republic Boursicot wielded the full extent of his powers. Chaintron,
the prefect, seconded him effectively. Mayor Chaudier had created
unity within his municipal council. In the name of France, I made
the pilgrimage to Oradour-sur-Glane. The next day, I travelled
through the Gascony countryside. At Périgueux the trip ended in a
reception which radiated patriotic pride.

Paris on April 2nd closed the series of manifestations which served
as a prelude to the victory. In the morning, in the Place de la Concorde fairly curtained with the Cross of Lorraine, in the presence of
the Government, the members of the state bodies, those of the
Assembly, and the diplomatic corps, I formally presented the 134
flags and standards to the colonels of the newly recruited regiments.
Then, from the Arc de Triomphe, where a huge flag floated, along
the Champs-Élysées, the Rue Royale, and the great boulevards to
the Place de la République, 60,000 men paraded with a powerful
show of military vehicles. These were either new units or those from
the front. The enthusiasm of the people, discovering the resurrection
of our military might, was indescribable.

E

That afternoon, on the porch of the Hôtel de Ville, André le Troquer received from my hands the Cross of the Liberation, awarded to the City of Paris. Earlier I had replied to the eloquent address of the President of the Municipal Council by a speech concerning our duties. 'France,' I said, 'is discovering with a clear mind the efforts she must make in order to repair what this war, begun more than thirty years ago, has destroyed of her substance . . . . We will re-establish ourselves only by arduous work, and severe national discipline . . . . Let the rivalry of political parties be silenced!' Referring to 'the difficult world to which our country has awakened', I declared, 'It is good that the realities are rigorous and uncomfortable. To a people like ours, rejecting the infamous caresses of decadence, asperities are worth more than the soft slopes of luxury.'

That day, as always at such ceremonies, I left the official cortège now and then in order to approach the crowd and join its ranks. Shaking hands, listening to cheers, I tried to make this contact into an exchange. 'Here I am, as God made me!' is what I tried to communicate to those around me. 'As you see, I am your brother, at home among the members of his family, but also a leader who cannot compromise with duty nor bend under his burden.' Beneath the cheers and behind the stares, I saw the image of the people's soul. For the great majority, what mattered was the emotion provoked by this spectacle, exalted by this presence, and expressed with smiles and tears by *Vive de Gaulle!* Many revealed their anxiety that new disturbances would soon threaten their national and individual lives, and seemed to be saying, 'We cheer you because you represent power, order, security.' But how grave was the mute question I read on certain faces, 'De Gaulle! How will the greatness you have restored to us resist tomorrow's rising tide of expedience?'

In the heart of the multitude I was imbued with its joys and its cares. I felt especially close to those who, celebrating France's salvation but conscious that her inner demons had reawakened, suffered on her behalf the lucid anxiety of love!

IV. VICTORY

AFTER THE GREAT spring and summer battles, the western front was established near the Reich's border, in order to prepare the decisive blows on both sides. Taking account of the huge offensive the Russians would soon launch, the western Allies were regrouping in mid-autumn with a view to concluding their campaign during the course of the winter. Hitler, on his side, still hoped to crush the Allies' assault by a supreme effort and even regain the advantage. As for France, these imminent events would give her an opportunity of winning her share of the victory and restoring lustre to her arms. Therefore my goals were clear, I intended our forces to be coordinated with those of our allies. I hoped that their new glory would revive throughout the nation the pride it so desperately needed. I wanted their action to produce specific results of direct interest to France on national territory.

Naturally, for operations, our campaign forces were placed within the inter-Allied strategic system. General Eisenhower, who exercised the supreme command, was equal to his task; fair, methodical and skilful enough to maintain his authority over his difficult lieutenants and to show flexibility towards the Governments which entrusted their armies to him. I decided not to complicate his task and arranged that his control of the major units we transferred to him was as complete as possible. Apart from our mutual interest in winning the battle, there was also the French national interest. That was my concern; to fulfil the requirements, I was obliged to intervene in the strategic domain on several occasions in the course of the fighting.

This would not have been the case had France been granted her rightful place in the leadership of the common effort, if the Paris Government, like its great allies, had been in a position to present its

war aims to the coalition, and if the French general staff had also
been allowed to co-operate in the Allied military decisions. But
Washington and London claimed exclusive rights to strategic leadership, and the 'combined' Anglo-American command jealously retained a monopoly of operational plans. As France's whole destiny
was at stake, as the French Army ultimately furnished nearly a
quarter of the troops under Eisenhower's orders, as the battle's
operational base was on French soil, and it used French roads, railways, ports and communications, the insistence of the Anglo-American forces on holding all the reins of command was unjustifiable
indeed. To compensate for this abuse, I had to force their hands
occasionally and even employ our troops outside the Allied framework.

I was helped in the military aspects of my task by the General
Staff of the Office of National Defence, set up in Algiers and directed
by General Juin, whose intelligence and assiduity had made him
skilful at easing my contacts with the Allies and reducing the shocks
to which my manner occasionally exposed my subordinates. Juin
carried out my operational decisions. In administration, armament,
equipment and personnel, the Ministers of War, the Navy and the
Air Force—Diethelm, Jacquinot and Tillon—with their chiefs of
staff—Leyer, Lemonnier and Valin—performed the same function.
But it was for me to decide the most important measures. I did so in
consultation with the Office of National Defence, in the presence of
the three ministers and their seconds. After which the latter went to
their offices and their telephones to deal with the problems inherent
in a nation stripped of its means of making war, yet which it was our
task to restore to battle with its sword in its hand.

I thought Eisenhower's general plan for the resumption of the
offensive during October well conceived. The Supreme Commander
wanted to move his main force in the direction of the Ruhr, sending
General Bradley's army group as far as the Rhine. Montgomery's
group would advance in the Low Countries to support the American
left flank while, to cover their right, the two armies in Devers' group
would drive into Alsace: Patch through Saverne, de Lattre through
Belfort. It would also be de Lattre's task to cover these positions
along the Alps.

Secondary operations were also provided for. The supply services
needed in a major battle required the landing of enormous amounts

of material, and since the liberated French and Belgian ports were in
the worst possible condition, the Supreme Commander decided to
raise the blockade of Antwerp. The British therefore seized the
islands of the Scheldt. Since the port of Bordeaux was also relatively
intact, and since its use would greatly facilitate the supply of French
equipment, I urged Eisenhower to provide us with the means to get
rid of the German pockets on both sides of the Gironde. He agreed
to do so on principle. The French were also to blockade—until they
could capture—the other Atlantic pockets: La Rochelle, St-Nazaire
and Lorient.

In October, I had decided on a redistribution of our forces to
correspond to the probable eventualities. The First Army, retaining
seven divisions—the 1st 'Free French', the 3rd North African, the
2nd and 4th Moroccan, the 9th Colonial, and the 1st and 5th
Armoured, as well as the two army corps and the reserve units which
had been assigned to it since Africa and Italy, also absorbed numerous reinforcements from the resistance groups. It brought the
striking force of its units to maximum strength, formed new regiments
and was soon to constitute an additional division, the 14th. General
de Lattre was therefore to have a total of more than eight divisions
under his command, with all corresponding services, supports and
flying columns, in order to reach and cross the Rhine.

The 2nd Armoured Division was also to take part in the battle of
Alsace. On my instructions, this division was initially reassigned to
the American Seventh Army with the general task of liberating
Strasbourg. The 27th Alpine Division and two mountain brigades
remained in the Alps to cover the Rhône valley through which the
communications services of de Lattre's and Patch's armies would
pass. Along the Atlantic coast, I entrusted de Larminat with the
command of the 'western forces', which were attached, for munitions
and fuel supply, to General Devers' army group. Larminat was
facing some 90,000 solidly entrenched German soldiers. Since there
were some maquis troops in the area, supported by several North
African and Colonial regiments and batteries of diverse origin, he
was to comprise three divisions—the 19th, the 23rd and the 25th.
Moreover, as soon as the necessary troops could be taken from the
Rhine front, the western forces would take the offensive in order to
liquidate the German pockets. Lastly, two divisions now being
formed—the 10th and the 1st—would temporarily remain at the

Government's disposal, one near Paris, the other close to Bourges. They, too, would be engaged as soon as possible. In the war's final phase, there would ultimately be more than fifteen French divisions in the line. This was all that was possible, at present and in our state of destitution. For France, unfortunately, it was little indeed, compared with the past. 'Allah! Who will restore to me my terrible army?'

All the air forces we possessed were to fly in the battle. On September 30th, we formed the 1st Air Corps under General Gerardot's orders. This corps, which included twenty groups divided equally between bombers and reconnaissance planes, was deployed around Dijon to support the French First Army, while actually comprising part of the air forces commanded by Air Marshal Tedder. Another seven groups remained based in England, five of these assisting in Allied operations in Belgium and Holland, while two heavy bomber groups contributed, with those in western France, to the annihilation of Germany's industrial centres. Six groups under the command of General Corniglion-Molinier were formed to support our western forces. Several squadrons helped the units engaged in the Alps. A few others in North Africa maintained the security of our Mediterranean bases and convoys. On the Russian front, two French groups continued to fight alongside the Soviet pursuit planes. All in all, a thousand French planes were in the line at the same time.

As for our Navy, its escort and pursuit vessels and submarines accomplished their ceaseless task of protecting the convoys, destroying German submarines, scout craft and freighters, and laying mines along enemy-held coasts. Admiral d'Argenlieu, stationed at Cherbourg, directed their operations in the Atlantic, the Channel and the North Sea. At the same time a squadron consisting of the cruisers *Montcalm*, *Georges-Leygues*, *Gloire*, *Emile-Bertin*, *Jeanne-d'Arc*, *Duguay-Trouin*, of seven light cruisers, and of smaller craft, under the successive orders of Admirals Auboyneau and Jaujard, bombarded the shores of the Gulf of Genoa, still in the hands of Kesselring's troops, and covered the southern French coast against the raids of the last enemy ships. Another squadron, commanded by Admiral Rue and comprising, in particular, the battleship *Lorraine* and the cruiser *Duquèsne*, blockaded the German Atlantic pockets until they could be taken. Several naval air squadrons were operating in the same areas. The Navy had furthermore formed three armoured rifle regiments, a regiment of gunners and several battalions of marines and commandos which took part in the land army's battles. It should be added that our minesweepers were completing the clearing of our ports and roadsteads. Lastly, in the Pacific, the battleship *Richelieu*, operating in the Allied fleet, was fighting against the Japanese. However reduced our enemy's naval power, everything, until the war's end, would depend on what happened at sea. It was therefore essential that whatever was left of our Navy maintain the honour of the arms of France.

The month of November saw the launching of the western Allies' general offensive. From north to south, the armies entered action one after the other. On the fourteenth, came the turn of the French First Army. Its mission was to force the Belfort Gap and drive through into Haute-Alsace.

General de Lattre had assigned the I Army Corps to the major operation, while in the north the II Army Corps was to seize the Vosges passes. This objective was to be achieved after fifteen days of battle fought in mud, in snow, and despite the stubborn resistance of eight German divisions of the Nineteenth Army. Béthouart was able to bring his left wing toward Belfort quickly—the 2nd Moroccan Division, the 5th Armoured Division and various resistance units crossed the Lisaine causing heavy enemy losses, including General Ochsmann, commanding the defence of this sector—then to drive his right wing, consisting of the 9th Colonial Division and the 1st Armoured Division, towards the Rhine. The river was reached on November 19th, at Rosenau and at St-Louis, by General du Vigier's tanks, so that the French were therefore the first of the Allied troops to take up a position there. Our troops liberated Mulhouse and Altkirch on the twenty-first, nevertheless the enemy lines held fast. Entrenched in fortified positions around Belfort, they several times launched counterattacks that cut off our forces advancing along the Swiss frontier.

Lastly, it was the progress of the II Army Corps in the Vosges which allowed the I Army Corps to achieve supremacy on the plain. The 1st 'Free French' Division, forming Monsabert's right wing, managed to cross the southern spurs of the range at Giromagny and Masevaux. Its chief, General Brosset, a legendary fighter, died in the course of this advance. But Garbay, who succeeded him, effected a junction with Béthouart's troops in the vicinity of Burnhaupt. Thus the encirclement of the last German resistance between Belfort and Mulhouse was complete. Further north, Guillaume's 3rd North African Division was able to take Gérardmer and Cornimont, and afterward the passes of Schlucht and Bussang. In fifteen days, the French First Army killed 10,000 Germans and captured 18,000 prisoners and 120 large guns. By the end of November, de Lattre was in a position to turn the entire strength of his army toward Colmar.

While he was strongly engaged there, his neighbour General Patch penetrated into Basse-Alsace. Having broken the first German position on the Lunéville-Blamont line, the American Seventh Army was approaching the Rhine from Strasbourg to Lauterbourg. This was the occasion for the French 2nd Armoured Division to liberate the capital of Alsace.

On November 18th this division received orders to advance toward Saverne in order to take advantage of the American success which had broken the enemy line. Leclerc rapidly moved up his forces. Advancing methodically, resolved to bring his soldiers to Strasbourg first, he manoeuvred so as not to be checked by successive German counter attacks. Therefore one of his groups outflanked Sarrebourg to the north, then Phalsbourg, site of the enemy positions. But to the south he would have to cross the Vosges. The roads Leclerc chose to bring his artillery, tanks and trucks to the front were in the worst condition and presented the most risks, but gave him the best opportunity of passing without meeting with resistance. So swift was the advance of our forces, so unexpected their lines of march, through Cirey, Voyer, Rehtal and Dabo, that the enemy units he met were virtually all surprised, captured, or routed, so that our columns often passed the fugitives on the road. On November 22nd, Saverne and Phalsbourg fell into our hands, with many German prisoners, including General Bruhn, the regional commander.

Now Leclerc and his men had only Strasbourg ahead of them. To reach it, they must cross 35 kilometres of open country, then reduce the approaches. Inside the position they had to face resistance from a garrison whose fighting strength was greater than their own and which was entrenched in secure positions. But our men felt the wind of victory rising. Leclerc asked for orders to march on Strasbourg. General Patch knew why the French 2nd Armoured Division had been attached to his army; he also understood the importance of striking while the iron is hot—he assigned Leclerc to the objective he deserved.

On November 23rd, one of the most brilliant episodes of our military history was brought to its conclusion. In five columns—one for each road—the 2nd Armoured Division charged on Strasbourg. The Germans, surprised on all sides, were not able to organize their defence. Only the position they had established in front of the Kehl bridges held fast, and their men retreated in disorder, with our combat vehicles in pursuit. The barracks and public buildings, occupied by 12,000 soldiers and 20,000 German civilians, surrendered almost immediately. By the middle of the afternoon, our troops had restored the entire city to France. The inhabitants exulted in the streets. The exterior fortifications were taken within forty-eight hours. General von Vaterrodt, the German governor of Strasbourg, after retreating to Fort Ney, capitulated on November 25th. Leclerc's success was complete, having been established by forethought, masterful execution and the attraction which Alsace and its capital holds over the French spirit properly translated as an irresistible effort on the part of our soldiers.

A message from General Leclerc informed me of our troops' entry into Strasbourg when they had scarcely penetrated the city. At the beginning of that day's session, I arrived to announce the news to the Consultative Assembly. A single impulse ran through those present, suddenly raised above partisan considerations. Battles occasionally have the virtue of creating French unanimity.

Yet the success of the French and American forces in the Haut-Rhin and around Strasbourg did not persuade the enemy to abandon Alsace. On the contrary, the Germans made enormous efforts to hold fast in the south, the west and the north of Colmar, until they could resume the offensive and regain what had been lost. Hitler intervened, ordered Himmler to assume political, military and police command in Alsace, reinforced the seven divisions of his Nineteenth Army with a mountain division from Norway, a Panzer division equipped with new Panther tanks that outmanoeuvred the Shermans of our own units, and with many contingents hurriedly sent from the interior. The Colmar pocket offered him good defensive conditions. The Germans immediately installed their right wing there, south of Strasbourg in a region which the Ill, the Rhine and the canal between the Rhine and the Rhône made difficult of access;

on their left they were covered by the dense Hardt Forest, while in
the centre, the rampart formed by the crest and the slopes of the
Vosges was still in their hands. While French material brought up
to the lines had to move around the mountains by long and rough
roads, the Germans, in order to shift troops and material north or
south, could do so over flat ground along the chord of the arc. In
their rear, along the Baden bank, the heights of the Black Forest
provided emplacements for their artillery and excellent observation
points over the plain below. During the first days of December, there
was every reason to suppose that our First Army would not seize
Colmar without new and arduous battles.

Furthermore, the Allies were meeting the same fierce resistance
along the entire front. In the Montgomery group, Crerar's Canadian
and Polish army succeeded in clearing Antwerp only with great
difficulty, and Dempsey's English army made the same inchworm
progress around Nijmegen. In Bradley's group, the Simpson and
Hodges armies advanced only step by step in the north and south
of Aix-la-Chapelle. Patton's army, having liberated Metz, slowly
pushed on to the Saar. Devers succeeded in advancing Patch as far
as Lauterbourg. Obliged, however, to act on his left in order to aid
his northern flank, he extended de Lattre's front without reinforcing
it proportionately, which made the French First Army's progress
still more difficult. Moreover, the winter, which was exceptionally
harsh this year, exhausted the troops, froze and blocked the roads
and slowed all circulation of materials. Supply services, manoeuvres
and attacks all suffered in consequence. At sea, the German submarines' desperate efforts still decimated Allied convoys and equipment was unloaded in the ruined ports late and with great difficulty.

In spite of everything, the First Army attempted to accomplish its
mission by completing the liberation of Alsace. Its zone of action was
now extended, in an arc, from the Swiss frontier to the approaches
to Strasbourg, the Alsatian capital being still included in the American Seventh Army's sector, though the garrison there was formed by
the 'Alsace-Lorraine' Brigade. General de Lattre's army was joined
by the Leclerc division regrouped south of Strasbourg and by the
American 36th Division. On the other hand, Devers withdrew the
21st 'Free French' Division, which was shifted toward Royan.

At the beginning of December, the First Army began to advance
on Colmar. Fifteen days of stubborn fighting achieved some success

to the north toward Thann, which it liberated, and in the region of
Sélestat and Ribeauvillé. At the same time, along the crest of the
Vosges, it attacked the Hohneck and the Bonhomme pass. But in
an advance of this kind, deployed simultaneously at every point
along a huge front, de Lattre had not the means to win a decisive
victory.

Suddenly the Germans launched a powerful offensive in the
Ardennes. As a consequence, the Allied munitions supplies and air
support, always given extremely sparingly, were almost completely
withdrawn and transferred to the sector of the German attack. The
French First Army was therefore obliged to suspend its advance.
Seeing the victory they had glimpsed fade before their eyes, leaders
and soldiers alike were bitterly disappointed. After expending so
many efforts, their present uncertainty doubled their exhaustion.

It was upon my return from Russia, in the middle of December,
that I realized what was happening to our army's morale in Alsace.
I was concerned, though not surprised. Knowing the martial energy
Germans are capable of, I had never doubted they could hold the
western powers in check for months to come. I should add that from
the national point of view, I did not deplore these setbacks in which
France's importance could make itself increasingly felt among our
allies. Yet it was essential that our men's morale be maintained.

Matters would soon be under control if the Army felt supported
by public opinion. But in this regard, there was much to be desired.
Not that the French people were theoretically unaware of the merits
of the men fighting in its service. But the latter too often seemed
remote and almost alien to them. For many, the Liberation meant
the war's end, and what happened afterwards on the battlefield
offered no immediate interest. Moreover, it was the Allies who
exercised the command and furnished the majority of the forces.
Many Frenchmen, deeply wounded by our collapse of five years
before, were scarcely enthusiastic over battles in which the French
Army no longer played the leading role. Then too, the disaster of
1940, the military character of the capitulation 'government', Vichy's
abuse of conformism and discipline, had provoked a certain dis-
affection towards professional soldiers in general. Finally, in the
world of politics, public interest and the press the majority of the
leaders focused their attention on subjects other than a campaign
which they regarded as won in advance and which would certainly

lead to demobilization. Noticing the limited space and the insipid commentaries the newspapers devoted to our troops, I called a meeting of the directors of the press to encourage them to give more prominence to events at the front. Their answer was: 'We'll do our best. But we must take public taste into account. Military subjects aren't of much interest now.'

Indeed, on December 18th, General de Lattre informed me of his concern for his army's morale. He wrote that he had asked General Devers to put at least two new divisions at his disposal, to furnish him air support and to allot him additional munitions, for otherwise his troops could not take Colmar. At the same time, the First Army's commander described the depression prevalent among his subordinates, attributing it less to losses, fatigue and the hardships caused by the winter than to spiritual isolation from the nation. 'From one end of the hierarchy to the other, particularly among the officers,' he wrote, 'the general impression is that the nation has neglected and abandoned us.' De Lattre continued: 'Some have even gone so far as to imagine that the regular overseas army is being deliberately sacrificed.' He added, 'The real root of this problem is the nation's non-participation in the war.'

I made every allowance for the disappointments General de Lattre and his army were encountering, following upon a phase of operations in which victories, trophies and recognition had been the rule; I assured him that his troops would in no way be abandoned and urged him to make this known to them; I indicated confidence and my encouragement by this message—'Like all the Allied armies, you are going through a difficult period, but you will emerge from it to your glory'—nevertheless I took steps to reinforce the First Army in view of the coming strategic crisis.

On December 18th, orders were given to incorporate into the front units the 10,000 young soldiers training in the military depots. On the nineteenth, I informed the Allied command that because of the new German offensive in Belgium, I was approving the suspension of the Royan drive, enabling the 1st 'Free French' Division to return to Alsace at once. These orders were carried out immediately. A few days afterwards, I went to inspect the 10th Division, a large new unit in training near Fontainebleau. Under General Billotte's command, this division consisted largely of Parisians who had fought in the streets of the capital during the Liberation. Reviewing them,

I was once more reminded that skilful gardeners can always restore the military stalk to bloom. Although the 10th Division's training and equipment were still incomplete, I decided to send it to the front and announced this news to the division on the spot. Then its young regiments paraded across the frozen snow; fifteen thousand proud pairs of eyes met mine, one after another.

Christmas Eve and Christmas Day, accompanied by Diethelm and Juin, I spent with the First Army. Following the lines, I entered Alsace, proceeding first to Strasbourg. The great city hailed my arrival, though it was in a virtual state of siege—for the Germans still held Kehl and maintained a constant bombardment—and though the garrison, under General Schwartz's orders, was extremely reduced and badly armed. Commissioner of the Republic Blondel, Prefect Haelling and Mayor Frey discussed with me their difficulties in re-establishing French administration. To accomplish what was necessary, it was evident that the future would have to be assured. And it was just as evident that this was not the case.

I next visited the 2nd Army Corps. After hearing Monsabert's report, I decided that all his ardour was no substitute for what he lacked in order to take the enemy positions between the Rhine at Rhinau and the Vosges at La Poutraye. Then I joined the 2nd Armoured Division. For weeks on end it had been thrown back, around Wittenheim, by defences it could not penetrate; its units were exhausted; the local inhabitants anxious. At Erstein, with Leclerc and many soldiers, I attended midnight Mass. The atmosphere was one of hope, not joy. The next day I inspected the valiant American 3rd Division, which had relieved the 36th; O'Daniel, its lively and sympathetic general, informed me of the slow progress his troops were making around Kaisersberg. On my visit to the 3rd North African Division, Guillaume reported on his painful advance in the vicinity of Orbey.

By way of Gérardmer and Belfort, I reached the 1st Army Corps' sector, where Béthouart explained to me that, given the morale of his men, he was paralysed along his entire front as far as Cernay. Near Thann, then at Altkirch, Generals Carpentier and Sudre presented to me the units of their respective divisions—the 2nd Moroccan and the 1st Armoured. Both men informed me that their means were insufficient for them to advance. At Mulhouse, Magnan's division paraded before me. But the Germans were still holding the northern edge of the city, and there seemed to be no means of driving them back.

Yet here as elsewhere, the people were vehement in their demonstrations of patriotism, and their expressions of faith made it impossible to forget how severely the war had chastened every Alsatian hearth. Receiving the authorities and delegations presented by Prefect Fonlupt-Esperabier, I remarked on the seriousness of the ordeals imposed by the occupation, the establishment of the enemy's laws, the herding of so many men into the Reich's armies, the loss of many among these, and the agony which the fate of those now in Soviet captivity inspired. Further, I noticed considerable concern over the possible results of an enemy advance from positions that were still quite near. Returning to Paris, I drew up a balance-sheet of my impressions: the Army was firm, but fatigued; Alsace loyal, but alarmed. I concluded that if anything untoward happened, I should have to intervene vigorously and immediately in order to forestall the gravest consequences.

At precisely this moment a regrettable incident occurred—after the German breakthrough in the Ardennes, the Allied Command decided to evacuate Alsace, withdrawing Patch's and de Lattre's armies to the Vosges.

Marshal von Rundstedt's offensive, launched between Echternach and Malmedy with twenty-four divisions, ten of which were armoured, had in fact made considerable progress. By December 25th, the Germans had almost reached the Meuse on either side of Dinant. They were then in a position to break through the rear lines of the Low Countries front by way of Namur and Liège. Therefore General Eisenhower decided that everything must be subordinated to the necessity of stopping and driving back the enemy advance, which was already eighty kilometres deep. He ordered Montgomery to take command of the defence of the Allied lines on the northern flank and in the Colmar pocket, and directed Bradley to launch Patton's counter-attack on the southern flank. But Patch's army on Patton's right gave signs of weakness in the region around Forbach, obliging Devers to bring in support in the form of the French 2nd Armoured Division, withdrawn from de Lattre's forces. Further, the enemy gave signs of new offensive activity around the Colmar pocket. The situation in Alsace was perilous, and the Supreme Commander supposed that if the enemy attacked here as well, there was nothing else to do but retreat to the Vosges. And it was Strasbourg which would be abandoned first of all. Eisenhower issued directives to this effect.

The evacuation of Alsace, and particularly of its capital, appeared logical from the point of view of Allied strategy, but to France it was not acceptable. That the French Army should abandon one of our provinces, and this province in particular, without even engaging in a battle to defend it; that the German troops, followed by Himmler and his Gestapo, should return in triumph to Strasbourg, to Mulhouse, to Sélestat, would be a terrible wound inflicted on the honour of our country and its soldiers, a terrible cause for the Alsatians to despair of France, a profound blow to the nation's confidence in de Gaulle. Naturally, I did not agree to it. The excuse a policy of acceptance might find in the fact that the Allied command was responsible for military operations had, in this case, no validity. If the French Government entrusted its forces to the command of a foreign leader, it was on the formal condition that the use made of those forces accord with the nation's interest. If not, the French Government was obliged to resume command of its forces. This is what I determined to do, with all the less scruple since Allied headquarters had not even deigned to inform me of a matter which touched France to the quick.

Actually, despite the silence maintained by the Allied command, various indications had alerted me to what was occurring. On December 19th, it was reported that Devers had replied when de Lattre asked him for reinforcements to resume the attack on Colmar that he had none to give, that the entire army group was in danger, and that consequently it was retreat which should be considered, not advance. At Christmas, during my inspection of the front, I had learned that de Lattre, upon orders from the command, had ordered the preparation of a retreat position opposite Giromagny across the Belfort Gap, and had withdrawn the 4th Moroccan Division toward Luxeuil. On December 27th, it came to my knowledge that General Devers was withdrawing his command post from Phalsbourg and establishing it at Vittel, 120 kilometres to the rear. The next day, Devers sent the forces under his command a directive requiring them to fall back to the Vosges in case of enemy attack. Consequently, on December 30th, General de Lattre ordered the First Army 'to establish successive lines of defence in order to retard the enemy as much as possible, in case he manages to break through the initial position . . .'

As a matter of fact, our intelligence reports indicated enemy preparations for a drive on Saverne between Bitche and Wissembourg. Our liaison officers at general headquarters observed that the German offensive was producing concern if not dismay there. On the front, in the rear and in Paris, alarming rumours circulated as to the progress of Rundstedt's troops, reports of Darnand's militiamen and enemy commandos being parachuted into various regions of France, and Hitler's boasts of returning to Brussels and restoring Strasbourg to the Reich by the New Year.

It was time to act. On December 30th I ordered General du Vigier, who had been appointed governor of Strasbourg and was about to return to his post, to proceed at once to de Lattre at Montbéliard and to Devers at Vittel, and to inform both from me that whatever happened, Strasbourg must and would be defended. He was to notify them of the imminent arrival of the 10th Division, which I was assigning to the French First Army. At the same time, I ordered General Dody, governor of Metz and commander of the north-east sector, to hold the Meuse crossings at Givet, Mézières and Sedan, so that in case of a sudden retreat on the part of the American forces operating in the area, French territory would nevertheless be protected. Units from the interior, summarily armed, it is true, but totalling 50,000 men, were immediately sent to Dody for this purpose.

On January 1st, with du Vigier on his way, Juin came to discuss the immediate danger that threatened Alsace. The National Defence Chief of Staff had been informed by Supreme Headquarters in Versailles that the immediate transfer of all Allied reserves to the Ardennes was obligatory, and that consequently the German attack on Saverne was greatly endangering Devers' army group, and that General Eisenhower was therefore ordering him to fall back to the Vosges in order to shorten his front. This decision had been made because of a successful enemy air operation. Dozens of swastikaed rocket planes—the first in the world—had appeared that day in the sky over the Ardennes, had swept the American pursuit planes from the air and destroyed many planes on the ground. Incidental though it was, the episode inclined headquarters to a pessimism which might demand the sacrifice of Alsace. I would have to intervene.

My first task was to make certain Strasbourg was protected. To
guarantee its defence, I had no other recourse than to assign the
French First Army there myself. Such action would contradict the
instructions of the inter-Allied command and, moreover, extend the
First Army's sector northward to include Strasbourg, which belonged
to the American Seventh Army zone. If, as I hoped, Eisenhower
wished to maintain the military unity of the Allied forces under his
command, he would have to agree to the modification I had brought
about in the measures he had described. On the afternoon of January
1st I sent my orders to General de Lattre. Referring to the High
Command's decision to fall back along the Vosges front, I wrote:
'Naturally the French Army cannot consent to the abandonment of
Strasbourg . . . In case the Allied forces retire from their present
positions north of the French First Army lines, I order you to take
matters into your own hands and to guarantee the defence of Strasbourg.'

At the same time, I sent an explicit letter to General Eisenhower.
I told the Supreme Commander that the strategic reasons for his
retreat did not escape me. But, I declared that 'the French Government, for its part, can obviously not let Strasbourg fall into enemy
hands again without first doing everything possible to prevent it'. I
formulated the notion that, in case the Americans did not hold the
Wissembourg salient, 'Strasbourg, at least, could be defended by
holding the line along the canal from the Marne to the Rhine', and
I declared myself ready to 'push all French forces that were being
mustered in this direction, first of all the 10th Division under General
Billotte'.

'Whatever happens,' I wrote in conclusion, 'the French will
defend Strasbourg.' Furthermore, I telegraphed Roosevelt and
Churchill to keep them informed of the High Command's views on
the evacuation of Alsace, to draw their attention to the extremely
serious consequences which would result for France, and to inform
them that I was not in agreement with such strategy.

On the morning of January 2nd I confirmed to de Lattre by
telegram the order I had sent him by letter the night before. Towards
noon, du Vigier, having flown back to Paris, gave me an account of
his mission. Three hours before he had been in Vittel, general headquarters of the Southern Army Group. There, Devers had told him
that since the enemy was attacking around Saverne, the order to

retreat had been given to de Lattre and Patch, and that the American troops had already begun moving. On hearing this I ordered Juin to confirm to Eisenhower that France alone would defend Alsace with all the means she had at her disposal. Juin was also to announce to general headquarters that I would pay them a visit next day.

I knew as well as anyone else that the mission I had assigned General de Lattre involved great risks. Moreover, the fact of withdrawing in the middle of battle from the inter-Allied community could only be painful to the First Army commander, who naturally saw the risky character of such a manoeuvre and who disliked seeing the rupture of the strategic solidarity which had hitherto distinguished his service. Nevertheless, he was forced to admit that in such a conflict of duties, that of serving France directly—in other words, of obeying me—was far more urgent than the other.

Moreover, on his own accord, he had already mentally prepared himself to do what I ordered. General du Vigier's visit on the night of December 31st, the messages from the Commissioner of the Republic and the Mayor of Strasbourg, and above all his own reactions, had made him aware of the disastrous nature of the envisaged retreat. On the morning of January 2nd, he had written to General Devers to express his views: 'Because of the extent of its sector and the weakness of its means, the French First Army is not in a position to defend Strasbourg directly. But it has determined to do everything in its power to cover the city from the south.' And he went on to urge Devers to have 'the American Seventh Army defend Strasbourg down to its last resources'. Therefore, when de Lattre received my letter of January 2nd assigning him his mission, he found nothing in it that was not in agreement with his own feelings. Yet there remained General Devers' imperative order to fall back along the Vosges front and to establish new lines there by the morning of January 5th.

General de Lattre answered my letter on January 3rd. He communicated to me the text of the order of retreat that Devers had given him. He discussed his intention to shift the 3rd North African Division to Strasbourg, moving the 10th Division into its present position. However, he appeared to think that the execution of what I had ordered him to do should be suspended until the Allied High Command had given its consent, alleging 'the necessity of being covered on his left by the American Seventh Army' and also 'the pivotal role played by the French First Army in the Allied position'.

I was, of course, extremely eager to have Eisenhower share my views. But whether he did so or not, I intended the French Army to do what I had ordered. A new letter, telegraphed by me to General de Lattre on the morning of January 3rd, clearly established what was to be done. 'I cannot accept your last communication . . .' I wrote. 'The First Army under your command forms part of the Allied positions for one reason only: that the French Government ordered it, only until it might decide otherwise . . . Had you been obliged to evacuate Alsace, the Government could not admit of your doing so without a major engagement, even—and I repeat—even if your left wing were exposed by the retreat of the troops in the adjoining sector.'

The responsibilities of the Government being thus assumed and its will made known, de Lattre immediately undertook to carry out what I expected of him. He would do so with all his heart and all his ability. The evening of that same day, he telegraphed me that an infantry regiment would occupy Strasbourg during the night and that the Guillaume division would be in a position to defend the city on January 5th.

During the afternoon of January 3rd, accompanied by Juin, I went to Versailles. Mr Churchill, alerted by my message, had also decided to come, and was apparently disposed to use his good offices. General Eisenhower explained the situation, which was certainly a serious one. He did not conceal that the extent and the energy of the German offensive in the Ardennes as well as the sudden appearance of new enemy arms—robot planes, Panther tanks, etc.—had morally shaken the Allied forces and even surprised himself. 'At the present time,' he said, 'the greatest danger seems to have been averted. But we must regain the ground we have lost and then resume the initiative. I must therefore reconstitute reserve units. In Alsace, where the enemy has extended his attack for two days, the Colmar pocket makes our position a precarious one. That is why I ordered the troops to establish another line, further back and shorter.'

'If we were at Kriegspiel,' I declared to Eisenhower, 'I should say you were right. But I must consider the matter from another point of view. Retreat in Alsace would yield French territory to the enemy. In the realm of strategy, this would be only a manoeuvre. For France, it would be a national disaster for Alsace is sacred ground.

Furthermore, since the Germans claim that this province belongs to them, they will not hesitate to seek revenge, should they retake it, for the patriotism its inhabitants have so tirelessly revealed. The French Government does not want to allow the enemy to return to Alsace. At the present moment, we are concerned with Strasbourg. I have ordered the French First Army to defend the city. It will therefore do so, in any case. But it would be deplorable if this entailed a dispersion of Allied forces, perhaps even a rupture in the system of command. That is why I urge you to reconsider your plan and to order General Devers to stand fast in Alsace.'

The Supreme Commander seemed impressed. Nevertheless he felt it his duty to formulate an objection in principle. 'You give political reasons,' said this excellent soldier, 'for me to change military orders.'

'Armies,' I replied, 'are created to serve the policy of states. And no one knows better than you yourself that strategy should include not only the circumstances of military technique, but also the spiritual elements. For the French people and French soldiers, the fate of Strasbourg is of an extreme spiritual importance.'

On this point, Mr Churchill expressed a similar opinion. 'All my life,' he said, 'I have known what significance Alsace had for the French. I agree with General de Gaulle that this fact must be taken into consideration.'

Before agreeing to what I wished, General Eisenhower asked me to consider the situation of the French First Army were it to operate independently of the Allied armies. He went so far as to imply that in such a case, the Americans might cut off our fuel and munitions supply services. I pointed out, in return, that by allowing the enemy to defeat French troops in an isolated sector, the High Command would provoke a rupture in the balance of forces that would perhaps be irreparable, and that by depriving our lines of the means of defence he exposed himself to the risk of seeing the outraged French people forbid him the use of its railways and communications which were indispensable to operations. Rather than contemplate the consequences of such possibilities, I felt I should rely on General Eisenhower's strategic talent and on his devotion to the service of the coalition of which France constituted a part.

Finally the Supreme Commander came round to my point of view. He did so with the frankness which was one of the most appealing qualities of his sympathetic character, telephoning to General Devers that the retreat was to be cancelled at once and that new orders would be sent. These orders were taken to Devers during the following day by General Bedell Smith. I agreed with Eisenhower that Juin should accompany Bedell Smith, which would be an additional guarantee for me and, for the executants, proof that agreement had been reached.

While we were taking tea together after this friendly discussion, Eisenhower told me how greatly his task was complicated, during the worst of the crisis the armies were passing through, by the requirements of various Governments in the coalition, by the touchy claims of the different categories of forces—the armies, navies and air forces of several countries—and by the personal susceptibilities of their chiefs. 'At this very moment,' he said, 'I am having a lot of trouble with Montgomery, a general of great ability, but a bitter critic and a mistrustful subordinate.'

'Glory has its price,' I replied. 'Now you are going to be a conqueror.' We parted good friends at the door of the Hotel Trianon.

The next two weeks were filled with the vicissitudes of the fierce battle for Strasbourg. The German First Army developed its offensive, driving through the Haguenau Forest toward Saverne, while the Ninth Army crossed the Rhine north and south of the Alsatian capital. In the Haguenau sector, the Americans yielded to the German impact but finally halted the attack along the Moder. At Gambsheim, the Guillaume division, and at Erstein the Garbay division and the Malraux Brigade also gave ground before re-establishing their lines. But Strasbourg remained in our hands. By January 20th, the enemy seemed to have reached the end of his strength, and of his hope as well. The same was true in the Ardennes, where all that the Germans had gained was won back again. On the eastern front, the Russians were launching their winter offensive. Over the whole of German territory, Allied bombers were sowing loads of destruction. At sea, the damages inflicted on Allied convoys began to diminish. Hitler could probably prolong the resistance of a great people and of a great army another few months, but fate's decree had obviously been drawn up and the necessary seals affixed. It was in Alsace that France attached hers.

Yesterday, the defeat before Colmar shook the First Army's morale; today, satisfaction at having saved Strasbourg rekindled every heart. General de Lattre, in particular, felt inclined to take an optimistic view and consequently the offensive. By mid-January, he had made his arrangements to resume the effort against the German pocket in Alsace.

At the same moment, the Allied command determined to begin decisive operations on the other side of the Rhine. Before crossing the river, however, they would have to reach it, and this had only been accomplished in the French sector near Strasbourg and St-Louis. Eisenhower therefore ordered Montgomery and Bradley to advance and seize the entire left bank along the Wesel-Coblenz-Mainz line. Naturally he approved of taking Colmar as well. But the First Army zone now extended over two hundred kilometres, in other words, a quarter of the total Allied front. To put de Lattre in a position to achieve his objective, and also perhaps to counteract the effect of the recent crisis in relations, the Supreme Commander decided to reinforce the French First Army. The Leclerc division, transferred from the Saar border, as well as several American divisions and a considerable complement of artillery, joined its ranks.

Yet such was the enemy's fury that it took the First Army three weeks of constant combat to complete its task. After January 19th, the French I Army Corps advanced step by step against the pocket's southern flank. On February 4th it reached Rouffach, near Colmar, having engaged a large part of the German units in many hard-fought battles. On the northern flank, the II Army Corps had also advanced. But by the end of January it had moved closer to the Rhine in order to make room on its right for the American XXI Army Corps, for it was to General Milburn's large unit that de Lattre ceded the principal effort. This time there was to be a sufficient concentration of forces at the right time and in the right place. On January 30th, Milburn, commanding the 3rd, 28th, and 75th American infantry divisions and three armoured divisions—the 12th American and the 2nd and 5th French—and operating in a narrow sector, penetrated the enemy lines north-east of Colmar. On February 2nd he ordered the city to be liberated by General de Vernejoul's tanks. On the fourth, he reached Breisach. During this period, the French I and II Army Corps, supported by well-equipped artillery under Chaillet's able command, liquidated the enemy slopes of the Vosges. On the ninth, our troops completed the conquest of the Hardt Forest and seized Chalempé. Consequently, save in the Haguenau and Wissembourg regions, no Germans remained in Alsace except for the 22,000 prisoners captured there.

On February 11th I visited Mulhouse and then Colmar. I cannot begin to describe the joy and the emotion all of us felt, whether administrators, officers, soldiers or citizens. But another element of enthusiasm was mixed with that day's patriotic zeal—the French and American soldiers' comradeship in arms. It was evident that this brotherhood had been raised to its highest pitch by the mutual success won within the framework of our army and on this very terrain. Beneath the regiments' motionless silence I sensed the pulse of friendship that links two peoples. In the centre of the Place Rapp, now choked with tricolours and star-spangled banners, before our troops and those of our allies ranged proudly side by side, to the cheers of the Alsatian people, more responsive than all others to military spectacles and apter to grasp the significance of such events, I decorated General de Lattre, the victor of Colmar; then it was the turn of Generals Milburn, Leclerc and Dahlquist. During the evening, Strasbourg celebrated the liberation of Alsace in my presence and sang in its cathedral the *Te Deum* intoned by Monsignor Ruch. The following day, in Saverne, Generals Devers, Bradley and Patch received the symbols of the honours I had granted them from my hands.

In this way, and temporarily, we surmounted the obstacles which had damaged our strategic relations with the Americans. But we had to anticipate encountering still others. In the immediate future one ticklish and crucial question was to arise, that of French participation in the German campaign. I wanted our army to enter enemy territory, to have its own sector of operations there, to conquer cities, land and trophies, and to receive the surrender of the vanquished. This was, of course, a condition dictated by my concern for our prestige. But it was also the only means we had of being included in the capitulation, the occupation and the administration of the Reich. Once a zone of German soil was in our hands, the fate of Germany itself could not be decided without us. If this were not the case, our right to participate in the victory would remain at others' discretion. In short, I intended that we should cross the Rhine and advance the French military machine as far as possible into the southern German states.

Early in March the Montgomery and Bradley army groups pene-

trated the Reich at various points. The moment of crossing the
frontier would therefore soon be at hand for us. Naturally I was
keeping a vigilant eye on the sequel, for knowing that the Allies'
chief effort was being made toward the Ruhr and would move down-
stream from Coblenz, I suspected that the Supreme Commander
would scarcely be interested in launching the French First Army into
the Black Forest in isolation. It seemed more likely to me that he
would leave it on the bank of the Rhine, which, perhaps, seemed a
justifiable solution to the general staffs, but made me fear that if we
accepted it the French Army would play only a passive role in the
final battle. Since my policy was at variance with this strategy, I
made my own decisions. Our troops, too, would have to cross the
border. They would do so, if possible, within the inter-Allied framework. If this was not possible, they would do so on our own account.
In any case, they would seize a French zone of occupation on the
right bank of the Rhine.

We soon learned that the Allied command's intentions justified all
our fears. Under the title 'Operation Eclipse', which seemed pecu-
liarly significant as far as we were concerned, Eisenhower's plans for
the crossing of the Rhine and the advance into Germany gave the
French First Army a strictly defensive mission. At best it was presumed, in case of the Wehrmacht's total collapse, that one of our
army corps could reach the right bank behind the American Seventh
Army in order to second the latter in its task of occupying Württemberg. But the First Army's crossing of the Rhine in its own sector was
not provided for. Reports from the front indicated further that the
inter-Allied command had withdrawn the bridgehead crews from the
French armoured division for use elsewhere, which meant depriving
our forces of a large part of their autonomous means of crossing the
river into Germany.

On March 4th I received General de Lattre in Paris and explained
that for reasons of national interest his army must cross the Rhine.
De Lattre asked nothing better but observed—and rightly—that his
sector, lying opposite the mountainous Black Forest region for its
entire length along the right bank, was poorly equipped to effect a
crossing by force. The operation would be a hazardous one against
an enemy occupying the fortifications of the Siegfried line in the
valley and entrenched in dominating positions further to the rear;
particularly since the Allied command was going to allocate the

French forces only a minimum of munitions. Furthermore, even if our men succeeded in surmounting this first obstacle, they would then have to penetrate a most difficult region, rising in successive ramparts of peaks and forests and ill suited for manoeuvring and strategy.

'On the other hand,' de Lattre pointed out, 'once the French front is enlarged towards the north to include both Lauterbourg and Speyer along the Rhine, we shall have better prospects. Actually, my army would find an advantageous base in this area, the right bank would be relatively easy to reach, and once the river was crossed, my left wing would be able to drive through the Pforzheim gap toward Stuttgart and bypass the natural fortress of the Black Forest on the north and east.' Preparing in advance arguments which he drew from comradeship as well as from tactics in order to convince the Allied command, de Lattre assured me that in the next few days he would extend his sector as far as Speyer.

Furthermore, as frequently happens in arguments among allies, the enemy himself was to make matters easier for us. On March 7th, General Bradley's troops had seized the bridge at Remagen, between Coblenz and Bonn, astonishingly enough still intact, and had immediately assured a bridgehead on the right bank. Consequently the Germans now opposed us on the left bank below Coblenz with only scattered resistance, and by the twelfth the Allies had reached the Rhine everywhere north of the Moselle. But south of this river the situation was not the same. The vast Saar salient remained in German hands. The enemy, covered on his right by the course of the Moselle, held the Siegfried line along the Treves-Saarbrücken-Lauterbourg front, which was deeper and better fortified in this sector than in any other. Before he could bring his army groups to the right bank, General Eisenhower would first have to liquidate this pocket. The battle was to be a hard one; although the French First Army was not asked to do so, since the engagement occurred outside its normal zone, it nevertheless found means of participating, operating along the Rhine on the Americans' right and also seizing, on the river's Palatine bank, the desired base of operations from which to invade Baden and Württemberg.

Nevertheless, according to the Allied command's orders, the attack on the Saar salient was exclusively the responsibility of Patton's army forming Bradley's right wing on the one hand, and

of Patch's army forming Devers' left on the other. But Patch's task
was particularly difficult, for his forces were directly opposite the
fortifications of the Siegfried line. Therefore de Lattre had no
difficulty persuading Devers that the assistance of the French forces
would be of value. Our II Army Corps therefore took part in
the offensive. Between March 15th and 24th, Monsabert, advancing along the Rhine, penetrated German territory, forced the Siegfried line north of Lauterbourg, and reached Leimersheim. At the
same time, our allies had pushed as far as Worms and liquidated the
last German resistance on the left bank of the Rhine.

Henceforth, in order for our First Army to have the necessary
crossing area in the Palatinate at its disposal, it had only to extend
its front as far as Speyer. I had taken care to make several insistent
representations to General Eisenhower as to the price my Government attached to seeing the French Army satisfied on this point.
Moreover, General Devers, a good ally and a good comrade,
sympathized with General de Lattre's desires. And besides, it was
at Worms that the American Seventh Army was effecting its crossing; Speyer was of no use in the operation, why not let the French
enter the city? On March 28th the matter was decided, Speyer and
its vicinity was incorporated into our First Army's sector. The
necessary base for operations had been acquired, and all that
remained to be done was the one essential thing—that is, to cross the
Rhine.

I was impatient to see this accomplished, for the British and
Americans were already rushing their forces on to the right bank.
This was a tremendous operation; since March 21st, Allied aviation
had crushed the enemy's communications, supply dumps and air
fields throughout western Germany, functioning with all the greater
accuracy since pursuit planes, now able to use advance bases in the
north and the east of France, were in a position to accompany the
bombers on all missions. The raids were therefore made by daylight without meeting any opposition in the air. On the twenty-
third, beneath colossal air protection, Montgomery crossed the
Rhine below Wesel. A few days later, Bradley advanced over the
Remagen bridge and others built further south. On March 26th,
the American Seventh Army established a bridgehead in the vicinity
of Mannheim.

I was eager to see our men on the other side too, not only in a

spirit of national emulation, but also because reasons of high policy
made it essential that de Lattre have time to drive as far as Stuttgart before his neighbour Patch reached the city himself. A personal telegram which I sent on the twenty-ninth to the commander
of our First Army urged him to make all possible haste. 'My dear
General,' I wrote, 'you must cross the Rhine, even if the Americans
do not help you and you are obliged to use boats. The matter is one
of the highest national interest. Karlsruhe and Stuttgart expect,
even if they do not desire you. . . .'

De Lattre answered at once that I would be satisfied, and in fact,
on the evening of March 30th, elements of the II Army Corps
began to effect the crossing—the 2nd Moroccan Division at Germersheim, which it had reached only the night before. At Leimersheim, on April 1st—Easter Sunday—the 9th Colonial Division undertook the crossing in its turn. The air support provided for all our
units was meagre, and they had at their disposal only an extremely
reduced amount of special apparatus for the crossing. But by in-
genious planning, several boats proved to be enough to move the
advance guards across. As for bridges, General Dromard, in
command of the Army Engineers, had prepared them far in advance. Foreseeing that he would have to construct them eventually
and that when the occasion arose he could count only on himself,
Dromard had collected the necessary material beforehand on our
own territory. At Speyer, a French ten-ton bridge was opened. On
the fourth, 130,000 French troops and 20,000 vehicles were already
on the right bank. Karlsruhe was taken the same day. On April
7th, accompanied by Diethelm, de Lattre, Juin and Dromard,
I had the proud duty of crossing the Rhine and driving through
the ruined capital of Baden.

The eruption into central Germany of some eighty American,
British, French, Polish and Canadian divisions, supported by 12,000
planes, supplied by convoys totalling 25,000,000 tons and navigat-
ing on seas dominated by 1,000 combat vessels, could no longer
leave the Reich's master any illusion as to his chances of escaping
disaster. Particularly since by the beginning of April the Russians,
too, were advancing steadily, crossing the entire length of the Oder,
already threatening Berlin and about to enter Vienna. Should Hitler
prolong hostilities, it would mean further losses, ruin and suffering
for the German people without any compensation other than the

satisfaction of a desperate pride for a few more weeks. Yet the
Fuehrer continued to demand the supreme resistance of his people,
and it must be said that he obtained it. On the battlefields of the
Rhine, the Oder, the Danube or the Po, the wreck of the German
armies, badly supplied, scattered, hastily incorporating barely
trained men, boys and even invalids, alongside the last veterans,
still fought on under a sky thick with enemy aircraft, and in a battle
which could have no other outcome but death or captivity. In the
ruined cities and the panic-stricken villages, the populace maintained perfect discipline in the execution of a labour which henceforth would have no effect upon its fate.

But since it was damned, the Fuehrer probably preferred his
creation to meet its destruction in apocalypse. Whenever I happened
to listen to the German radio during this period, I was struck by
the frenzied character of its broadcasts. Heroic and funereal music,
senseless accounts made by soldiers and workers, mad speeches by
Goebbels proclaiming to the end that Germany would triumph—all
enveloped the German catastrophe in a kind of phantasmagoria. I
regarded it as necessary, for history's sake, to record the feelings such
a spectacle inspired in France. In a broadcast on April 25th, I
declared:

'Philosophers and historians will some day argue over the motives
for this desperation which is leading a great people to complete
ruin—a guilty people, certainly, and one that must be punished as
justice demands, but whose destruction the higher rationality of
Europe would deplore. As for France, for the moment she can do
nothing better than to redouble her efforts, side by side with her
allies, in order to bring the conflict to an end as soon and as completely as possible.'

Moreover, there was justification for wondering if the Nazi
leaders would not attempt to prolong the struggle in the natural redoubt offered by the Bavarian and Austrian Alps. According to our
information, they had already set aside huge amounts of material.
Reports of certain movements of their pathetic columns seemed to
indicate that they were concentrating the mass of prisoners, deported men and forced labour in the interior of this fortress. It was
not inconceivable that the Fuehrer would attempt here a supreme
strategic and political manoeuvre.

How long would a defensive battle last in these mountains, one

waged under his command by all the forces he still possessed? Long
enough to force the eastern and western Allies, no longer operating
on two fronts, but side by side on the same terrain, to inflict upon
each other all the friction inherent in such contiguity? If the fighting
dragged on, would not the behaviour of the Soviets in the states of
the Vistula, the Elbe and the Danube, that of the Americans in the
Pacific, in Indochina and in Indonesia, and that of the British in the
Middle East provoke many dissensions among the Allies? Would not
the postponement of the reconstruction of France, of the Low Countries, of Italy caused by the continuation of the war and of the misery
that gripped the German, Czech and Balkan peoples result in
social upheavals which might hurl the entire western world into
revolution? Universal chaos would therefore be Hitler's last chance
of at least his supreme vengeance.

While the First Army was advancing in Germany beside our
allies, other French forces were executing autonomous operations on
the Atlantic coast. Here it was a matter of capturing the enclaves
where the enemy was still entrenched. After months of waiting,
I was now eager to see the task accomplished soon, for the war's
days were numbered.

The spirit of facility, of course, might counsel us to remain in-
active on this front, for once the Reich had capitulated the fruit
would fall from the tree by themselves. But in war, the policy of
least exertion always runs the risk of being paid for dearly. Here, as
everywhere, we had to strike. The blows we would inflict upon the
Germans in this theatre would have their repercussions elsewhere.
Besides, should Hitler continue the struggle in the mountains of
Bavaria and Austria, our army would have to fight there with all its
forces; which made the prior liquidation of the inopportune pockets
essential. In any case, I would not permit German units to remain
intact until the war's end upon French soil jeering at us behind their
ramparts.

My feelings were shared by the troops of the 'Atlantic Army
Detachment'. These 70,000 former maquisards, like the regiments
from Algeria, the Antilles, Equatorial Africa and Somaliland, which
had come to support them, were eager not to lay down their arms
before they had won some distinguished victory. Their leader,
General de Larminat, outstripped all others in this respect. Since
October 14th, when I had appointed him to the command of the

western forces, he had devoted himself to organizing, training and equipping the ardent but chaotic and badly supplied military group out of which he was to forge an army. He had succeeded in doing so in so far as this was at all possible. Knowing what he wanted, and wanting it with determination and method, experienced at his task yet burning with inspiration, an authoritative yet human and generous leader, a difficult yet unshakably loyal subordinate, he had created, out of miscellaneous bits and pieces, three divisions, reserves, artillery, an air group and supply services—all, as they now proved, ready to give battle.

Yet whatever de Larminat's achievements, his group was not in a position to take the steel- and concrete-clad fortifications in which the Germans were entrenched. We needed the reinforcement of at least one army. In October I requested the inter-Allied command to send our 1st 'Free French' Division to the Atlantic at the earliest opportunity. The inter-Allied command had agreed to this arrangement, but only after tergiversations which delayed the move until December—that is, too late or too soon for the occasion to be profitable. No sooner had the Garbay division reached the Gironde, in fact, than it had had to be recalled to the east because of the German offensive in the Ardennes and in Alsace. The crisis over, this large unit had been assigned to the Alps on operations which also concerned me deeply. Finally, I chose the 2nd Armoured Division to participate in the seacoast offensive. Headquarters made no objection to this, and was even willing to provide our Western Army Detachment with a brigade of American artillery. During the first days of April, all the forces selected for the attack were brought to fighting strength and prepared to begin the campaign.

General de Larminat had chosen the enemy positions at the mouth of the Gironde for his first objective. On the right bank Royan and its environs, on the left the Pointe de Grave, and offshore the Île d'Oléron formed a powerful and solidly held complex. It was true that three months before, the American bombers had come on orders of their own to inflict heavy damage throughout the area in a single night. But this hurried operation, while ravaging the houses and property of Royan, had left the military installations virtually intact. At the time time of the attack, 15,000 Germans, commanded by Admiral Michahelles, were entrenched in the fortifications supported by 200 heavy guns. If his offensive succeeded, de Larminat would turn his forces towards La Rochelle, while we undertook to open the port of Bordeaux.

On April 14th our troops came under fire, supported on the ground by Jacobson's 300 artillery pieces, in the air by Corniglion-Molinier's 100 planes, and offshore by Rue's ships. General d'Anselme was in charge of the attack, commanding his 23rd Division, a large part of the 2nd Armoured Division, and reinforcement units. On every level our men conducted the campaign skilfully and with great spirit. On the eighteenth, after bitter fighting, the enemy's major resistance centre, located between the Seudre and the Gironde, was entirely in our hands, including the Coubre redoubt. Simultaneously, on the other bank, Milleret's troops attacked the Pointe de Grave, which was stubbornly defended. But by April 20th they had reached the end of the last islets. Immediately the landing on the Île d'Oléron was prepared and on the thirtieth General Marchand's army group, supported by the naval squadron, gained a foothold there. By the following day, the battle was finished, though the enemy had struggled bitterly to the very end. Thousands of Germans were killed; 12,000 more were taken prisoner, including Admiral Michahelles. The operation in the Gironde was a French victory; I lost no time consecrating it as such, visiting Royan and the Pointe de Grave among its beaming conquerors on April 21st.

Nevertheless, Larminat did not rest on his laurels, but moved on to strike at the La Rochelle pocket which, with the island of Ré, formed a huge defensive complex. During the last days of April, d'Anselme established positions for the attacking troops. On the thirtieth, the assault was begun. In three days, our men took the line of peaks—Pointe du Rocher, Thairé, Aigrefeuille—and threw back the German garrison to the outskirts of the city. Admiral Schirlitz then opened negotiations for the surrender of his 18,000 men. Soon afterward I hastened to La Rochelle to congratulate the victors, greet the cheering populace and inspect the port which the Germans had left intact.

Once Charente was liberated, positions were established to take the fortified zones of St-Nazaire and Lorient. But the Reich's capitulation occurred before this operation could be concluded, and General Fahrenbacher lay down his arms. Ahead of the Borgnis-Desbordes and Chomel Divisions which had besieged the two areas for months, and the 8th American Division maintained in Brittany since the fall of Brest, paraded long files of prisoners. Of the 90,000 Germans who manned the western pockets, 5,000 were dead, the rest in French captivity. This chapter of the great battle had come to a suitable close.

The same was true, and at the same time, of events in the Alps. Here too, I was extremely eager that the hostilities should not end indecisively; before the cease-fire. it was necessary that we obliterate the outrages lately endured on this terrain, recover in combat the fragments of our territory which the enemy still held, and seize the enclaves in Italy's possession along the Little Saint Bernard, Iseran, Mont Cénis and Genèvre passes, as well as the cantons of Tenda and Briga that had been artificially detached from Savoy in 1860. Afterward, our Alpine troops would be free for other assignments. Should Hitler then intend to prolong the conflict in his 'National Redoubt', these forces would be in a position to provide highly qualified reinforcements for the First Army.

In March, we had in the Alps the 27th Division, a large and spirited unit including a number of mountain resistance fighters, particularly the survivors of Les Glières and the Vercors Massif, who formed its nucleus but who had received only haphazard arms. Under General Molle's orders, this division engaged the enemy along the approaches to the passes from Lake Leman to Mont Thabor. Farther south, an incompletely-equipped brigade held the high valleys of the Durance and the Ubaye. The region around Nice was held by an American brigade, but the latter, summoned to the Rhine, was preparing to withdraw.

For our men to take the offensive, they would have to have a command and reinforcements. On March 1st I created the 'Alpine Army Detachment' and placed General Doyen at its head. The latter, experienced in mountain warfare, was to conduct battle with great ability. Apart from the units already in the region, I put under his orders the 1st 'Free French' Division, which I had restored to my command after the Colmar incident. I added to it two African regiments, unfortunately quite badly equipped, artillery, engineering and supply service units. In agreement with Eisenhower's arrangements, the Doyen army detachment, like de Larminat's, was theoretically attached to the Devers army group. But the latter, engaged in an altogether different theatre, paid little attention to their operations, though it did furnish them with a minimum supply of ammunition and fuel.

The attack began at the end of March. General Doyen was facing four divisions. The 5th Mountain Division was holding the Little Saint Bernard, Iseran and Mont Cénis passes; the 34th was occupying the fortified Aution Massif above Nice and blockading the Corniche road along the coast; both these divisions were German. Two Italian Fascist divisions, 'Monte Rosa' and 'Littorio', garrisoned the intervening areas. Doyen wanted to engage the German 5th Division, which included the best enemy troops, and then storm the Aution Massif. Taking advantage of the advance of Alexander's armies, which were to take the offensive in Lombardy, he then intended to drive ahead into Italian territory.

At more than 2,000 metres above sea level, in the snow and cold which still enveloped the mountains, General Molle's division engaged the installations of the Little Saint Bernard and Mont Cénis passes. Several fortifications were taken; others were not. But the German garrisons, distracted and decimated, could not go to the aid of the Aution defenders. It was the 1st 'Free French' Division which was assigned the task of taking this massif. The task was difficult and ungrateful, for the officers and soldiers of this exemplary division found it painful to abandon to others the laurels which strewed the soil of Germany and to conclude in this isolated sector the epic combat they had waged since the darkest days on the most brilliant battlefields.

On April 8th, leaving the Rhine, I reached the Alps. Receiving General Doyen's report at Grenoble, then reviewing part of Molle's troops at St-Pierre d'Albigny, I finally reached Menton where Garbay's men were stationed. To these comrades, the first to answer my call to honour and subsequently indefatigable in their loyalty, I stressed the importance which this last effort asked of them assumed for France. Then, wishing to give a national resonance to their operation, I went to Nice on the ninth, and from the balcony of the *hôtel de ville*, announced to the crowd that 'our forces are about to cross our Alps'. The voice of the people acclaimed this decision. On April 10th, our troops began the assault of the Aution Massif.

They fought there for seven days, scaled the steepest slopes, seized the Forclaz, Mille Fourches, Sept Communes and Plan Caval forts dominating the mountain, and cleared the slopes above La Roya pass. The Larche and Lombarde passes were also taken after fierce fighting, and the French entered Tenda and Briga, where

F

the inhabitants cheered for joy. Shortly afterwards, a virtually unanimous plebiscite was to consecrate their annexation to France. On April 28th, the Alpine Army Detachment announced a general advance: while its left drove toward Cuneo and dashed through the Val d'Aosta, brilliant with tricolours, its centre descended from the Mont Cénis and Genèvre passes, and its right pushed through the Stura and along the Corniche. By May 2nd, the day when the German forces and the Italian Fascists laid down their arms, our soldiers were nearing Turin at Ivrea, Lanzo and Bussoleno, had reached Cuneo and occupied Imperia. In this war it was established that the battles in the Alps, begun in 1940, later continued by the resistance, and finally resumed by our revived army, concluded in a French victory.

War is like certain plays in which, as the denouement approaches, all the actors appear on the stage at once. While the French forces were heavily engaged in the Alps and on the Atlantic as well as on the Rhine and the Danube, fighting broke out in Indochina. On March 9th Japanese troops which had occupied Tonkin, Annam and Cochin China attacked our garrisons.

This event was inevitable. The Nipponese, driven out of the Philippines and Indonesia, hard pressed in Burma, powerless to reduce China and in no condition to maintain their communications by sea, could no longer tolerate the presence in the midst of their positions of an alien force which threatened to become hostile. Despite the Tokyo-Vichy agreement on the 'common defence of Indochina', Japan had no doubt that if the Allies approached the Union's territory, the French there would join them. Moreover, Vichy had disappeared. De Gaulle was head of the Government in Paris. At the first opportunity, he would certainly give orders to attack the Japanese invader. Although the Indochinese Government had not officially rallied to the Republic, and although at Saigon an apparent 'collaboration' was maintained, the Japanese could no longer rely on such fictions. We could be sure that from one day to the next they would begin the liquidation of the French forces and administration, and that they would do so in the most sudden and brutal manner imaginable.

Yet, however painful the immediate results of such issue, I must admit that from the point of view of national interest, I was not distressed by the prospect of taking up arms in Indochina. Measuring

the shock inflicted on France's prestige by Vichy's policy, knowing
the state of public opinion throughout the Union, foreseeing the outbreak of nationalist passions in Asia and Australasia, aware of the
hostility of the Allies—particularly the Americans—to our Far
Eastern position, I regarded it as essential that the conflict should
not come to an end without our participation in that theatre as well.
Otherwise every policy, every army, every aspect of public opinion
would certainly insist upon our abdication in Indochina. On the
other hand, if we took part in the battle—even though the latter
were near its conclusion—French blood shed on the soil of Indochina would constitute an impressive claim. Since I was certain the
Japanese would fight to the very end, I wanted our troops to join
the battle despite the desperate nature of their situation.

In order to lead this resistance, the Government could not, of
course, turn to Admiral Decoux. Doubtless the Governor General
had secretly altered his allegiance since Vichy's collapse; probably
his orders, his observations, the tone of his radio broadcasts bore no
resemblance to what they had been previously. But for four years,
he had so stubbornly vilified Fighting France that he was now too
compromised to return to command. Furthermore, the Admiral,
unable to rouse himself from his old-man's complacency, refused to
believe in Japanese aggression. Therefore in 1943 I had entrusted to
General Mordant, High Commander of the Troops, the task of
leading an eventual action. Admiral Decoux, moreover, had been
notified of this; discreet telegrams, as well as the instructions which
Governor de Langlade, twice parachuted into Indochina, had
brought him on my behalf, informed him what was expected of him.

In order not to provoke the Japanese attack too soon, Decoux was
apparently to remain in office, but Mordant would become the man
in power once the battle started. Although Vichy in the spring of
1944 had replaced Mordant as Commander of the Troops with
General Aymé—which made matters more complicated—I had
left Mordant his service letter as delegate general. Aymé, moreover,
shared his views. Furthermore, in Calcutta, General Blaizot and the
personnel of our special services, whose presence in the East Indies
the British had agreed to, had been able to organize the many
loyalties available to us in Indochina into clandestine networks for
information and action. For months, it was our services that provided information for the American air action launched from

Chinese territory and for the British raids from Burmese bases against Japanese installations, ships and planes.

French troops in Indochina consisted of some 50,000 men, including about 12,000 Europeans. Numerically this force was weak, though it was actually much more so than the figures indicated, for the native troops, often capable of holding positions to the degree their loyalty remained certain, could generally not be used in the field. As for the French units, unrelieved in six years, they were more or less devastated by the difficult climate. Moreover, our men had only worn and outdated arms and equipment and were almost totally without planes, armour and trucks. Lastly, they were scattered throughout a tremendous territory without being able to change their positions, watched as they were by an enemy ready to assail them at any moment.

My instructions to General Mordant as to the steps to take in case of an attack were intended to prolong the resistance of French troops on Indochinese territory as much as possible. Those meagre forces garrisoned in Annam, Cambodia and Cochin China were too isolated to operate in the field; they would therefore defend their posts as long as they had the means, then fall back in small groups to difficult terrain in order to form guerrilla units there. But the principal force, stationed in Tonkin, received orders to retreat towards the Chinese frontier along the Hanoi—Lai-Chau line, continuing the battle as long as possible. During these operations, they might be supported, or at least given supplies, by the American aviation deployed in Chinese territory and assigned to Chiang Kai-Chek's troops. On the basis of these instructions, General Mordant had explained to his subordinate commands the eventual orders for the alert and for operations. On February 21st I renewed my directives and admonitions by telegram.

This was how matters stood when, on the evening of March 9th, the Japanese ordered Admiral Decoux in Saigon and General Aymé in Hanoi to surrender their command and place all French forces under immediate Japanese control until they were disarmed. Upon the High Commissioner's and the High Commander's refusal, they were immediately arrested and our garrisons attacked.

Unfortunately, General Mordant was discovered and taken prisoner almost at once. This decapitation of the resistance greatly compromised its functioning; yet almost everywhere, our officers and our soldiers, knowing that they were fighting a hopeless battle, in some cases abandoned by the native auxiliaries or deciding to release them, courageously did their duty. In particular the citadels of Hanoi and Haiphong, the garrison of Hué and the posts of Langson, Hagiang, Laokay and Thatkhé defended themselves with great energy. At Monkay, the attacks inflicted by the Japanese, at high cost in human life, were repulsed for over fifteen days. Vinh fought on until March 24th. In the Bassac region, the resistance did not stop until April 1st. Columns formed in various parts of upper Tonkin reached Chinese territory; a few small ships and customs vessels reached the Kwangsi coast. But above all, an important group, constituted ahead of time in the Sontay region under General Alessandri's orders with the Foreign Legion as its core, valiantly carried out its mission. These few thousand men, manoeuvring and fighting first between the Red River and the Black, then to the west of the latter, resisted the Japanese for fifty-seven days before falling back, with their wretched arms, to join the Allied forces in China.

On the occasion of these operations, American prejudices stood clearly revealed. Despite the incessant representations of the French Government, Washington still refused to send to the Far East the troops we were training in Africa and Madagascar. The battles waged in Indochina wrought no change in the United States attitude. Yet the presence in Burma of a French Expeditionary Corps would certainly have encouraged Indochinese resistance, and air transport of detachments to our Tonkin and Laos columns would have been of great assistance there. Even the American aviation based in China, within immediate reach of the Alessandri group, gave it no assistance. General Sabattier, who had been appointed delegate general after Mordant's disappearance from the scene and who had been able to escape from Hanoi, reach Lai-Chau and make contact with the American command in China, was refused all support. Having long discerned the stakes of the game, I felt no surprise at discovering what others' intentions were. But I was all the more resolved to bring France back to Indochina when, once the victory was assured, our hands would be free in regard to the Allies.

In any case it was henceforth certain that the French forces in Indochina would also have contributed to this victory. Two hundred officers and 4,000 soldiers had been killed by the enemy. During the month of May 6,000 soldiers, mostly Europeans, were

regrouped in Yunnan. The battles, suddenly yielding to a prolonged period of doubts, disappointments and humiliations, had
been waged under the bitterest of circumstances—surprise, isolation,
lack of supplies, the impression that God was too high and France
too far. But such efforts and sacrifices were all the more meritor-
ious: in the spiritual development of a people, the efforts of its
soldiers are never wasted.

Despite my attention to the development of affairs along the
Atlantic, in the Alps and in Indochina, it was what was happening
in Germany that particularly concerned me. Here, in fact, destiny
was in the making, fate was being sealed. Then too, the operations
of the various Allied armies on German soil, their objectives, their
directions, the limits of their sectors, created a succession of *faits
accomplis* which were to wield a practical influence on the period
following the armistice. It was my responsibility to be sure that the
role of the French Army, the relative dimension of its successes and
the extent of the territory it would be allowed to conquer were
large enough for France to assert herself in the discussions and
decisions that followed hostilities. In order that no one should be
unaware of this, I proclaimed it on the occasion of a ceremony
organized in Paris on April 2nd in the Place de la Concorde during
which the colonels of the new or reconstituted regiments received
flags and standards from my hands.

In the mind of the Allied command, obviously orientated by Washington, it was the American forces which were to assume for themselves almost all the action in this last phase of the conflict. Supreme
Headquarters entrusted to the Americans alone the task of seizing
the Ruhr, a region more essential than any other, then of driving
towards the Elbe as well as towards the Danube in order to submerge
the body of Germany, and finally of making contact, near Berlin,
Prague and Vienna, with the Soviet troops. The British were allowed to devote themselves to the coast of the North Sea. As for the
French, an initial effort was made to keep them on the left bank of
the Rhine. Since they nevertheless found means of crossing the
river, attempts were now being made to keep them as close to it as
possible. Naturally at the very moment when perspectives were
widening before us, we would not consent to such a diminution.

While General Bradley's army group encircled Marshal Model's
German forces in the Ruhr Basin and brought them to capitulation,

then crossed the Weser in the central Reich, that of General Devers advanced southward from the Main. But Devers, instead of marching east as well, tended to bear towards the south. If the French let him continue, this movement would press Patch's army against de Lattre's, block the latter close to the Rhine, and limit the German territory we occupied to a few shreds of Baden. Here, operations also had a direct bearing on the political realm. Therefore I informed de Lattre, even before his troops began to cross the Rhine, to what extent his army's action would be serving the national interest. We had agreed that in any case the First Army should seize Stuttgart. The capital of Württemberg would be, in fact, the open door to the Danube, Bavaria and Austria for our troops. Its possession would assure us, furthermore, an important pledge to support our intentions as to the French zone of occupation.

But we also had to consider the enemy, whose Nineteenth Army was energetically fighting in the Black Forest massif. It was therefore in this difficult region, and not towards Stuttgart, that the brunt of the French Army's effort was turned during the first two weeks of April. It was true that the II Army Corps had crossed the Rhine in the Palatinate, had taken Karlsruhe and, on April 7th, invested Pforzheim. But before crossing the Neckar and driving towards the Danube, de Lattre felt he must assemble his army in the Black Forest and clear this natural fortress of Germans. He therefore moved Monasbert southward to penetrate into the heart of the massif and open a passage for Béthovart from the Rhine to Strasbourg; thus Rastatt, Baden-Baden, Kehl and Freudenstadt were captured and the German Nineteenth Army was driven into the wooded heights of the Black Forest. But the capital of Württemberg remained in enemy hands and within reach of our allies—it was high time for us to seize it. Without interfering in the arrangements of the First Army's commander, I informed him again, on April 15th, that the Government expected him to take Stuttgart.

And indeed on the very next day, General Devers sent his army group a contrary directive; according to his instructions it was the American Seventh Army, hitherto engaged further north, which was to seize Stuttgart and, later driving up the Neckar, reach the Swiss frontier near Schaffhausen. The French would be confined to mopping up the Black Forest and cut off from all the roads that might take them further east. 'I must warn you,' Devers

wrote de Lattre, 'against a premature advance of the French First
Army.'

General de Lattre realized that it was urgent to change direction.
He gave orders to the II Army Corps based on this realization.
Monsabert therefore turned towards Stuttgart and Ulm, then
Pforzheim and Freudenstadt, Guillaume's 3rd North African
Division, Linares' 2nd Moroccan Division, and Hesdin's and Vernejoul's 1st and 5th Armoured Divisions. On April 20th, French
tanks entered the capital of Württemberg, a huge city where 800,000
inhabitants awaited them in silence among the ruins. While this
part of the army drove swiftly eastwards, another, led by Béthouart,
advanced directly southwards. Carpentier's 4th Moroccan Division,
Valluy's 9th Colonial Division and Callies', Billotte's and Salan's
1st, 10th and 19th Divisions were used to complete the conquest of
the Black Forest.

As a matter of fact, General de Lattre, while seizing the objectives I had assigned him on the Neckar and the Danube, did not
want to leave any enemy forces of any size behind him. Moreover
General Guisan, Swiss commander-in-chief, fearing that the Germans, in their last extremity, might penetrate Swiss territory in
order to seek passage or refuge, had urgently requested the First
Army's command to send French troops along the Rhine frontier
from Basel to Lake Constance. At another period, the uncoupling
of our forces along two different axes, one to the east, the other to the
south, might have involved great risk; but the enemy had now
reached such a point of disorganization that every step taken against
him succeeded and justified itself. The report de Lattre gave me on
April 21st was a bulletin of victory: 'Complete success of operations
engaged the last fifteen days in Württemberg, in the Black Forest
and in Baden. The Danube has been crossed along a line of over
60 kilometres below Donaueschingen. We have entered Stuttgart
from the south, completing the encirclement of important enemy
forces. In the plain of Baden, Alt Breisach and Freiburg are in our
hands. The Black Forest is completely surrounded.'

It was, however, only a week later that the French First Army
managed to defeat the German Nineteenth Army. The latter, although surrounded, had grouped in the heavily wooded massif east
of Freiburg and was desperately attempting to clear a passage to
the east. Unable to manage this, the fractions finally laid down their

arms. While this affair was being settled, our advance guards were reaching Ulm and Konstanz. By the end of April, there was no further organized resistance ahead of the French forces. Since they had crossed the Rhine, 110,000 prisoners had fallen into their hands. Every day, thousands more were to surrender before the conclusion of hostilities.

But in the coalition, the roses of glory grew thorns as well. As we expected, the inter-Allied command opposed the presence of our troops in Stuttgart. On April 24th General Devers reminded the First Army that the city was not in its zone and that this communications centre was necessary for the American Seventh Army. On the twenty-eighth, he gave de Lattre formal orders to evacuate the city. I informed the latter, when he referred the matter to me, that none of my decisions had been altered. 'I order you,' my telegram specified, 'to maintain a French garrison in Stuttgart and to establish military government there at once. . . . To any possible American observations, you will reply that your Government's orders are to remain in the city and administer the territories conquered by your troops, until the French occupation zone has been established by agreement among the Governments concerned.' De Lattre therefore answered Devers that the question went beyond the two of them, since it was one to be decided by Governments. Without opposing the passage of Allied columns and convoys through Stuttgart, de Lattre maintained the garrison he had established in the city with General Chevillon as military governor.

The controversy, therefore, moved to a higher level. In doing so it lost a good deal of its sharpness. On April 28th, General Eisenhower sent me an acquiescent letter. Of course, he declared, by intervening in strategic matters for political reasons, my Government, in his opinion, was violating its agreements with regard to the rearmament of the French forces. However, he agreed that 'speaking personally', he could do nothing but accept the situation, for he rejected the notion of suspending the supplies furnished by his services to the French First Army and wished to do nothing which might alter the 'exemplary spirit of co-operation between French and American forces in battle'.

Well and good! I replied in friendly tones to the Supreme Commander that the difficulty just encountered derived from a situation not at all of his making—'the lack of agreement between the American and British Governments, on the one hand, concerning the policies of the war in general and the occupation of German territory in particular'. On May 2nd, Eisenhower wrote that he understood my position and was pleased to discover that, on my side, I understood his. As the last echo of the affair I received from President Truman—who had been three weeks in office at the time—a message stamped with a certain acidity, that 'questions concerning France as closely as the occupation of German territory should be discussed with her, which, unfortunately, has not been the case'. The French remained in Stuttgart.

Like waves breaking one after another over a foundering ship, the Allied forces submerged a wrecked Germany. Their advance further cut off the enemy fractions, which circled in confusion. Pockets of resistance still courageously resisted; in certain completely isolated zones, unorganized troops accumulated by virtue of their very exhaustion. In many places, large or small units surrendered on their own account. If the appearance of the western powers was regarded by the populations as a kind of deliverance, where the Russians advanced panic-stricken crowds fled before them. Everywhere, the conquerors received groups of Allied prisoners who had liberated themselves. Here and there, stupefied with horror and indignation, they discovered the survivors and the charnel houses of the extermination camps. In blood and ruins, with a profound fatalism, the German people yielded to its destiny.

At the end of April, Bradley reached the Elbe and established contact, around Torgau, with Zhukov's troops, which had just taken Berlin. To the north, Montgomery had seized Hamburg and early in May took Kiel and Lubeck, within reach of Rokossovsky, who had succeeded Marshal Chernyakhovsky, killed in February, in the East Prussian theatre. Thus the German occupation forces in Denmark were cut off from the Reich, as were those who had remained in Holland under Blaskowitz. To the south, three Allied armies were marching on the redoubt in the Bavarian and Austrian Alps where the enemy might have hoped to hold fast. Patton penetrated into Czechoslovakia, where he seized Plzon, and, in Austria, reached Linz, close by Tolbukhin's Russians, who had taken and passed Vienna; Patch seized Munich and drove as far as Innsbruck; de Lattre launched his armoured units and his Moroccan divisions into the Tyrol, one column driving up the Iller, another bordering

Lake Constance. In the Vorarlberg, the French advance guards engaged the German Twenty-fifth Army, new in the order of battle but formed from a host of fragments and whose leader, General Schmidt, immediately offered to surrender. On May 6th the French flag was floating over the Arlberg pass. Meanwhile, Leclerc's division, hurriedly returning west and put at the head of Patch's army, had reached Berchtesgaden.

This was the end. The Axis was defeated. Its leaders capitulated. On May 1st the last broadcasts from the German wireless announced the news of Hitler's death. A few days before, Mussolini's murder had been made known.

the end

The latter, though he had persisted in the conflict until the very end, had already been effaced by events. Yet how much sound and fury the 'Duce' had caused in the universe, this ambitious, audacious, vainglorious statesman with broad views and dramatic gestures, this grandiloquent and excessive orator! He had seized Italy when the country was slipping into anarchy. But for him it was not enough to save and restore his country to order: he wanted to make it into an empire. Exiling liberty in order to do so, constructing his own dictatorship, he made his country look united and resolute by means of parades, fasces and lictors. Then, relying on appearances, he became a great star on the international stage.

His demands, at the time, were oriented towards Africa. Along the shores of the Mediterranean and the Red Sea, he claimed, or would have conquered, the lion's share. Soon it was in Europe too that he aspired to enlarge his territory. Savoy, Nice, Corsica, Croatia, Slovenia, Dalmatia, Albania—all these were to be his! Then he roused 'Fascist and proletarian Italy' against the decadent French, the impotent Yugoslavs. Lastly, while he saw the Panzer divisions roaring across France, while England fell back to her island, while Russia leaned on her guns and waited, while America remained neutral, the Duce joined the Fuehrer and rushed into the war, supposing it was about to end.

At the moment when a partisan's machine gun shot him down, Mussolini had lost all reason for living. Having tried to grasp too much, he now had nothing left to hold on to. Certainly, at the time of the Fascist apogee, his dictatorship had seemed a firm one. But fundamentally, how could it be when within it subsisted the monarchy, the Church and the interests of capitalism, and when its people, jaded by the centuries, remained what they had always been despite his fetishes and his rituals? Certainly there was some grandeur in claiming to revive the ancient primacy of Rome. But was this a realizable goal when the world was as large as the earth itself, and machine-made at that? To oppose to the west an Italy which was the mother of its genius, to associate the homeland of Latin culture with the explosion of German oppression, in short, to hurl an entire people into battle for a cause not its own—was this not to contradict the very nature of Rome? As long as Germany appeared to triumph, the Duce succeeded in bringing his ill-assured armies to the battlefields. But once his mighty ally began to weaken, the tie became indefensible and a tide of denials swept Mussolini away.

For Hitler, it was suicide, not treason, that brought his enterprise to its end. He himself had incarnated it, and himself terminated it. So as not to be bound, Prometheus cast himself into the abyss.

This man, starting from nothing, had offered himself to Germany at the moment when she awakened to a desire for a new lover. Tired of fallen Emperors, of beaten generals, of absurd politicians, she gave herself to an unknown man-in-the-street who represented adventure, promised domination, and whose hysterical voice stirred her secret desires. Moreover, despite the defeat recently inflicted at Versailles, this daring couple saw a long career opening before them. During the thirties, Europe, obnubilated here by the lure, there by the panic of Communism or Fascism, exasperated with democracy and encumbered with old men, offered many opportunities to German dynamism.

Adolf Hitler hoped to realize them all. Fascism combined with racialism gave him a doctrine. The totalitarian system allowed him to act without check or curb. Technological progress put into his hands the trump cards of shock and surprise. Certainly the system led to oppression and oppression led to crime. But for Moloch, all things are justified. Moreover, Hitler was strong; he was also cunning. He knew how to entice, and how to caress. Germany, profoundly seduced, followed her Fuehrer ecstatically. Until the very end, she was to serve him slavishly, with greater exertions than any people has ever served any leader.

Yet Hitler met the human obstacle, the one that cannot be surmounted. He based his colossal plan on the strength he attributed

to man's baseness. Yet men are made of souls as much as of clay. To
behave as if everyone else is without any courage is to venture too
far. According to the Fuehrer, the Reich, first of all, had to tear up
the Versailles Treaty, counting on the democracies' fear of war. It
would then proceed to the annexation of Austria, of Czechoslovakia, of
Poland, assured of the cowardly acquiescence of Paris and London and
the complicity of Moscow. After which, as occasion arose, the French
would be overpowered in the presence of the motionless Russians, or
else Russia struck down before a terrified France. This double goal
realized, England would be drawn beneath the yoke, thanks to the
sybaritic neutrality of the United States. With Europe entirely grouped
willy-nilly under the ferule of the New Order, and Japan serving as
an ally, America outflanked and isolated would yield in her turn.

At first, everything proceeded as planned. Nazi Germany, endowed with terrible weapons and armed with pitiless laws, marched
from one triumph to the next. Geneva, Munich and the Nazi-Soviet
pact justified Hitler's contemptuous reliance on his neighbours. But,
suddenly, courage and honour flamed forth. Paris and London could
not accept the murder of Poland. At that very moment it seemed as if
the Fuehrer, in his lucid moments, knew the charm was broken. His
armour-clad army thundered across a France without a state and without a command; but England, beyond the Channel, refused to yield,
and the flame of resistance was lit among the French. Henceforth, the
struggle spread from ocean to ocean, to Africa, to the Middle East, and
to the clandestine recesses of France. When the Wehrmacht attacked
Russia, it lacked precisely those German troops it needed to reduce
the Soviets because they were engaged elsewhere. Thereafter,
America, flung into the war by Japan's aggression, could deploy
her forces to certain effect. Despite the phenomenal energy of
Germany and her Fuehrer, their fate was sealed.

Hitler's attempt was superhuman and inhuman. He maintained
it without stint, without respite. Until the final hours of agony in
the depths of a Berlin bunker, he remained unquestioned, inflexible,
pitiless, as he had been during his days of supreme glory. For the
terrible greatness of his conflict and his memory, he had chosen never
to hesitate, compromise or retreat. The Titan that tries to lift the
world can neither bow nor bend. But conquered and crushed,
perhaps he becomes a man again, just long enough for one secret
tear at the moment when all is at an end.

The German capitulation was now only a matter of formalities. Still, they had to be executed. Even before Hitler's death, Goering, whom he had designated as his possible heir and who believed the Chancellor could no longer make himself obeyed, attempted negotiation, but was immediately condemned by the Fuehrer. Himmler, second in the order of succession, made contact with Count Bernadotte, President of the Swedish Red Cross, and through Stockholm sent an armistice proposal to the western Governments. Apparently Himmler hoped that if hostilities ceased on the western front and continued in the east, a fissure would be created in the Allied bloc of which the Reich could take advantage. The master of the Gestapo's action was accompanied by some gestures intended to reduce the abominable reputation his crimes had won for him. It was thus, in extremis, that he authorized the International Red Cross to distribute supplies to the deported prisoners. As soon as we were notified by this organization, we sent foodstuffs on our own trucks, driven by Swiss chauffeurs starting from Berne and Zurich, to the concentration camps and the starving columns the Germans drove along the roads of southern Germany.

To myself, Himmler sent a semi-official memorandum which betrayed its guile beneath its anguish: 'Agreed! You have won,' the document admitted. 'Considering where you started from, one bows low indeed to you, General de Gaulle. . . . But now what will you do? Rely on the Americans and the British? They will treat you as a satellite, and you will lose all the honour you have won. Ally yourself with the Soviets? They will restore France to their own pattern and liquidate you. . . . Actually, the only road that can lead your people to greatness and to independence is that of an entente with defeated Germany. Proclaim it at once! Lose no time in entering into relations with those men in the Reich who still possess de facto power and are willing to lead their country in a new direction. . . . They are ready to do so. They invite you to command them. . . . If you overcome the spirit of vengeance, if you seize the opportunity history offers you today, you will be the greatest man of all time.'

Apart from the personal flattery that decorated this message from the brink of the grave, there was certainly an element of truth in the picture it sketched. But the desperate tempter, being what he was, received no reply from me, nor from the Washington and London Governments. Moreover, he had nothing to offer. As a matter of fact, Hitler, who probably got wind of these schemes, disinherited Himmler in his turn. It was to Admiral Doenitz that the Fuehrer transmitted his powers after his own suicide. The Admiral was therefore invested by an ultimate telegram sent from the subterranean refuge of the Reich's chancellery.

Until the end, the last possessors of the Reich's authority made every effort to come to some separate arrangement with the western powers. In vain! The latter excluded any issue save unconditional surrender received simultaneously by all the Allies. It was true that on May 9th Admiral Friedeburg surrendered the north-west armies, as well as those of Denmark and Holland, to Montgomery; but this was merely a convention between local military leaders, not a surrender binding the Reich itself. Finally, Doenitz capitulated. General Jodl, sent by Doenitz to Reims, brought Eisenhower the unconditional surrender. The latter was signed on May 7th at two in the morning. The cease-fire was set for midnight the following day. Since the act was signed in the headquarters of the western commander-in-chief, it was understood that a corresponding ratification would occur on May 9th at the Soviet command post in Berlin.

Naturally, I had arranged with our allies for the French to participate in the signing of these two documents. The text, of an extreme and terrible simplicity, aroused no objection on our part. I must say that the Allies asked us to do so of their own accord, with no circumlocutions. At Reims, as had been agreed, General Bedell Smith, chief of General Eisenhower's general staff, presided at the ceremony in the name of the Supreme Commander and signed, first, with Jodl as Doenitz's representative. Next, for the Russians, General Suslaparov, for the French General Sevez, Assistant Chief of the General Staff of National Defence—Juin being at San Francisco—affixed their signatures. The Berlin surrender was to involve a greater degree of formality—not that it added anything to the one signed at Reims, but the Soviets were extremely eager to give it prominence. I designated General de Lattre to represent France at the signing.

The latter, received by the Russians with all suitable regard, nevertheless ran up against protocol objection. Marshal Zhukov being the delegate of the Soviet command and the British Air Marshal Tedder that of the western command, the Russians declared that in principle they were in agreement that General de

Lattre should also be present. But since the Americans had sent General Spaatz to sign with de Lattre, the high handed Mr. Vishinsky, rushing forward to 'advise' Zhukov, pointed out that the American general was duplicating Tedder's function and could not participate. The French would consequently be excluded. With skill and firmness de Lattre claimed to the contrary the right to fulfil his mission. The incident was soon settled. On May 9th General de Lattre took his place alongside the military delegates of the major Allied powers beneath a panoply in which the tricolour figured among the other flags. At the final act of the German capitulation, the representative of France was a signatory with those of Russia, the United States and Great Britain. Field Marshal Keitel, exclaiming, 'What? The French too?' thereby paid tribute to the *tour de force* which had brought France and her army to such a recovery.

'The war is won. Victory is ours! It is the victory of the United Nations and the victory of France!' I broadcast this announcement on May 8th at three in the afternoon. In London Winston Churchill, in Washington Harry Truman spoke at the same time. A little later, I went to the Place de l'Étoile; it was filled with a crowd which became enormous a few seconds after my arrival. No sooner had I paid my respects to the Tomb of the Unknown Soldier than the throng thundered its cheers as it pressed against the barricades. With difficulty, I extricated myself from the torrent. Yet this manifestation, the parades, the sound of bells, the salvos of artillery and the official speeches did not prevent the people's joy, like my own, from remaining sober and contained.

It was true that for months now there had been no doubt of the issue and that for weeks it had been considered imminent. There was nothing surprising about the news to provoke an explosion of feeling. The latter, moreover, had already been given free rein on the occasion of the Liberation. Then too, the ordeal, if it was marked for the French by a glory won from the depths of the abyss, had nevertheless involved disastrous lapses at its start. For all the satisfaction of its denouement, it had left—and for ever!—a secret grief in the depths of the national conscience. Elsewhere, from one end of the world to the other, the salute of guns was of course heard with an enormous relief, since death and misery were fading away with them, yet it was heard without transports of joy, for the struggle had been sullied with crimes that shamed the human race. Every man, whoever or wherever he was, felt anew the hope that springs eternal, but feared once again lest 'war, the mother of all things', had given birth to peace.

The mission to which I was prompted by France's distress was now accomplished. By incredible luck, it had been granted to me to lead my country to the conclusion of a combat in which it had risked everything. Now France was revived, respected, recovering her territory and her status, engaged alongside the greatest powers in settling the world's fate. With what dazzling light the day, now ending, was gilded! But how dim were the future dawns of France! And already all was settling, slackening, sinking. How would we keep alive the flame of national ambition, relit beneath the ashes by the storm, now that the wind had fallen?

V. DISCORD

No sooner had the sound of gunfire faded than the world's appearance changed. The strength and spirit of the peoples mobilized for the war suddenly lost their unifying object, while the ambition of states reappeared in all its virulence. The Allies revoked the considerations and concessions they had necessarily granted each other in time of peril, when they were confronting a common enemy. Yesterday was the time for battle; the hour for settling accounts had come.

This moment of truth revealed France's continuing weakness in relation to her own aims and to the partisan calculations of other states. The latter, of course, would take advantage of the situation to try to force our hand on those issues still undecided, or else to relegate us to a secondary place among nations responsible for constructing the peace. But I had no intention of letting this happen. Considering, in fact, that Germany's collapse, Europe's laceration and Anglo-American friction offered a miraculously saved France exceptional opportunities for action, it seemed likely that the new period would allow me to achieve the great plan I had conceived for my country.

I intended to guarantee France primacy in western Europe by preventing the rise of a new Reich that might again threaten its safety; to co-operate with East and West and if need be contract the necessary alliances on one side or the other without ever accepting any kind of dependency; to transform the French Union into a free association in order to avoid the as yet unspecified dangers of upheaval; to persuade the states along the Rhine, the Alps and the Pyrenees to form a political, economic and strategic bloc; to establish this organization as one of the three world powers and, should it become necessary, as the arbiter between the Soviet and Anglo-American camps. Since 1940, my every word and act had been dedicated to establishing these possibilities; now that France was on her feet again, I tried to realize them.

The means were poor indeed! Yet if France had not yet been dealt the trump of her ultimate power, she still held a number of good cards: first of all, the singular and century-old prestige which her miraculous return from the brink of the abyss had partially restored; then the fact that her co-operation was no longer to be despised amid the disequilibrium that burdened the entire human race; and lastly, the solid units constituted by her territories, her people and her overseas extensions. Even before we had recovered all our strength, these elements put us in a position to act and to make ourselves respected.

On condition we put them to good use. Here, indeed, lay my task. But to compensate for all we lacked, I required bold support from the nation. This granted, I could promise that no one would ignore or defy the will of France. Naturally, our allies expected the situation to be otherwise: whatever their regard for General de Gaulle, they orientated their nostalgia towards the old, political France, so malleable and so convenient, and watched for the inevitable discords to appear between myself and those who anticipated a return to yesterday's regime.

Immediately after the victory, a serious incident occurred over the establishment of our Alpine frontier. Our Government had long since clarified its intentions in the matter: we intended to extend the boundary of our territory to the very crest of the range, taking in the several Italian enclaves on the French side near the passes; we also intended to incorporate the formerly Savoyard cantons of Tenda and Briga, and perhaps Ventimiglia as well, if it was the wish of the latter's inhabitants. We certainly had every ethnic and religious justification to claim Val d'Aosta, particularly when our advancing troops met with an almost unanimous desire to join the French camp. But for eight months of the year the snows of Mont Blanc cut off all communications between France and the Valdôtains. Their existence was consequently linked to Italy's so we decided not to claim possession of the valley; we would be satisfied with Rome's recognition of its autonomy. Further, the Government of Bonomi and Sforza indicated to our representatives that it was willing to accept our considerations. The latter, indeed, could seem only moderate in relation to the ordeals Italy had inflicted on us and to the advantages she would acquire from reconciliation.

The final offensive launched in the Alps by General Doyen's troops had reached its assigned objectives. The enclaves, the Val d'Aosta and the cantons of La Roya were in our hands by May 2nd, when the German and Fascist forces in Italy surrendered. From the administrative point of view, Tenda, Briga and Ventimiglia were at once reattached to the Alpes-Maritimes Department, while at Aosta we transferred the administration to local committees.

This was how matters stood when, during the month of May, the Americans expressed their desire to have our troops withdraw inside the 1939 frontier and be replaced in the evacuated territories by Allied forces. The Quai d'Orsay was informed of this desire by Mr Caffery; General Doyen was notified by General Grittenberg, commanding the American Occupation Corps in Piedmont, and Bidault was told as much by Truman during the former's visit to the American President in Washington. In demanding our retreat, the Americans could instance no agreement drawn up with us, nor henceforth allege any military necessities. They merely referred to their own decision not to allow the settlement of any territorial questions affecting prewar boundaries before the signing of the final peace treaties. Of course, Washington formulated this claim with regard to the French alone, and only for the Alpine communes.

To a certain extent the source of this affair was the United States' desire for hegemony, which they readily manifested and which I had not failed to discern on every occasion. But above all, I saw in their demand the effect of British influence. For at the same moment, England was preparing her decisive manoeuvre in the Levant. For London to inspire Washington to find a source of friction with Paris was a strategic move. Various facts indicated that this was indeed the case.

General Alexander, Commander-in-Chief in Italy, obeying Mr Churchill's orders, sent to Tenda, Briga and Ventimiglia Italian troops under his order which, if we allowed them to do so, would effectively re-establish Rome's sovereignty there. Since harsh exchanges had taken place between Grittenberg, who wished to replace us, and Doyen, who would not agree to such a move, and since the French general, more experienced in fighting than in political manoeuvres, had notified his interlocuter in writing that 'if need be he would extend his refusal to extreme consequences, in accord with General de Gaulle's order', Allied headquarters in Italy lost no time in informing the correspondents of every newspaper that French troops were preparing to fire on American soldiers on my orders. Lastly, secret observers obtained copies of the telegrams the Prime Minister was sending to the President. In them, Mr Churchill characterized me as an 'enemy of the Allies', urged Mr Truman to behave towards me, politically speaking, in the most intransigent manner, and declared to him 'on the basis of information obtained in French political circles, that such behaviour would be enough to provoke the immediate fall of General de Gaulle's Government'.

Although Truman had less prejudice and more discretion he decided to intervene. On June 6th Ambassador Caffery delivered a note to the Ministry of Foreign Affairs expressing the concern of his Government as to the maintenance of French forces in certain parts of north-west Italy, protesting against Doyen's attitude, and demanding the retreat of our troops. Next Duff Cooper appeared to say that 'His Majesty's Government are in entire agreement with the position taken by the United States'. The next day, a personal message from the President reached me, expressing the distress General Doyen's threat had occasioned him; he urged me to order the evacuation of our forces 'until the settlement of the claims which the French Government wishes to formulate with regard to the frontier can be effected normally and rationally'. Unless I was willing to act in accordance with his requests, he would be obliged 'to suspend the distribution of equipment and munitions allocated to the French Army by American services'. 'However,' he added, oddly enough, 'food supplies will continue.'

I did not take Truman's communication too seriously. However, it seemed wise to lubricate the machinery of Franco-American relations at a moment when the British were officially letting it be known that they were ready to attack French troops in Syria. I replied to the President that 'of course neither the French Government's intentions nor General Doyen's orders ever opposed the presence of American troops in the Alpine zone', that there were American troops in this zone as well as French forces, and that both were living together there, 'as everywhere else, on extremely good terms'. What was in question was not the coexistence of the French

and their allies, but indeed 'the eviction of the French by their allies
from a territory conquered by our soldiers against the German and
Italian Fascist enemies. Furthermore, several villages have populations of French origin'. I informed Harry Truman that 'our compulsory expulsion from this region, coinciding with British treatment
of our interests in Syria, would have the gravest consequences as to
the feelings of the French people'. Lastly, I wrote that to give Truman himself 'satisfaction insofar as was possible', I was sending
Juin to Alexander so that they could reach an agreement together.

Ultimately, this solution provided that we remain in possession of
what we wished to have. At first, of course, the draft agreement between Alexander's general staff and General Carpentier, Juin's
representative, provided that our troops would gradually retire to
the 1939 frontier. But save for the Val d'Aosta, which we had no
intention of keeping, I refused to agree to such an arrangement,
conceding only that small Allied detachments have access to the
contested communes without in any way participating in their
administration or government. Furthermore, while deliberations
were proceeding, we created several *faits accomplis:* the cantons of
Tenda and Briga elected municipalities which proclaimed their
reattachment to France; in the formerly Italian enclaves of the
Little Saint Bernard, Isern, Mont Cénis and Genèvre passes, we
accorded woods and fields to the nearest French villages. The
Valdôtains, supported by the liaison officers we had sent them and a
militia they had formed themselves, instituted an autonomous
government by the intermediary of their 'Committee of Liberation'.
It was only in Ventimiglia that we let matters take their course, for
here feelings seemed to be mixed. Besides, the few American and
British soldiers present on the disputed territory withdrew at once
after Mr Churchill's electoral defeat at the end of July. When, on
September 25th, M. Alcide de Gasperi, appointed Minister of
Foreign Affairs in Rome after Count Sforza's death, visited me in
Paris, he urged me to specify what conditions we would stipulate
at the imminent signing of the peace treaty. I could tell him, as I
had informed Ambassador Saragat, that we wished to see recognized
by law only what had been realized in fact. Gasperi agreed, with a
few sighs, that the treaty might include such clauses and that Italy
would subscribe to them without rancour. This was what occurred.

While these difficulties were looming and consequently subsiding like a sort of side show, a major crisis exploded in the Levant. For some time the frenzy of the Arab nationalists and the desire of the British to remain the exclusive Western power in the Middle East had been uniting against us there. Hitherto, our adversaries had been obliged to take precautions; now it was no longer worth their while to do so. Once the Reich had capitulated, they united to assault France's position.

It was Syria which was to be their theatre of operations. After the 1943 elections, M. Choukri Kouatly, President of the Republic, and his successive cabinets increased their aggressive claims towards us all the more virulently since, in this unstable country subject to the chronic agitation of politicians, the Government constantly tended to turn the flood of discontent against us. Yet in 1941 we had proclaimed Syria's independence of our own accord. Quite recently, the country had been invited to the San Francisco conference as a sovereign state as a result of France's intervention. For four years, the instruments of our authority—administration, finance, economy, police, diplomacy—had gradually been transferred to the state. But since we still remained the mandatory power and consequently responsible in the realms of defence and the maintenance of order, we had kept the local troops under our command and left minor French garrisons at several points. Thanks to which there had been no upheavals in Syria since 1941, whereas serious disturbances had occurred in Egypt, Palestine, Transjordan and Iraq, which were all under British domination.

Nevertheless, we were eager to establish France's relations with Syria and Lebanon on a secure basis. Supposing that the United Nations would soon establish a system of world security, we intended to transfer the mandate the old League of Nations had entrusted to us, to maintain two military bases in the area, to withdraw our troops from the territory, and to leave to the Damascus and Beirut Governments the control of their own troops. Further, agreements with both states would determine the help we were to give them and the fate of our remaining economic and cultural interests. This was the plan I had originally conceived, which I had subsequently pursued in all weathers, and which seemed close to realization, except that England's sudden intervention brought all my efforts to nothing. It was at this very moment that this intervention occurred.

I had always expected it, for the national ambitions masked by the

world conflict included British plans to dominate the Middle East.
How many times I had already confronted this passionate resolve
that was prepared to shatter any barrier that stood in its way! With
the war's end in Europe, its occasion had come. In an exhausted
France, the invasion and its consequences had obliterated our former
power. As for the Arabs, a political programme as subtle as it was
costly had rendered a number of their leaders accessible to British
influence. Above all, the economic organization established by Great
Britain, with the help of the blockade, the mastery of the sea, and the
monopoly of shipping, had put at her discretion the trade, in other
words, the existence of the Middle Eastern states, while 700,000
British soldiers and many air squadrons dominated land and sky
alike. Lastly, during the bargaining at Yalta, Churchill had managed
to persuade Roosevelt and Stalin to leave him a free hand at Damascus and Beirut.

I had no illusions as to the means we could muster to weather the
storm. In Syria and Lebanon, our forces were reduced to 5,000 men
—that is, five Senegalese battalions, a nucleus of service groups and
one squadron of eight planes. In addition, the 'special' troops—
18,000 native soldiers and officers—were under our command. This
was enough to maintain and, if need be, re-establish order, for the
great majority of the population was not at all hostile to us. But if
these minor units should be engaged by riots in various parts of the
country and simultaneously assailed by the British forces, there could
be no doubt as to the result. Confronted by this evidence, I had
already clarified my intentions: should such a situation arise, we
would not fight both revolution and the English unless absolutely
forced to do so.

I wanted to avoid any conflict between ourselves and our allies
but I had no intention of subscribing to a policy of renunciation.
Such a refusal would be enough to oblige the London Government
to come to terms. On condition, of course, that I was supported by
my own country. If France seemed as determined as I was not to
yield to intimidation, there was every likelihood that Great Britain
would not push matters to extremes, for the exposure of her ambitions and the threat of a break with France would soon have made
her position untenable. I therefore hoped that in case of a crisis,
public opinion would support me. Conversely, the British, particularly Churchill, counted on the anxiety and interests of influential

French circles to frustrate de Gaulle and perhaps cause his fall. And, as a matter of fact, I was to find in political, diplomatic and press circles alike an extremely inconsistent policy of support, or else one of outright disapproval.

In Syria, at the end of April, many signs indicated that agitation was brewing, particularly in Damascus, Aleppo, Homs, Hama and Deir-ez-Zor. At the same time, the Syrian Government grew more insistent in its protests, demanding the return of the 'special' troops and encouraging the leaders of agitation. Our Council of Ministers, on the request of General Beynet, decided to send three battalions to the Levant, two of which would relieve an equivalent force of Senegalese Rifles who were to be repatriated. The cruisers *Montcalm* and *Jeanne d'Arc* undertook to transport them, since we had not yet been able to recover the steamers and freighters we had lent to the inter-Allied 'pool'. This minor rearrangement of troops was all the more justified in that a British division stationed in Palestine had just received orders to proceed to Beirut, although an entire English army, the Ninth, was already stationed on Syrian and Lebanese territory.

No sooner had the movement of French reinforcements started than the English ambassador called on me, on April 30th. He was obliged to ask me, on his Government's behalf, to stop sending troops into the area because 'General Paget, the British Commander-in-Chief in the Middle East, regarded such movements as likely to cause difficulties'. London proposed that our reinforcements be sent not to Beirut but to Alexandria, on merchant ships to be furnished by British services. It was evident that under these conditions our units would not reach their destination.

'We feel more secure,' I replied to Duff Cooper, 'transporting our troops ourselves. Furthermore, you know, the maintenance of order in the Levant is incumbent upon the French and upon them alone. Neither the British command in the Middle East nor the London Government is qualified to intervene in the matter.'

'However,' the British ambassador said, 'General Paget commands all the Allied forces in the Middle East, including yours.'

'We have consented to this organization,' I declared, 'only in the case of military operations, and the common enemy was driven out of the Middle East over two years ago. Our Levant troops are therefore no longer subordinate to the British command in any way.'

'The situation in Syria,' Duff Cooper objected, 'is linked to that of the entire Arab world in which the British have a superior responsibility.'

'In the states of the Levant,' I told him, 'no responsibility is superior to that of France, the mandatory power. Your conduct proves that despite the assurances lavished by your Government and despite Spears' departure after his recall in December, British policy has not changed. You persist in interfering between France and the states under her mandate. We are therefore justified in supposing that your purpose is our eviction.' Shrugging and murmuring that he feared complications were inevitable, Duff Cooper withdrew.

The complications, as a matter of fact, developed in the expected way. On May 5th Mr Churchill sent me a message conforming in both style and spirit with those he had issued on the same subject over the last four years. The Prime Minister declared, once again, that he 'recognized France's special position in the Levant'. But having said as much, he let it be understood that England must nevertheless concern herself with matters in the area, 'by reason of her commitments and duties'. Since Mr Churchill could no longer, as once before, justify this interference by alleging his obligations to defend the Suez Canal zone against Hitler and Mussolini, he now invoked the necessities of the war with Japan and declared: 'This struggle obliges that the Allied land, sea and air communications, as well as the free passage of oil, be protected in the direction of the Indian and Pacific theatres of war. . . . The British must therefore remain on guard with regard to any disorders likely to occur at any point in the Middle East.'

Then, specifying his demands, Mr Churchill urged me to stop sending reinforcements to our bases, to restore the 'special' troops to the Damascus and Beirut Governments, and to make an immediate declaration on this point. He concluded by expressing the hope that I would help him 'to prevent a new trial from being added to our difficulties'.

I did not deceive myself as to what the sequel would be. If Mr Churchill sent me a reprimand with regard to a reinforcement of 2,500 French soldiers sent into a region in which 60,000 British soldiers were stationed and about to be joined by 15,000 others, and 2,000 combat planes were ready to support, it was because the English were about to provoke a tremendous upheaval.

In replying to the Prime Minister, I felt it wise to expose the responsibility England was assuming by interfering in our affairs and the obstacle she herself was raising against any possibility of an agreement between London and Paris. 'We have recognized,' I wrote, 'the independence of the Levant States, as you have done in Egypt and Iraq, and we seek only to reconcile this independent regime with our interests in the region. These interests are of an economic and cultural order. They are also of a strategic order . . . . Like you, we are interested in communications with the Far East. We are also interested in the free control of our share of Iraq oil.' I added that once these various points were settled, we would end the mandate.

Then, assuming the offensive on the epistolary battlefield, the only one where I possessed the means to do so, I declared to Churchill: 'I believe this matter could have been settled long since if the Damascus and Beirut Governments had not been led to suppose they could avoid all commitment by relying on your support against us. The presence of your troops and the advice of your agents is encouraging them in this unfortunately negative attitude.' I continued, with some insistence: 'I must tell you that the entry into Lebanon of a new British division from Palestine is extremely regrettable and inopportune from our point of view.' Lastly, informing the Prime Minister that General Beynet was opening negotiations in Damascus and in Beirut, I asked him 'to assure us that the situation will not be complicated, during this period, from the English side . . . . This,' I concluded, 'is one of the items which, from our point of view, keeps the two countries from establishing the harmony in their policies which in my opinion would be extremely useful to Europe and to the world.'

Everything was clear, and ill-omened. What followed was no less so. Two days after this exchange, the trial by strength began. It opened on May 8th, in Beirut, during the victory celebrations. Troops of Arab soldiers attached to the British Division from Palestine paraded through the streets, insulting France. During the days that followed, many outrages were committed against the French in Syrian localities without the police taking steps to prevent them. It must be added that this police force, which had proved exemplary while attached to French authority, had entirely altered since we had transferred it to the Syrian Government two years before. Since the

British command had continued to give arms to the police despite
our representatives' repeated admonitions, M. Choukri Kouatly and
his ministers had some 10,000 men equipped with the latest weapons
at their disposal. They were to use them to foment and support
disturbances. Naturally, the negotiations General Beynet attempted
to open in Damascus came to nothing.

Nevertheless, on May 27th, the French forces and special troops
had quelled the upheavals in every region of the country except
Jebel Druze, where we had only a few isolated units. It was then that
the Syrian ministers and their British advisers, seeing that the game
was turning to their disadvantage, laid their trump cards on the
table. On May 28th, in Damascus, all our posts were attacked by
bands of rioters and units of the Syrian police, all armed with
machine guns, automatic rifles and British grenades. For twenty-four
hours, the sound of gunfire crackled through Damascus. But on the
twentieth, it appeared that our men had held fast. In fact, the rebels,
hard pressed, had had to take refuge in such public buildings as the
Houses of Parliament, the Hôtel de Ville, Police Headquarters, the
Seraglio, the Bank of Syria, etc. To bring the matter to an end,
General Oliva-Roget, French delegate in Syria, ordered that these
centres of insurrection be captured. This was accomplished in
twenty-four hours by Senegalese troops and several Syrian companies;
two heavy guns and one aeroplane were also used. By the evening of
May 30th, French authority was in control of the situation and the
Syrian ministers, taken by car from the British legation, prudently
withdrew outside the capital.

During the three weeks of rioting, the British had not stirred. In
Cairo, Sir Edward Grigg, Secretary of State in charge of Middle
Eastern Affairs, and General Paget, Commander-in-Chief, had remained impassive. In the Levant, General Pilleau, commanding the
British Ninth Army, had made no move to alert the considerable
forces at his disposal throughout the region. In London, silence
reigned. In Paris, on the twenty-seventh, the reception given by the
city and myself to General Montgomery, whom I formally decorated
in Les Invalides, took place without incident. Everything indicated,
in fact, that our 'allies' were merely marking time while they supposed the 'special' troops would refuse to obey us and we would
therefore lose control of events. For twenty-three days, the reasons
which, according to Churchill, would have justified the British in

halting the conflict—'the necessities of the war with Japan', the obligation to protect 'Allied communications as well as the passage of oil, in the direction of the Indian and Pacific theatres of war', and even the duty of preventing 'disorders likely to occur at any point in the Middle East'—did not determine them to abandon their passivity. Moreover, we did not ask them to take any such steps. But once they saw that the uprising had collapsed, their attitude suddenly changed. Britannia Militant pitted herself against France.

On the evening of May 30th, Massigli, our ambassador in London, was summoned by Mr Churchill, in the presence of Mr Eden, to receive a serious communication. Through the lips of the Prime Minister, the British Government asked the French Government to order a cease-fire in Damascus and announced that if the fighting continued His Majesty's forces could not remain indifferent.

When I learned of this, I was obliged to recognize that our men, simultaneously attacked by British troops and Syrian insurgents, would be in an untenable position. Moreover, Beynet's report, received at the very moment the British manoeuvre came to our knowledge, specified that French troops had occupied all the points in the city of Damascus from which shooting had been directed against our establishments. Our military action had therefore achieved its purpose. Whatever my indignation, I decided I must agree to a cease-fire in so far as there was any shooting still going on and, while maintaining our present positions, not oppose any movements the British troops decided to make. Georges Bidault, who was in charge of our delegation to the Levant and who ardently hoped that matters would not move towards catastrophe, telephoned this information to Beynet at eleven at night on May 30th, with my consent. The British embassy was informed and Massigli received instructions to inform Eden of the fact at once.

If, on the British side, action had been taken only to obtain the cease-fire, the affair would have ended here. But an altogether different aim was envisaged; hence London, learning that the French had decided on a cease-fire, hastened to stage a tableau prepared in advance in order to inflict a public humiliation upon France. Mr Churchill, apparently informed that the fighting was over in Damascus, subsequently launched a threatening ultimatum, certain that we could not respond to it by the appropriate means, eager to put himself up in a favourable light as protector of the Arabs, and hoping that in France the shock would involve a political defeat and perhaps even a loss of power for de Gaulle.

At four in the afternoon on May 31st, Mr Eden read to the House of Commons a message which I had apparently received from the Prime Minister. The British Foreign Minister knew that at that hour I had received no such thing. 'Because,' Mr Churchill informed me over the floor of the House of Commons, 'of the grave situation now obtaining between your troops and the Levant States and the resulting conflicts, we have the sad duty of ordering the Commander-in-Chief in the Middle East to intervene in order to prevent further bloodshed. We do so in the interest of security over the whole area and of communications in the war against Japan. With a view to avoiding any conflicts between British and French forces, we request you to give the French troops immediate orders to cease fire and to retire to their billets. When the fighting has stopped and order is re-established, we will agree to begin tripartite discussions in London.'

Thus the British Government displayed to the world not only the conflict which it had instigated against us, but also the insult it offered to France in a moment when she was not in a position to accept the challenge. It had also taken every possible occasion to ignore our official notification of the cease-fire before its own outrageous orders had been broadcast. In London, Mr Eden had managed not to receive Massigli before the Commons session, despite the requests for an audience which our ambassador had been making since that morning. As for Mr Churchill's message, it was delivered to me at five—that is, an hour after it had been read to British parliamentarians. This delay, which added a breach of normal usage to the insolence of the text, could have no other purpose than to keep me from making known in time that the fighting had stopped in Damascus and that there was no excuse for the British 'ultimatum'. I should say that Mr Duff Cooper, unwilling to associate himself with such a manoeuvre, abstained from delivering his Prime Minister's statement himself; it was brought to me by the Counsellor of the British embassy, who addressed himself to Gaston Palewski.

I naturally made no reply whatever to the British Prime Minister. During the night, I sent Beynet explicit instructions about the future conduct of our troops: 'Do not resume the fight unless forced to; retain positions in any eventuality; do not in any case accept orders from the British command.' On June 1st, our Council of Ministers met and was informed of all dispatches and information received and sent during the preceding days. The Council unanimously approved what had been done and ordered. I might add that the feeling among the ministers was not at all one of fear that we might be drawn into an armed conflict, since we were disposed to avoid any such likelihood and since the degree of bluff in the British threats was evident. All shared the irritation and regret that I myself felt at seeing Great Britain spoil—perhaps for ever—the foundations of our alliance. Soon afterward, I made public what had happened, in Damascus as well as in London and Paris. My communiqué revealed the fact that the cease-fire had been ordered on the evening of May 30th and executed several hours before the British adopted their policy of intimidation. I pointed out that I had deliberately been informed of the latter only after it had been announced in London. Lastly, I repeated that the British Government had ordered French troops to stay in their barracks.

That same day, General Paget came to Beirut and delivered a detailed ultimatum to General Beynet. According to the terms of this document, the Englishman who called himself 'Supreme Commander in the Middle Eastern Theatre', though for an area of 10,000 square miles there was no longer a single enemy soldier in sight, declared that he had received orders from his Government to assume command in Syria and the Lebanon. He therefore ordered the French authorities to execute without opposition any orders he gave them. To begin with, he directed our troops to cease fighting and withdraw to their barracks. On the occasion of this visit, General Paget employed an outrageous military display. Several pursuit squadrons escorted the plane that brought him to Beirut; between the airport and the residence of the French Delegate General, he was preceded by a column of tanks and followed by a long line of armoured vehicles whose occupants, as they crossed the city and passed our posts, held their rifles in firing position.

General Beynet informed General Paget that he took orders only from General de Gaulle and his Government. He pointed out that the cease-fire had already been executed on the orders he himself had given in accordance with my instructions. At present, our troops would remain where they were. The British forces, they could come and go as they chose, now as previously: we raised no objection to that. The Delegate General added, however, that he trusted that

Paget and his men would refrain from any attempt to force orders on our troops and from taking responsibility for a deplorable conflict. For his part, he remained ready to settle, as previously and in agreement with the British command, all questions of billets, supplies and traffic common to the two armies. General Paget, his tanks, his armoured vehicles and his air squadrons then withdrew undisturbed.

Beynet was soon informed that he was supported; when I was told of the communication that had been made to him, I immediately reassured him. 'I repeat the orders I gave you . . . Our troops are to be concentrated in the positions fixed by the French command and to remain there on the alert. Under no conditions can they be subordinated to the British command . . . We hope that the necessity of opposing British troops by force will not arise. But you should not give way to the point where we lose the possibility of using our arms, which the behaviour of the British may render necessary. If they threaten to fire on us, in whatever circumstances, we must threaten to fire on them. If they do fire, so must we. Indicate this very clearly to the British command, for nothing could be worse than a misunderstanding in this matter.'

In order that there should be no misunderstanding in world and national public opinion, I held a press conference on June 2nd. Never before had the crowd of French and foreign journalists been so large. I explained matters objectively, but without mincing words about our former allies. Then, on June 4th, I sent for the British ambassador, asked him to sit down, and said, 'We are not, I admit, in a position to open hostilities against you at the present time. But you have insulted France and betrayed the West. This cannot be forgotten.' Duff Cooper stood up and walked out.

Mr Churchill, stung to the quick, spoke the next day in the House of Commons, declaring that he would answer me. He insisted that his Government sincerely wished to maintain the alliance between England and France, as if the abuse of force it had just perpetrated did not inflict a festering wound upon the friendship the French felt toward the British nation. He claimed, once again, that British intervention in the Levant was justified by the responsibility which his country, he declared, assumed in the entire Middle East. He did not say a word about the formal commitment made by Great Britain on July 25th, 1941, under the signature of her Minister of State, Oliver Lyttelton, to respect France's position in Syria and the

Lebanon, not to interfere in our political position, and not to play
any part in the administration of public order. He admitted that the
Syrian police had received the arms they were now using against the
French from the British, but felt he must point out—absurdly
enough—that the French Government had approved this British
initiative. He expressed regret at not having known that the French
Government had ordered a cease-fire before London launched its
ultimatum, and offered his apologies for not having sent the text to
me until an hour after reading it to the House of Commons. But he
gave no explanation whatsoever for this delay, and with good reason!
Moreover, if the Prime Minister claimed to have been unaware until
four in the afternoon of May 31st that the battle was over this lacuna
in his information services was certainly remedied by June 1st. Yet
it was on June 1st that Paget, on Churchill's orders, had come to
notify Beynet, with all the backing of a military demonstration ready
to be transferred into action, of the details of his 'diktat'.

If the Prime Minister counted on the crisis to isolate de Gaulle
from leading French circles, he was quite justified in doing so. As in
the case of Roosevelt's summons to me immediately after the Yalta
Conference, the Levant incident left me with no effective support
among the majority of the men who held public office. Masked by
the precautions still considered necessary in dealing with me, it was
either distress or downright disapproval which my action provoked
among almost all influential men and articulate public figures.

First of all, the staff of our diplomatic corps concurred only
remotely with the attitude I adopted. For many of the men in charge
of foreign relations, good relations with England was a kind of principle. When the unity was broken on the British side, it seemed
essential to them to re-establish it by negotiating at any price to
reach a favourable conclusion. The Levant question was therefore
regarded by these specialists as a kind of explosive which must be
handled with particular care in order to avoid a rift with Great
Britain. Between the impulse I was trying to transmit and the behaviour of those who actually wrote the notes, maintained the contacts and established the communications, the discrepancy was too
apparent to escape our associates, thereby weakening the effect of
my own determination.

The same was true of the tone adopted by the French press. I
confess that in this crisis, convinced as I was that a categoric attitude

G

on the part of French public opinion would have made the British retreat, the tone of our newspapers greatly disappointed me. Instead of voicing national resolution, they revealed only their inclination to diminish the affair's significance. The articles they devoted to it, brief and of little prominence, made it clear that for French journalists the matter was settled—that is, lost—and that they were therefore eager to move on to something else. Resentment was occasionally expressed, but towards General de Gaulle, whose tenacity appeared temerarious and ill-advised.

The Consultative Assembly gave no greater support. It was only on June 17th—three weeks after the British intervention—that it broached the subject. The Minister of Foreign Affairs explained the series of events to a small group of members; then several speakers took their turn on the tribunal. Maurice Schumann and Father Carrière condemned the riots agitators had provoked against us, praised France's accomplishments in the Middle East and deplored the attitude adopted by Great Britain in explicit terms. However, they were only relatively successful. Georges Gorse also referred to the unacceptable nature of British intervention, but addressed no fewer reproaches to the Government. After which, Florimond Bonte, André Hauriou, Marcel Astier and, in particular, Pierre Cot bitterly criticized both France and myself and received the approval of almost the whole audience.

Judging from their remarks and from the applause lavished upon them, what was happening in Syria was the result of an abusive policy we had pursued from the start. To modify its excesses, our only recourse was to present ourselves to the people of the Levant in the guise of liberating, educating and revolutionary France, while leaving them to govern themselves. There was a contradiction here which these peculiar Jacobins were not prepared to resolve, nor would their ideology take into account the realities of the riots, the murder of our nationals, the obligations of the mandate, and the British intention of driving us out of the area. They had no good word to say about the civilizing function France had performed in Syria and the Lebanon, the independence which I myself had given both states, the place my Government had just got them in the United Nations, and the efforts of our soldiers who during the first World War had helped liberate them from the yoke of the Ottoman Empire and during the second had protected them against Hitler's domination.

Personally, I had anticipated that out of this entire gathering of men devoted to political affairs, someone—if only one man—would stand up and say: 'The honour and the interests of our country are at stake. In an area where both are endangered, it is true that we are not immediately the strongest. But we shall not renounce our rights. Let those who have contravened them know that they have also gravely offended the alliance which united us. Let them know that France will come to the appropriate conclusions when she recovers her power and her influence.'

No one spoke in these terms except myself at the end of the session. The Assembly listened to me with close attention and applauded, as usual, when I left the tribunal; after which, it voted a motion lacking all vigour and expressing nothing but renunciation. I was obliged to declare that the text was not binding on the Government. This led me to realize the profound lack of unity which, beneath appearances, separated me from the political parties with regard to foreign affairs.

Meanwhile, the British intervention in Syria had succeeded in unleashing a new wave of anti-French agitation, but our few forces, threatened as they were by the British, were not, this time, able to control the situation. General Beynet therefore decided to regroup them outside the large cities, whereupon the latter were immediately occupied by the British. This resulted in many and bloody attacks, whose victims were our nationals. Upon which our 'allies', on the pretext of avoiding further incidents, expelled all remaining French citizens from Damascus, Aleppo, Homs, Hama and Deir-ez-Zor. Further, our inability to maintain order as well as the general agitation risked throwing the Syrian troops into chaos too. The French authority therefore renounced its command of these units.

During the summer, a state of fragile equilibrium was established in Syrian territory between the French, who still held certain points —the regions around Aleppo and Damascus, the port of Latakia, the air base of Rayak—the English, who had established themselves in most of the cities and were unsuccessfully trying to restore order, and the nationalists, who had now turned on the British and were asking for the withdrawal of all foreign forces. In the Lebanon, on the other hand, the populace remained calm, though at Beirut the leaders added their claims to those of the Damascus Government.

Under such conditions, I felt no need for haste in proceeding to a

settlement. Therefore Mr Churchill's suggestion for a tripartite conference involving France, England and the United States received no
reply from us. But the way in which the Anglo-American powers
were behaving towards us justified our throwing a pebble in their
diplomatic pond. Since on June 1st Soviet Russia had sent us a note
expressing concern over the incidents in the Levant, as well as those
in Egypt, Palestine and Iraq, all of which were eager to be free of the
British, I publicly declared on June 2nd that the question should be
studied by a conference of the five 'great powers'—France, England,
the United States, the Soviet Union and China. The note we sent on
this subject pointed out that these five states had just been recognized
as permanent members of the United Nations Security Council and
that until this organization was set in operation, it was the responsibility of these nations to settle a problem which concerned the peace
of the entire world. Our programme was, of course, rejected by the
British and the Americans with sullen resentment. The same reaction
was accorded our next proposal to bring the entire Levant affair
before the recently constituted United Nations.

Everything, therefore, remained in suspense. As matters stood, this
was the most favourable situation for us. I was, indeed, convinced
that the British attempt to replace us in Damascus and Beirut would
end in failure. Moreover, the day would soon come when a functioning United Nations would assume the responsibility the League of
Nations had previously entrusted to France in Syria and Lebanon.
We would then be justified in removing the last vestiges of our
authority from the Levant, without having abandoned this area to
any other power. Of course, and in any case, our troops would not
leave the area so long as the British forces remained there. As for
what would happen then, I did not doubt that the agitation supported in the Levant by our former allies would spread through the
entire Middle East to the detriment of these sorcerer's apprentices,
and that eventually the British and Americans would pay dearly for
the enterprise they had launched against France.

But while the British were abusing us in the Levant, the general
consent of nations nevertheless restored France to the place she had
once occupied among the primary states. It was as if the world
hailed our resurrection as a kind of miracle, hastened to take advantage of it to give us once more the place we had always had, and
believed that with all its new anxieties it would need us. The demon-

stration took place in San Francisco, where the conference met on April 25th and ended on June 26th, after adopting the United Nations Charter. Franklin Roosevelt had died a week before its opening. (What man ever lived to see his triumph complete?) But the plan which the unanimous delegations had adopted was that of the great American leader.

Reviving an idea which had haunted the minds of many philosophers and several statesmen, had given birth to the League of Nations and then foundered because of the defection of the United States and the weakness of the democracies, Roosevelt had wanted a world peace organization to emerge from the conflict. In our conversations in Washington the year before, the President had made me understand how close this monumental edifice was to his heart. In his ideology, international democracy was a sort of panacea; he felt that the nations, thus confronting each other, would examine their grievances and in each case take the measures necessary to keep matters from reaching a state of war. They would also co-operate on behalf of the progress of the human race. 'Thanks to this institution,' he told me, 'the old American isolationism will come to an end and we will also be able to associate Russia, long isolated from us, with the rest of the Western world.' Although he did not mention it, Roosevelt expected that the crowd of small nations would force the hand of the 'colonialist' powers and assure the United States an enormous political and economic clientele.

First at Dumbarton Oaks and later at Yalta, America, Great Britain and Russia had reached agreements on a constitution for the United Nations. China's consent had been obtained. When the Crimean conference was over, France's approval was sought, and Paris was invited to join Washington, London, Moscow and Chungking in issuing invitations to the San Francisco Conference. After careful consideration, we had declined the offer the other four 'big powers' had made to us to be a sponsoring power along with them. It was not suitable for us to recommend to fifty-one nations that they subscribe to articles drawn up without our participation.

On my part, it was with sympathy but circumspection that I watched the nascent organization. Of course its universal object was highly estimable in itself and consonant with the genius of France. It was salutary that cases of imminent conflict be referred to international intervention, and that the latter be employed to effect compromises. In any case, it was good that the states make contact with each other periodically, in full view of world opinion. Nevertheless, despite what Roosevelt thought, what Churchill implied and what Stalin appeared to believe, I did not allow myself to exaggerate the value of the United Nations.

Its members would be states, that is, the least impartial and the most partisan bodies in the world. Their meeting could, assuredly, formulate political motions, but not give decisions. Yet it was inevitable that such an organization would claim to be as qualified for the one as for the other. Furthermore, its more or less tumultuous debates, developed in the presence of innumerable transcribers, broadcasters and cameramen, ran the risk of baulking genuine diplomatic negotiation which is almost always fruitful only when characterized by precision and discretion. Lastly, it was to be presumed that many small countries would automatically oppose the great powers, whose presence and territories extended the world over, touched many frontiers and inspired frequent envy or anxiety. America and Russia certainly had strength enough to inspire more than respect. England, relatively intact, retained its manoeuvrability. But France, terribly damaged by the war and assailed by all kinds of claims from Africa and Asia—what hearing would she obtain in her difficulties?

This was why I instructed our delegation not to give way to highsounding declarations, as many of our representatives had once done in Geneva, but instead to observe an attitude of restraint. This was done, and done well, under the successive leadership of Georges Bidault, participating for the first time at an international conference, and President Paul-Boncour, whose experience with the League of Nations made him a master of such subjects. The discretion shown by our representatives did not, of course, keep France from taking her place in the Areopagus of the five 'big powers' which conducted the affair. It achieved, in San Francisco, all that we were most eager to obtain. Thus, despite a certain amount of opposition, French was recognized as one of the three official languages of the United Nations. Further, beyond the right of veto appertaining to France as to the other great powers, the Charter's original draft was amended so as to make the 'General Assembly' counterbalance the 'Security Council' and, at the same time, to control the tendencies of the Assembly by requiring a two-thirds majority for its motions. It was further specified that the examination of litigation by the organization would in no way impede the drafting and signing of treaties of alliance. Lastly, the system of 'trusteeship', under which malevolent intentions with regard to the French Union were apparent, would be subject to severe restrictions.

The United Nations was born, but its first session, devoted to its constitution, did not deal with the problems raised by the war's end. Americans and British rushed without us to Potsdam intending to meet with the Russians there and to establish what must be done in the practical sphere. The conference began on July 17th. In Truman's mind and Churchill's, it was a matter of concluding with Stalin what had been proposed at Teheran and decided at Yalta in regard to Germany, Poland, Central Europe and the Balkans. The Americans and British hoped to recover in practice what they had conceded in principle. The 'Big Three' would also confer on the conditions under which Soviet Russia would participate *in extremis* in the war against Japan.

That our allies of yesterday should convene yet again in our absence—for the last time, moreover—could only cause us renewed irritation. Yet fundamentally we considered it preferable not to be introduced into discussions which could henceforth be nothing but supererogatory.

For the facts were decided. The enormous chunk of Europe which the Yalta agreements had abandoned in advance to the Soviets was now in their hands. Even the American armies, after having overrun the frontiers established for them in Germany during the last days of the fighting, had fallen back 150 kilometres. The Russians alone occupied Prussia and Saxony. Without further delay they had annexed all of Poland east of the Curzon line, transferred the inhabitants along the Oder and the western Neisse, and driven the German population of Silesia, Poznan and Pomerania west. All frontiers were thus decided quite simply by the Soviets. Furthermore, in Warsaw, Budapest, Sofia, Belgrade and Tirana, the Governments installed were at their discretion and almost all at their beck and call. The rapidity of the Sovietization was the inevitable result of what had been agreed upon at the Crimea conference. The regrets the British and Americans now expressed were quite uncalled for.

What purpose could Soviet intervention in the Pacific theatre serve? The atom bombs were ready. Arriving in Potsdam, Truman and Churchill announced the success of the New Mexico experiments. From one day to the next, Japan was to suffer the terrible explosions and consequently surrender. Any commitments the Russians now made about the war in the Pacific involved no military consequences, but resulted in the Kremlin's recognized right to participate as victor in Far Eastern affairs. For Asia and for Europe, there was every reason to predict that the Potsdam conference would realize no durable entente on any issue, but would, instead, provoke unlimited friction between the Soviet and the Anglo-American participants.

This prospect convinced me that it was wiser not to climb on the band wagon at this point. Naturally I regretted that I had not been present at Teheran. There, as a matter of fact, I would have defended the equilibrium of Europe while there would still have been some point in doing so. Subsequently, I was sorry not to have been allowed to take part in the Yalta Conference, since there were still some chances of preventing the iron curtain from cutting Europe in two. Now everything had been arranged—what could I have done at Potsdam?

Once the communiqué published by the conference appeared, we learned that it had concluded in a kind of uproar. Despite the wealth of conciliation lavished by Mr Truman, despite Mr Churchill's vehement protest, Generalissimo Stalin had agreed to no compromises of any kind. In Poland particularly, the appearance of Mikolajczyk, Grabski, Witos and Stanczyk in the cabinet formed on the basis of the Lublin Committee had induced Washington and London, and obliged Paris as well, to recognize the Government directed by Bierut and Osubka-Morawski. It was soon apparent that the totalitarian character of the Warsaw Government was in no way diminished thereby. In Asia, Stalin, in exchange for his promise to declare war on Japan, managed to obtain for Russia the Kurile Archipelago and half of Sakhalin, induced the Allies to accord Korea to the Soviets north of the 38th parallel, and forced Chiang Kai-shek to withdraw from Outer Mongolia. The latter became a 'People's Republic'. At this price the Generalissimo promised not to intervene in China's internal affairs, but he was nonetheless allowed to furnish support and arms to Mao Tse-tung's Communists who were soon to seize the country. On the whole, far from consecrating the world-wide co-operation of America and Russia, to which Roose-

velt had sacrificed the equilibrium of Europe, the Potsdam conference
whetted their opposition.

Mr Churchill left before the end, thrust from power by the British
electors. Upon the Reich's surrender, Great Britain had broken up
a national coalition which had lasted for over five years. Elections
had been held and on July 25th, a breakdown of the votes gave the
Labour Party a majority in the House of Commons. The Prime
Minister, head of the Conservative Party, was therefore obliged to
resign.

To minds inclined towards sentimentality, this sudden disgrace
inflicted by the British nation upon the great man who had led it to
salvation and glorious victory might seem surprising. Yet there was
nothing in the occasion which was not in accordance with the order
of human affairs. Once the war was over, public opinion and policy
alike cast off the psychology of union, energy and sacrifice and turned
once more to interest, prejudice and antagonism. Winston Churchill
lost neither his glory nor his popularity thereby, but only the general
adherence he had won as a guide and symbol of a nation in peril.
His nature, identified with magnificent enterprises, his countenance,
etched by the fires and frosts of great events, had become inappropriate in the era of mediocrity.

In some respects, Churchill's departure facilitated the conduct of
French affairs; in others, it did not. In any case, I saw it with
melancholy. Certainly within the alliance itself Churchill had not
dealt gently with me, and lately, in the Levant, his behaviour had
been that of an enemy. In general, he had supported me for as long
as he took me for the head of a French minority which favoured him
and which he could put to good use. This great politician had always
been convinced that France was necessary to the free world; and
this exceptional artist was certainly conscious of the dramatic character of my mission. But when he saw France represented by me as an
ambitious state apparently eager to recover her power in Europe and
the world, Churchill had quite naturally felt something of Pitt's
spirit in his soul. In spite of everything, the essential and ineffaceable
fact remained that without him my efforts would have been futile
from the start, and that by lending me a strong and willing hand
when he did, Churchill had vitally aided the cause of France.

Having seen a great deal of him, I had greatly admired though
quite as often envied him. His task was colossal but at least he found

himself legally invested with power by the state. He was given all
the powers and provided with all the levers of legal authority, set at
the head of a unanimous people, of a territory still intact, of a tremendous Empire, and of formidable armies. At the time I was
condemned by apparently official powers, reduced to nothing but
the fragments of an army and the vestiges of national interest—I had
had to answer, alone, for the destiny of a nation in the enemy's hands
and torn to its vitals. Different though the conditions were under
which Churchill and de Gaulle had had to operate, fierce though
their disputes had been, for more than five years they had nonetheless sailed side by side, guiding themselves by the same stars on the
raging sea of history. The ship that Churchill had captained had not
been moored fast. And even as I stood at the helm of mine, we had
come in sight of port. Learning that England had asked her captain
to leave the command to which she had called him when the tempest
rose, I foresaw the moment when I would relinquish the helm of
France, of my own accord, as I had taken it.

During the final sessions of the Potsdam Conference, Mr Churchill's replacement by Mr Attlee, who became Prime Minister, resolved
none of the hostile tensions among the Big Three. Settlements concerning Europe and, above all, the Reich could therefore not be
concluded. For my part, I was convinced that this would be the case
for a long time. For Germany would henceforth be the object of
Russo-American rivalry, until, perhaps, it became the stake of their
future conflict. For the moment, no arrangement appeared practi-
cable save some sort of *modus vivendi* relative to the occupation and
the administration of the national zones, the feeding of the inhabitants and the trials of the war criminals. Before separating, Truman,
Stalin and Attlee, admitting their impotence, had arranged for their
foreign ministers to convene in London, under less tense circumstances, and attempt to determine the bases of the peace treaties.
This time, France was invited to participate. We accepted—on
principle, but without illusions.

It should be said that at this point one matter was settled in a
manner which afforded relative satisfaction. In July the London
'European Commission', on which France was represented along
with Great Britain, the United States and Russia, had established
the boundaries of the French zones of occupation. I myself had
determined the territories we would control. In Austria, where

Béthouart was in command, it was the Tyrol which fell to us, as well
as responsibility in Vienna one month out of every four; in Germany,
it was the left bank of the Rhine from Cologne to the Swiss frontier
and, on the right bank, the state of Baden and a sector of Württemberg; we were to be as responsible for the occupation of Berlin as
were the other powers. The Allies had subscribed to these conditions
save for Cologne, which the British held and insisted on keeping. In
regard to our status, the future of Europe and the human relations
between French and Germans, the occupation of the zone was an
extremely essential but delicate task, since the reactions which the
German atrocities might have provoked amongst our men were the
responsibility of the French Army. Yet that Army was to acquit
itself with dignity, moderation and discipline which were an honour
to France.

Immediately after the Reich's surrender, I had gone to salute this
Army on its field of victory, to decorate General de Lattre and
several of his lieutenants, and to give them instructions. On May
19th and 20th, in a totally ruined though still heavily populated
Stuttgart, later at the foot of the Arlberg, and finally under the
walls of Konstanz, the commander of the 'Rhine and Danube'
offered me splendid reviews of his troops. Among the victorious
Frenchmen filing before de Gaulle, there certainly subsisted differences of outlook. But unity was now assured regarding the subject
that had lately provoked so many divisions: today every soldier was
certain that it had been his duty to oppose the invader and that, if
France now had a future, it was because he had fought for her.

During my inspection, I visited, in particular, the 2nd Armoured
Division. Across the Augsburg plain, this entire great unit paraded
swiftly before me in battle array. Before this spectacle, I was proud to
realize that thanks to such units, this war and my undertaking had
reached their end in honour. But at the same time I recalled—
infandum dolorem!—that if we had only had seven such divisions at our
disposal six years before, and a command capable of putting them to
use, the arms of France would have changed the face of the world.

The face Germany showed was certainly lamentable in any case.
Observing the mountains of ruins to which cities were reduced,
passing through flattened villages, receiving the prayers of despairing
burgomasters, seeing populations from which male adults had almost
entirely disappeared made me, as a European, gasp in horror. But I

also saw that the cataclysm, having reached such a degree, would profoundly modify the psychology of the Germans.

It would be a long time before we would see again that victorious Reich which thrice during one man's lifetime had rushed to domination. For many years, the ambitions of the German nation and the aims of its policy would necessarily be reduced to the level of survival and reconstruction. Moreover, I scarcely suspected that it must remain severed and that Soviet Russia would insist on keeping at its disposal those very German territories which had nourished the impulses toward *Lebensraum*. Thus, amid the ruins, mourning and humiliation which had submerged Germany in her turn, I felt my sense of distrust and severity fade within me. I even glimpsed possibilities of understanding which the past had never offered; moreover, it seemed to me that the same feeling was spreading amongst our soldiers. The thirst for vengeance which had spurred them on at first had abated as they advanced across this ravaged earth. Today I saw them merciful before the misery of the vanquished.

But with the Reich annihilated and the Allies not yet in agreement as to its destiny, each of us would have to assume the administration of his own zone. According to the instructions of their Governments, this was what Eisenhower, Zhukov, Montgomery and de Lattre had agreed upon, meeting in Berlin to settle matters as soon as possible. Further, it was agreed that the four commanders-in-chief would constitute an Allied Control Commission for the whole of German territory. At the end of July, our troops occupied Saarbrücken, Treves, Coblenz, Mainz, Neustadt and their suburbs, from which the Americans withdrew in exchange for the French evacuation of Stuttgart. On the right bank of the Rhine, we remained in the regions of Freiburg, Konstanz and Tübingen.

General de Lattre then regretfully left his command to assume the highest post in our Army, that of Chief of the General Staff. General Koenig replaced him as Commander-in-Chief in Germany. An administrative staff was constituted under his orders; Émile Laffon was appointed adjutant to the Commander-in-Chief and to the French delegates in charge of the various territories—Grandval in the Saar, Billotte in the Rhineland and Hesse-Nassau, Boulay in the Palatinate, Widmer in Württemberg, Schwartz in the state of Baden. They chose administrators and officials amongst those German citizens who seemed to be qualified.

Before the opening of the London Conference, where the ministers of foreign affairs were to seek a basis of understanding, I went to Washington. For three months, Harry Truman had been inviting me. Probably the new President wanted firsthand information as to France's intentions in this early phase of a difficult peace.

The collapse of Germany, soon followed by that of Japan, left the United States in a kind of political void. Hitherto, the war had dictated its plans, its efforts and its alliances. All had had no other object beyond victory. Now the universe was changing, and at an ultrarapid tempo. Yet America, the only one of the great powers to remain completely intact, was invested in peace with the same responsibility she had finally had to assume in war. She was to enter into national and ideological rivalry with a state that was her equal in size and power. Confronting the Soviet Union, the United States wondered which course to take, which foreign causes to espouse or reject, which peoples to help, which to ignore. In short, isolationism had become impossible. When one is powerful and undamaged, one must accept the encumbrances of a great policy.

It was natural for President Truman to lose no time in consulting France. The latter, despite the ordeals she had just survived, was the only nation on the European continent on which Western policy could count. She remained, moreover, a major African reality. Her sovereignty stretched as far as America and Oceania. She had not left the Middle East. Nothing could prevent her from returning to the Far East. Her prestige and her influence were gaining ground all over the world. Whether America tried to organize the peace by the collaboration of nations, attempted to institute a balance of power, or was merely obliged to prepare her own defence, how could she do so without France?

This was why, at the end of May, Truman had requested Georges Bidault, whom the San Francisco Conference had brought to the United States, to tell me that he hoped to meet me soon. My reply was favourable. I invited Truman to come to France if he was able to. Otherwise, I would gladly pay him a visit in the United States. But since the Potsdam Conference was already under discussion, I indicated to the President 'that because of the reactions of French public opinion, his arrival in Paris or mine in Washington should not immediately precede or follow the meeting which the "Big Three" were to hold in my absence'. Truman agreed that it would be better if he did not stop in France on his way to Berlin or upon his return. On July 3rd he telegraphed that 'he proposed that our meeting should take place in Washington at the end of August'. I replied: 'I accept your kind invitation with pleasure. . . .'

I flew to Washington on August 21st, accompanied by Bidault, Juin, Palewski and several diplomats. Stopping in the Azores and in Bermuda, we reached the capital of the United States on the afternoon of the twenty-second. Mr Byrnes, the Secretary of State, General Marshall and Mr Caffery met us at the airport with a large crowd of officials, onlookers and journalists. Along the road leading to the White House, Washington lavished its cheers on us. We started a series of talks immediately, our evenings were given over to a round of receptions and ceremonies, notably that during which I made Generals Marshall, Arnold and Somervell and Admirals King and Leahy (the latter somewhat embarrassed at being decorated by de Gaulle) officers in the Legion of Honour. Going through the same ritual in which I had figured a year before, listening to the remarks of the same statesmen, influential leaders, and officials, being interviewed by the same press representatives, I realized to what an extent France had recovered in the world's eyes. During my previous journey, she was still regarded as an enigmatic captive. Now she was considered as a great ally, wounded but victorious, and above all, needed.

This, certainly, was President Truman's sense of the situation. For seven hours on August 22nd, 23rd and 25th, I conferred with him, attended by James Byrnes and Georges Bidault and Ambassadors Jefferson Caffery and Henri Bonnet. Mr Truman, for all his simplicity of manner, proved to be an extremely positive man. His speech suggested an attitude remote from the vast idealism which his illustrious predecessor had developed in the same office. The new President had abandoned the plan of world harmony and admitted that the rivalry between the free world and the Soviet bloc now dominated every other international consideration. It was therefore essential to avoid dissension and revolutionary upheaval, so that states not yet dominated by the Communists would not be led to become so.

The complex problems of the Old World in no way intimidated Harry Truman, who regarded them from a position which simplified everything. For a nation to be happy, it need only institute a democracy like that of the New World; to put an end to the antagonisms which opposed neighbouring countries, for instance France and Germany, all that was necessary was to establish a federation of rivals, as the states of North America had done amongst themselves. There existed one infallible formula to influence the underdeveloped countries to favour the West, independence; the proof, America herself, who once free of her former possessors had become a pillar of civilization. Finally, confronted with its present danger, the free world could do nothing better, and nothing else, than adopt the 'leadership' of Washington.

President Truman, as a matter of fact, was convinced that the mission of serving as guide fell to the American people, exempt as they were from the exterior shackles and internal contradictions that encumbered all the other states. Moreover, to what power, to what wealth could America's be compared? I must admit that by the end of the summer of 1945, one was struck, at first contact with the United States, by the impression of an overpowering activity and an intense optimism that swept all before them. Among the former belligerents, this nation was the only one still intact. Its economy, based on apparently unlimited resources, quickly emerged from the wartime regime to produce enormous quantities of consumer goods. The avidity of the buyers and, abroad, the needs of a ravaged world guaranteed an outlet to the greatest enterprises, and full employment to the workers. Thus the United States was assured of being the most prosperous nation for some time. Then, too, it was the strongest! A few days before my visit to Washington, atom bombs had reduced Japan to capitulation.

The President, therefore, did not expect that Russia would risk actual war for a long time to come. This was why, he explained to me, the American forces were to be entirely withdrawn from Europe, with the exception of occupation forces in Germany and in Austria. But he considered that in many areas an extreme of devastation, poverty and disorder might result in the succession of Communism and afford the Soviets many victories without the need for battle. The peace problem, according to Truman, was therefore largely economic. The nations of western Europe, whether they had won or lost the war, had to resume the normal course of their existence as soon as possible. In Asia and Africa, the underdeveloped peoples should receive the means of raising their standard of living. This was what mattered, not frontiers, grievances and guarantees!

It was with these convictions that President Truman discussed the problems raised by victory with me. He let me explain how we French envisaged the fate of the German territories and made no direct objection to any of our proposals—termination of the centralized Reich, autonomy of the left bank of the Rhine, international government of the Ruhr. But he reserved his position on these points. On the other hand, he was categoric as to the necessity of helping Germany materially. While eager—like myself—to assist the Westphalian basin to resume coal production on a large scale and at once, he did not favour the idea of handing over certain quantities of its output to France, Belgium and Holland in compensation for the devastation of which they had been victims. At best, he suggested that these nations buy—in dollars—a share of the fuel. Similarly, the President opposed the withdrawal from Germany of raw materials, machinery and manufactured goods. Even the recovery of the machinery which the Germans had taken from France disturbed Harry Truman. On the other hand, he was quite favourable to the attachment of the Saar to France, since her coal and steel production would certainly be increased thereby.

I explained to the President why France saw the world less abstractly than the United States. 'You Americans,' I said, 'have taken part in two world wars with an effectiveness and courage which we certainly salute. Nevertheless, invasion, devastation and revolution are unknown ordeals for you. In France, the old men have seen our nation invaded three times during their own lives, the last time totally. The resulting amount of human loss, destruction and expense is actually incalculable. Each of these crises, particularly the last, has provoked divisions in our people whose profundity cannot even be estimated. Our inner unity and our international status will long be compromised. My Government and I must therefore take the necessary measures to prevent the German threat from ever reappearing. Our intention, of course, is not to drive the German people to despair. On the contrary, we want the people to live, to flourish and even to draw closer to us. But we must have guarantees. I have specified which ones. If, later on, it appears that our neighbours have changed their ways, we could modify these initial precautions. But at present, the reconstructed Germany must be pacific and it must be forged while the Lord's fire has rendered the iron malleable.'

I observed to Mr Truman that here lay the hope of one day re-establishing European equilibrium. 'This equilibrium has been shattered,' I said, 'because with the consent of America and Great Britain, the states of Central Europe and the Balkans are forced to serve as satellites to the Soviet Union. If these states have a national dread of seeing an ambitious Germany reappear in common with their "protector" the bonds which link them by force to Soviet policy will be all the stronger. If they realize, on the contrary, that the German menace no longer exists, their national interest will not fail to develop within the Soviet camp. Whence, between them and their suzerain, the inevitable discords which will turn the Kremlin from belligerent enterprises, particularly since Russia herself will be profoundly less inclined to such adventures. Even Germany will be able to take advantage of the new structure which must be established, for a truly federal regime would be her unique opportunity to induce the Soviets to permit the Prussian and Saxon territories to rejoin the common body. The road France proposes to the former Reich is the only one which can lead to European reorganization and regrouping.'

At the end of these exchanges between Truman and myself on the subject of Germany and of the complementary discussions between Byrnes and Bidault, it was agreed that at the London Conference, the American delegation would recommend that our proposals be taken into consideration. Without prejudice to the eventual decision relative to the Ruhr's status, it was agreed that a Franco-Anglo-American commission would immediately be established in the Basin to promote the rapid recovery of the mines and determine that France received a significant share of the coal produced, the terms of payment to be settled at the same time as those of reparations. The Americans announced that they would not oppose the measures we wished to adopt relative to the Saar. Finally, my trip to Washington was made the occasion to conclude negotiations, conducted for several months, by Jean Monnet, with regard to a long-term loan of 650 million dollars which America was making to us at the moment she was bringing 'lend-lease' to an end.

As for the more or less 'colonial' countries of Asia and Africa, I declared that in my opinion the new era would mark their accession to independence, though the means would inevitably be varied

and gradual. The West should understand and even desire this. But
it was essential that these changes be made with, not against us, or
else the transformation of peoples still primitive and ill-assured
states would launch a wave of xenophobia, poverty and anarchy. It
was easy to predict who would benefit from such a situation.

'We are determined,' I told the President, 'to forward those
countries which depend on us towards self-government. In some
cases, we can proceed rapidly; in others, less so. Obviously that is
France's affair. But in this domain nothing is so deplorable as the
appearance of rivalry among the Western powers. Unfortunately,
that is precisely what is happening in the Levant.' And I expressed
my irritation over the support America had just given to British
intervention there. 'Ultimately,' I declared, 'I predict that the
West will have to pay for this error and this injustice.'

Mr Truman agreed that Washington had given disproportionate
credit to British claims. 'In any case,' he said, 'my Government is
not opposed to the return of the French Army and French authority
in Indochina.'

I replied, 'Although France need ask no one for permission or
approval in an affair which is hers alone, I note your remarks with
satisfaction. The enemy recently seized Indochina. Thanks to the
victory in which America has played an incomparable part, France
is about to return there. She does so with the intention of establishing a regime in harmony with the will of the people. Nevertheless, in
this area too, we find ourselves hampered by the arrangements our
allies are making without consulting us first.'

I indicated to Mr Truman that we were not eager to see British
troops replace the Japanese in the southern part of Indochina or
Chinese troops in the north. Yet this was what was about to happen,
according to an agreement concluded in Cairo in 1943 between
Roosevelt, Churchill and Chiang Kai-shek and recently confirmed
by the Potsdam Conference. We were not unaware, furthermore,
that American agents, under General Wedemeyer, United States
delegate to the Chinese command, were preparing to infiltrate
Tonkin to establish contact with the revolutionary power. All this,
I pointed out, was not likely to facilitate matters for us. Thereupon
the President felt he should inform me once again that, from Washington's point of view, there would be absolutely no attempt to
hamper our undertakings in the Far East.

We parted on good terms. Between our two states there could not have been either understanding or confidence without some reservations. The Washington talks had shown that if necessary America would follow a path which was not the same as ours. But at least Harry Truman and I had discussed this frankly with each other. As Chief of State, Truman impressed me as equal to his task, his character firm, his mind orientated towards the practical side of affairs—in short, a man who, though he promised no miracles, could be counted on in a crisis. He certainly showed every consideration for me, and his statements following my visit went far beyond official praise. At our last meeting, he suddenly opened the doors of his office, behind which were standing some twenty photographers, and slipped a decoration around my neck, knowing that I would have declined any honour had I been informed beforehand; he then decorated Bidault as well. Upon my departure, in the name of the United States Truman presented me with a magnificent DC4. On subsequent occasions, no hard words ever passed between us.

To receive de Gaulle and his colleagues, New York lavished its torrential friendship upon us. We drove there on August 26th, by way of West Point, where I inspected the Military Academy, and Hyde Park, where I visited Roosevelt's tomb. It was Sunday and happened as well to be the first day when petrol was on sale without ration cards. The roads were jammed and a tremendous row of cars parked along the curb for about one hundred kilometres greeted our passage with an incredible racket of horns. Mayor Fiorello La Guardia, a marvel of energy and sympathy, received us as we entered the city. That evening, after various ceremonies, he took me to Central Park where Marian Anderson was to sing the 'Marseillaise'. There, in the darkness, twenty irresistible arms drew me on to the stage of the huge amphitheatre. The spotlights came on and I was revealed to the crowd sitting in the theatre. Once the storm of cheers had died away and the singer's superb voice had rendered our national anthem, I saluted the great city with all my heart.

The next day we attended the 'Victory Parade'. We drove through the city in state, the mayor beside me exultant with satisfaction while cheers filled the air and flags and banners fluttered at every window. We reached lower Broadway amid an indescribable storm of 'Long Live France!' 'Hurrah! de Gaulle!' 'Hello, Charlie!' beneath thick clouds of confetti and ticker tape thrown from

100,000 windows. At City Hall the reception took place. I decorated
La Guardia, who since June 1940 had proved one of the most ardent
and effective advocates in the United States of Fighting France.
Then I was awarded honorary citizenship of New York, and at the
colossal banquet which followed, the mayor declared in his toast,
'In raising my glass to the glory of General de Gaulle, I wanted to
salute him as New York's youngest citizen, for we inscribed his
name on the city register only an hour ago. But since then, the birth
of forty-five other babies has been announced!'

New York State's Governor Thomas Dewey declared: 'Calm
though I might have seemed, I was overwhelmed by the city's
emotion.' Certainly this quality of picturesqueness on a colossal
scale is characteristic of American public demonstrations. But the
explosion of enthusiasm which marked this occasion revealed the
extent of the city's extraordinary love of France.

Chicago gave evidence of the same affection. Unlike New York,
however, Chicago is not orientated towards Europe, and its population derives from the most various nations of the world. 'Here,'
Mayor Edward Kelly told me, 'you will be cheered in seventy-four
languages'. And in fact that evening going to the municipal banquet, and the next day when we drove through the avenues of
Chicago to visit the New Deal buildings, when we were received at
the city hall, or driving to a monster banquet given by the Chamber
of Commerce and the American Legion, we were surrounded by
a tremendous crowd which mingled all the races of the earth,
unanimous in their cheers.

Canada, in its turn, gave us a warm welcome. My hosts, Governor
General the Earl of Athlone and his wife, Princess Alice, said on
my arrival, 'When you were here last year, you could see what feelings public opinion in this country entertained toward you. Since
then the popularity of you and France has risen about three
hundred per cent.'

'Why?'

'Because then you were a question mark; now you are an ex-
clamation mark.'

In Ottawa, officials and people alike lavished every imaginable
evidence of their enthusiasm on us. 'Premier' Mackenzie King,
assisted by Minister of Foreign Affairs St. Laurent, Ambassador
Vanier and myself, accompanied by Bidault and our Ambassador

Jean de Hauteclocque, found we could discuss major issues with great candour, since France's interests were quite separate from those of Canada.

Mackenzie King, a veteran of Canadian politics and a resolute advocate of an independent Canada, told me quite candidly, 'This is our situation: Canada adjoins the United States for over five thousand kilometres—a frequently overwhelming contiguity. It is, besides, a member of the Commonwealth—an occasionally onerous responsibility. But we intend to act in complete independence. We are a nation of unlimited space, endowed with great natural resources. Our ambitions are to exploit these, and therefore they are internally oriented. We have no interest in opposing France in any of her fields of activity. On the contrary, we have every reason to lend our good offices to whatever degree that we can, whenever France feels the necessity of calling upon us.'

'As for us,' I said to Mackenzie King, 'two world wars have shown us the value of your co-operation. Certainly we shall need to rely on your friendship in peacetime. What you have just said convinces me that France was quite right in coming here long ago and planting the seed of civilization.'

We passed through Newfoundland in order to fly back to Paris. During the stopover at the American base at Gander, in the midst of a normally almost desert country, I heard my name shouted by a crowd of cheering men gathered along the fences. I walked over to them: they were inhabitants assembled from various parts of the island to greet General de Gaulle. Faithful to their Norman, Breton and Picardy ancestors who first settled Newfoundland, all spoke French. All, too, seized by an ancestral emotion, shouted '*Vive la France!*' as they held out their hands.

Almost immediately after our journey, the London Conference convened a last chance for agreement among the four Allies. From September 11th to October 3rd, Byrnes, Molotov, Bevin and Bidault examined the problems of Europe together. Yet the Big Four's discussions did nothing but sharpen the antagonism between the Russians and the Anglo-American powers. It was with the greatest difficulty, when Italy was discussed, that we were able to envisage the possibility of an agreement on the fate of Istria and Trieste. Georges Bidault specified the minor changes we expected to see made in our Alpine frontier, and got the agreement of his three

colleagues on this point. But when the question of the former Italian
colonies was breached, when the British and American ministers
spoke of making Libya into an independent state, while the French
minister proposed placing the territory under United Nations
control with Italy as 'trustee', Mr Bevin and Mr Byrnes were outraged, broke off the conversations and the Italian question reached
an impasse.

The same was true of the projected treaties with Hungary,
Rumania and Bulgaria. The Soviets let it be understood that it was
their responsibility to establish the terms and that they had the means
of doing so, since they were the sole occupiers. British and American
ministers protested against the political oppression all three states
were suffering, as if the latter were not the consequence of the
Teheran, Yalta and Potsdam agreements. The problem of Germany,
however, made the four powers' inability to reach any solution
particularly obvious.

France, however, and France alone, had formulated one. On the
eve of the London conference, I made public, in an interview with
Gerald Norman, Paris correspondent of *The Times* of London, what
our conditions for peace with Germany were. Then, during the conference, a memorandum from our delegation and a report by Bidault
specified our position. The conference did not give the French
programme a negative reception. The notion of replacing the Reich
by a federation of states was apparently regarded as extremely
reasonable; the conception of a Franco-Saarois economic union
aroused no objection; the projected transformation of the Palatinate, Hesse and the Rhineland into autonomous states and their
integration into a western economic and strategic system did not
seem unacceptable. At first our partners even sanctioned our
proposal to put the Ruhr under international control. But after Mr
Molotov had insisted that Russia participate in such a regime and
that Soviet troops join the detachments of western forces in Dusseldorf, Mr Byrnes strongly objected and Mr Bevin took up the refrain. The conference advanced no further in its examination of our
solution; no one, moreover, proposed any other, and the ministers
separated after twenty-three days of discussion as futile for the
present as they were depressing for the future.

Each power was consequently inclined to proceed in its own zone
as it judged best. In the east, the Soviets imposed their now familiar

political and social system upon Prussia and Saxony. In the west, the Americans, opposing certain 'autonomist' tendencies appearing in Bavaria, Lower Saxony and Württemberg, and the British, who were finding the direct responsibility for the Ruhr and the major North Sea ports a heavy one, proceeded to the kind of organization they found easiest—they merged their two zones into a single unit delegating authority to a college of German secretaries general. Thus a Reich Government was created after all, at least until general elections could be held. The prospect of a true German federation vanished in the hard light of fact. Later the British and Americans urged us to unite the territories we occupied to the zones where they were rebuilding the Reich, but I would not agree to this step.

For the moment, in any case, our zone was our own responsibility. Early in October, I visited the area to make contact with the German authorities and the people, and to determine the possibilities of realizing the policy to which I had committed France. Diethelm, Capitant, Dautry, Juin and Koenig accompanied me. Our first visit was to the Saar. On October 3rd, in ruined Saarbrücken, Dr Neureuther, president of the Government, and M. Heim, the Burgomaster, informed me of the difficulties they were struggling with. To them and to the other Saar officials and prominent citizens, all evidently devoured by apprehension and curiosity, I declared: 'I shall deliberately not refer here to the past events. But for the future's sake we must understand each other, for there is much for us to accomplish together.' Then I indicated that our task consisted in re-establishing normal life and eventually prosperity in the Saar. I concluded by expressing the hope that 'with the passing of time and the results of our collaboration, we French will discover excellent reasons for esteem and confidence in the people of the Saar, and that the latter will realize, humanly speaking, how close we are to them. If this is the case,' I added, 'so much the better for the West and for Europe, of whom you, like ourselves, are the children.' When I finished my speech, I saw tears in the eyes of my audience.

In Treves, I saw the same evidence of mute resignation and mountainous rubble. Yet the old Moselle city had preserved its characteristic appearance around the 'Porta Nigra', which had emerged intact from the cataclysm. The local dignitaries, including the bishop, Monsignor Bornewasser, told me of the extent of their demoralization. I made the same kind of speech I had made in

Saarbrücken. 'France,' I said, 'is not here to crush but to bring about a resurrection.' That evening, I visited Coblenz. M. Boden, president of the Government, and the prominent citizens who surrounded him, got encouragement from France from my words. Here, as elsewhere, my speech was received with respect and emotion.

This was the case the following day, in Mainz, where the crowd that received Charles de Gaulle was a large one. It was as if after centuries of terrible ordeals the souls of their Gallic and Frankish ancestors lived again in those present. The president of Hesse-Nassau, Dr Steffan, the burgomaster, Dr Kraus, and the bishop, Monsignor Stohr, mentioned this phenomenon in their speeches. I replied with words of hope, adding: 'As we stand here, we proceed from the same race. And as we stand today, we are Europeans, men of the West. Excellent reasons for us to stand by one another henceforward!'

Reaching the terribly ravaged Palatinate, I was given a striking reception in Neustadt. Around the president, Dr Eisenlaub, his adjutant, Dr Koch, and the bishop, Monsignor Wendel, crowded district councillors, burgomasters, priests, pastors, professors, representatives of the Bar, labour and management; all warmly applauded the head of their Government when he declared that the territory wanted to become what it had once been, that is, the Palatine State, to take its destiny into its own hands and to ally itself with France.

Freiburg, in the Black Forest, received de Gaulle with every element representative of the regions we occupied on the right bank of the Rhine. On October 4th, Dr Wohleb presented to me the prominent citizens of Baden. On the morning of the fifth, Mr Carlo Schmitt introduced those of Württemberg. Monsignor Groeber, Archbishop of Freiburg, as well as Monsignor Fisher of the diocese of Rotthausen, were among the visitors. Then these distinguished men, full of good will, gathered to hear me discuss 'the bonds which once linked the French and the southern Germans and which must now reappear in order to reconstruct "our" Europe and "our" West'. At these words the hall burst into the most enthusiastic cheers. In this surprising atmosphere I began wondering if so many battles fought and invasions endured for so many centuries by the two peoples struggling against each other, as well as so many fresh horrors committed to our detriment, were not merely bad dreams. It was difficult to believe that the Germans had ever entertained

anything but this cordiality of which I was being offered such striking proofs towards the Gauls. But when I left the ceremony to find
myself again in the ruined streets amid a grief-stricken crowd, I
could see what disasters this nation had had to endure before heed-
ing the counsels of reason at last.

Later that day, I went to Baden-Baden, where General Koenig
had his headquarters. Here, all who directed some branch of the
French administrative organization described the eagerness of the
Germans to obey our directives and their desire for a reconciliation.
One of the signs of this state of mind was the extraordinary success
of the Franco-German University of Mainz, as well as the schools,
lycées and study centres which we had just opened at various places.
Leaving Germany that afternoon, I reached Strasbourg, intending to
tell that city of the great goal toward which I was leading the
French nation, provided it would follow me. Émile Bollaert,
Commissioner of the Republic, Bernard Cornut-Gentille, Prefect
of the Bas-Rhin, and General du Vigier, the governor, escorted me
there by river. Having crossed the harbour, our boats entered the
city through canals whose banks and bridges were swarming with a
crowd who showed incomparable enthusiasm. I presided at the re-
opening of the University of Strasbourg, received the Alsatian
authorities at the Palais du Rhin, and finally, in the Place Broglie,
from the balcony of the *hôtel de ville*, I addressed the populace:

'I am here,' I said, 'to proclaim the great task of the French
Rhineland. Yesterday, the River Rhine, our river, was a barrier,
a frontier, a battle line. Now that the enemy has fallen as a result of
our victory, now that the fevered affinities which once united the
German states to such evil purpose have disappeared, the Rhine can
resume the role which nature and history have assigned it. It can
again become a western bulwark.' Then I exclaimed: 'Consider this
river! It bears upon its waters one of the greatest destinies in the
world. From its source in Switzerland, through Alsace, the Moselle
region, Baden, the basins of the Main and Ruhr, which are on its
banks; across the Low Countries, where it flows into the seas not
far from the coast of England, ships can henceforth ply up and down
and wealth spread freely from one end to the other. The same is true
of ideas and influences, of all that proceeds from the mind, the heart
and the soul. . . . Yes, the link of western Europe is here, in the
Rhine, which flows through Strasbourg!'

This conception of an organized group of western nations found an ardent hearing in Belgium. I realized this on my visit. The Prince Regent invited me, and I reached Brussels in his private train on October 10th, accompanied by Georges Bidault. At the station, the Prince had come to meet me and I was struck by the cheering which rolled over me like a tide. For two days in Brussels, which we spent visiting the royal palace, the Tomb of the Unknown Soldier, Ixelles, and Laeken—where we were received by the Queen Mother Elizabeth—the city hall, the University, the Ministry of Foreign Affairs, the French *lycée*, and the French Embassy, where Raymond Brugère was our host, each of our comings and goings gave rise to enthusiastic ovations. It was evident that the Belgians identified their joys and hopes with those of the French people.

Prince Charles told me as much, and I listened to his remarks with great attention because of my esteem for him. Amid the bitter divisions which the question of the King—who was still in Switzerland —provoked among the people and which made the Regent's task extremely difficult, I saw this clear-thinking prince, firm in the exercise of his duties safeguarding the throne and national unity, yet certain, though he made no mention of it, that he would not be given credit for it in any of the opposing camps. The ministers, particularly the robust Premier, M. van Acker, and the always well-informed and enterprising Minister for Foreign Affairs, M. Spaak, as well as the Presidents of the Assemblies, M. van Cauwelaert and M. Gillon, and Cardinal van Roey, all talked to me in similar terms, for all believed that Europe would have been lost if France had not been present at the victory. As for the future, the vital interest of the establishment of close relations among the states of western Europe dominated every hope.

The next day, Burgomaster Vandemeulebroek received us at the *hôtel de ville* while a huge crowd filled the splendid square, and then at the University of Brussels, whose President Fredrichs and Dean Cox made me a *Doctor Honoris Causa*, I proclaimed my faith in the efficacy of an eventual association of all the peoples of Europe and, in the immediate present, 'a western grouping having as its arteries the Rhine, the Channel and the Mediterranean'. On each occasion, this great French project was received by my audiences with transports of joy. On my return to Paris, I discussed it again at an enormous press conference.

Thus the idea was launched. Once the elections which were to take place in fifteen days had decided the fate of our institutions and so of my future role, the appropriate proposals would either be addressed by me to the other powers or would not. This immense plan seemed to provoke the passionate attention of the other interested nations but I got the impression that French political leaders did not, in fact, greatly favour it. From the day of the victory to that of the elections, not a single discussion in the Consultative Assembly referred to these problems. Except for vague formulas, the many congresses, party motions and meetings mentioned virtually nothing relating to France's effect and influence on other nations. The press, of course, reported General de Gaulle's speeches and journeys. But the aims the latter proposed gave rise to no campaign, nor even to a commentary, as if what was at stake were beyond the national interest. Everything occurred as if my conviction that France had the opportunity to play an independent role and my effort to lead her to do so was received by those preparing to represent the nation with unexpressed esteem but universal doubt.

I could not, moreover, overlook the fact that in order to realize such a European policy we must have our hands free elsewhere. If overseas territories cut themselves off from Metropolitan France, or if our forces were engaged there, what consequence would we have between the North Sea and the Mediterranean? Conversely, if those territories remained associated with us, we would have every opportunity for action on the continent! The age-old destiny of France! Yet after what had happened on the soil of our African and Asian possession, any attempt to maintain our Empire there as it had been would be perilous, particularly when new nationalist movements were springing up all over the world with Russia and America competing for their adherence. If the peoples for whom we were responsible were to remain with France tomorrow, we must take the initiative and transform a relation which at present was merely one of dependency for them. On condition, of course, that we remain firm, but insisting on loyalty to the word given it as well. I had inaugurated this policy in Brazzaville. Now we would have to apply it in Indochina and in North Africa.

In the Maghreb, matters could still be arranged peacefully and gradually. Although signs of agitation were already appearing there, we were still in control of the situation. In Tunisia, the popularity of the former Bey Moncef provoked little beyond Platonic regrets; the two experienced 'Destours' kept on the alert and Resident General Mast manoeuvred readily between plans for reform and authoritative action. In Algeria, an insurrection begun in the Constantinois and synchronized with the Syrian riots in May, was put down by Governor General Chataligneau. In Morocco, the proclamations spread by the 'Istiqlal' and the parades it organized had little effect on the people; moreover, Sultan Mohammed V, after some hesitations and upon the pressing request of Resident General Puaux, had repudiated such demonstrations. But if we still had time, it was not time to waste. I took immediate action.

Sovereignty in the Empire of Morocco and in the Regency of Tunis was identified with their sovereigns. I therefore wished to deal with them directly. I invited the Sultan of Morocco to France and received him as a chief of state entitled to great honours and a loyal friend who had shown his worth in the most trying circumstances. In addition to the usual receptions. I asked him to stand beside me during the great military ceremony of June 18th in Paris, and awarded him the Cross of the Liberation. Later he accompanied me on a trip to Auvergne, receiving the cheers of enthusiastic crowds in the cities and the heartfelt welcome of the country people. He then visited Germany with the First Army and reviewed its splendid Moroccan troops. Finally, he visited our great hydroelectric installations. He was universally acclaimed, which created a favourable atmosphere for our personal meetings.

I asked the Sultan to express quite frankly his considered opinion as to the relations between France and Morocco. 'I am profoundly aware,' he declared, 'that the protectorate has brought my country order, justice, a basis of prosperity, elementary education for the masses and the formation of an elite. But this regime was accepted by my uncle, Moulay-Hafid, then by my father, Moulay-Youssef, and accepted today by me as a transition between the Morocco of the past and a free and modern state. After the recent events of this war, and before those that will occur tomorrow, I believe this is the moment to take a further step along this road. That is what my people are waiting for.'

'The objective you envisage,' I said, 'is the one which France has adopted, which the Treaty of Fez and the Act of Algeciras formulate, and which Lyautey, the founder of modern Morocco, never ceased to pursue. Like yourself, I am convinced that we must modify the bases of our relationship in this way. But as things stand now, such liberty can be only relative for anyone. Is this not particularly true of Morocco, which has still so much to accomplish before it can exist by its own means as a nation? It is France's duty to lend you her assistance, in return for your loyalty. Who else could do so honourably? When President Roosevelt jingled the marvels of independence before your Majesty at Anfa, what did he offer you beyond cash and a place among his customers?'

'It is quite true,' Mohammed V declared, 'that the progress of my country must be accomplished with France's aid. Of all the powers that can lend us their support, France, best situated and best endowed, is the one we prefer. You have learned, during the war, that our help too, is not without value. The result of the new agreements we could negotiate would be the contractual association of our countries from economic, diplomatic, cultural and military points of view.'

I indicated to the Sultan that, pending actual terms, which must be closely studied, I agreed with him on all essential points. As to a suitable date for opening negotiations, I proposed the day following the Fourth Republic's adoption of its own constitution. Surely the latter could not fail to define the federal or confederated links applicable to certain territories or states whose self-government and participation in a common structure must be provided for. I proposed to Mohammed V that we keep in personal touch concerning all matters that related to the union of our two countries, assuming, of course, that I remained in office. He acquiesced immediately and, I believe, enthusiastically. To begin with, the Sultan indicated his approval of my Government's initiative in re-establishing at Tangier the Sherifian authority and the international status abolished in 1940 by a Spanish *coup de force*. This was achieved in September, following a Paris conference of French, English, American and Russian representatives whose settlements the Madrid Government agreed to recognize.

Next, the Bey of Tunis came to France at my invitation. Sidi Lamine was the object of a reception as brilliant as circumstances allowed. In Paris, on July 14th, he attended the imposing review of our victorious Army. Many receptions and gatherings gave him the opportunity to see French leaders of all circles. During our conversations the sovereign made clear to me what, in his opinion, the Regency should become in order to correspond to the aspirations of its people and the demands of the times. In general, the Bey's notions coincided with the Sultan's. Sidi Lamine's tone, of course, was less clarion clear than that of Mohammed V because of a difference in age and temperament, as well as of a less assured popularity and the fact that he was speaking in the name of a kingdom weaker than Morocco. But the general tenor was the same, as was that of my reply. The Bey received it with great friendliness.

From the remarks exchanged with Maghreb sovereigns, I drew the conclusion that it was possible and necessary to reach agreements of co-operation with both states that accorded with the demands of the time, agreements which, in a changing world, would settle the relations among our countries for at least a generation.

If North African questions appeared in a more or less encouraging light, affairs in Indochina offered the greatest difficulties. Since the liquidation of our military posts and our administration by the Japanese and the retreat into Chinese territory of our remaining free detachments, nothing was left of France's authority in Cochin China, Annam, Tonkin, Cambodia and Laos. The surviving soldiers were in captivity; the officials interned; the private citizens closely watched; all were subject to the most odious treatment. In the states of the French Union the Japanese had supported the native Governments under their sway, while a resistance movement appeared, directed by Communists resolved to seek eventual independence. This league organized a clandestine government which was preparing to become public. The French were reduced to sending a small advance guard to Ceylon in view of the possibility that the Allies would agree to transport our Expeditionary Corps; we also organized a skeleton information service operating throughout Indochina and attempted to persuade the Chungking Government and its American military advisers to facilitate the regrouping of our detachments retreating from Tonkin and Laos.

But the German capitulation determined the United States to bring an end to the Japanese conflict as well. In June their forces, advancing from island to island, had come close enough to Japanese territory to be able to effect a landing there. The Japanese fleet was swept from the seas by Nimitz's warships, and their aviation was too far reduced to hold its own against MacArthur's. In Tokyo, however, the party favouring war retained its influence. Yet it was with apprehension that the American President, military command and Congress envisaged the bloody conquest, foot by foot, cave by cave, of the territory of a people both gallant and made fanatical by its leaders. Consequently, we witnessed a singular reversal of Washington's attitude toward the value of French military aid. Early in July the Pentagon even asked us if we would be disposed to send two divisions to the Pacific. 'It is not out of the question,' I replied. 'But in that case, we should also want to send the necessary forces to Burma to take part in the Indochinese offensive.'

On June 15th I determined the composition of our Expeditionary Corps. General Leclerc was to take command, though I was obliged, on this occasion, to contravene his wishes. 'Send me to Morocco,' he asked me once. 'You will go to Indochina,' I told him, 'because that is more difficult.' Leclerc began to organize his units. By the beginning of August they were ready. It was with great enthusiasm that soldiers and officers alike prepared to restore the flag of France to the only one of her territories in which it had not yet reappeared.

Then, on August 6th and 9th, atom bombs were dropped on Hiroshima and Nagasaki. As a matter of fact, the Japanese had given indications, before the cataclysm, that they were prepared to make peace negotiations. But it was unconditional surrender the Americans wanted, certain as they were, following the success of the experiments conducted in Nevada, that they would obtain it. Emperor Hirohito capitulated immediately following the destruction of the two cities. It was agreed that the treaty by which the Empire of the Rising Sun would surrender to its conquerors would be signed on September 2nd, in Yokohama harbour, on the battleship *Missouri*.

I must say that the revelation of the terrible weapons stirred me deeply. Certainly I had long been aware that the Americans were in the process of perfecting irresistible explosives by smashing the atom. But though I was not surprised, I was no less tempted to despair at the birth of means that made possible the annihilation of the human race. Yet these bitter visions could not keep me from taking advantage of the situation created by the bombs' effect. For the capitulation destroyed both Japanese defence and the American veto which had kept us out of the Pacific. Indochina, from one day to the next, became accessible to us once again.

We wasted no time in returning there. Still, it was essential to do so as acknowledged participants in the victory. As soon as Tokyo had shown its intention of negotiating, we had insisted, in Washington, that the Allied reply bear the seal of France as well. This had been agreed to. Then, when Emperor Hirohito capitulated, it was agreed that the French command would receive the surrender along with the Allied chiefs. I delegated General Leclerc to the ceremony, and he signed the agreement on board the *Missouri*. Previously, on August 15th, I had appointed Admiral d'Argenlieu High Commissioner in Indochina.

The sending of troops was the condition on which everything else depended. Seventy thousand men had to be transported along with a great deal of material. This was a considerable undertaking, for we had to begin it in a period of demobilization and while we were maintaining an army in Germany. But it was essential, after yesterday's humiliating liquidation, that the arms of France give an impression of force and resolution. Moreover, a squadron consisting of the battleship *Richelieu*, already in those waters, the cruisers *Gloire*, *Suffren*, *Triomphant*, the transport vessel *Béarn*, and several smaller craft, all under Admiral Auboyneau's orders, would cover the Indochinese coast. Some hundred planes would operate in the skies over the Peninsula. Since the war's end allowed us to recover the freighters we had lent to the inter-Allied pool, we could control their movements, despite generally inadequate tonnage, in such a way that in three months the entire Expeditionary Corps reached its destination 14,000 kilometres away. Yet however rapidly it had arrived, the situation was still extremely difficult.

There were one hundred thousand Japanese soldiers in Indochina. They had ceased fighting and were waiting to be repatriated. But at present they were fraternizing with the units of the league that was to become the 'Vietminh'. The latter emerged from the brush, proclaimed its independence, demanded the union of the 'Three-Ky' and issued propaganda against the re-establishment of the French authority. In Tonkin, their political leader, Ho Chi Minh, and their military leader, Giap, both Communists, formed a committee which took on the appearance of a government. The Emperor Bao Dai had abdicated and now figured beside Ho Chi Minh as an 'adviser'. Our delegate to Tonkin, Jean Sainteny, landing at Hanoi on August 22nd, found Vietminh authority established in the

capital and on good terms with the Japanese. Throughout Indochina the population, which had recently seen the French lose face,
now appeared hostile towards our compatriots there. In Saigon on
September 2nd, several of the latter were massacred despite the
pacific efforts of Governor Cédile, who had been parachuted in on
August 23rd. Famine complicated the political difficulties, for since
the disappearance of the French authority, supply services had been
paralysed. Lastly, the Allies, applying their pre-established plan for
the occupation of the country—Chinese north of the 16th parallel,
British south, American missions everywhere—had fatally compromised the effect which the immediate arrival of French troops and
officials and the disarmament of the Japanese by our forces might
have produced.

Naturally we did not agree to this triple foreign intrusion. Not
that the presence of the British in Cochin China concerned us
particularly. We managed to arrive there at the same time as they.
Furthermore, the British Empire had its hands full in India, Ceylon, Malaya, Burma and Hong Kong, and was so eager to allay the
resentment provoked by the recent crisis in the Levant that we had
every reason to believe it would agree to an imminent withdrawal
of its forces. As a matter of fact, this proved to be the case. Then too,
we regarded the presence in the area of United States personnel for
the combined task of economic prospecting and political indoctrin-
ation as ungracious but, generally speaking, without great effect.
On the other hand, the occupation of Tonkin, as well as of a large
part of Annam and Laos by General Lu Han's Chinese army threatened the gravest consequences: our political and administrative
action would thereby be hampered for a long period; once the
Chinese were established, when would they leave, and at what price?

Nevertheless, the Chunking Government unceasingly lavished its
assurances of goodwill upon us. In October 1944 Marshal Chiang
Kai-shek received Ambassador Pechkoff and assured him: 'I
promise you that we have no interest in Indochina. If at any time
we can help you restore French authority there, we shall do so
gladly. Tell General de Gaulle that this is our policy. But let him
also consider it as a personal commitment to him on my part.'
During my stay in Washington, in August, I received Mr T. V.
Soong, who happened to be in the city at the time. The Minister of
Foreign Affairs of the Republic of China also made me formal

H

declarations. On September 19th, when the same Mr Soong visited me in Paris, accompanied by Ambassador Tsien-Tai, and I referred to the unfortunate behaviour of General Lu Han's troops, the minister promised me that his Government 'would bring this state of affairs to a halt and withdraw its forces from Indochina'. But whatever the intentions, not to mention the orders, of the central Government, the fact of the matter was that Lu Han had established himself as master of Tonkin.

The arrival of our soldiers, the departure of the Japanese, the withdrawal of foreign troops—these conditions would have to be fulfilled for France to recover her status in Indochina. But above all, she had to know what she wanted to accomplish there. I could not, of course, determine my policy as long as the situation in the area remained as confused as it was. But I knew enough to be certain that our direct administration could not be re-established. Henceforth our goal would be the association of the French Republic with each of the countries which constituted the Union. The agreements should be negotiated by accepting as interlocutors those who seemed best to represent the states and the population and without the exclusion of any member. This was the plan I had settled on.

In regard to Laos and Cambodia, the presence of solid dynasties dispelled all incertitude. But in Vietnam matters were much more complicated. I decided to proceed step by step, ordering Leclerc to gain footholds first in Cochin China and Cambodia. He would not proceed into Annam until later. As for Tonkin, his forces would not enter the area except on my orders, and I had no intention of giving them until the situation was clarified, the population thoroughly exasperated by the presence of the Chinese, and relations settled between Sainteny and Ho Chi Minh. High Commissioner d'Argenlieu received my instructions to proceed first to French India. It was from Chandernagore that he would gain an adequate perspective of the situation. Then, when the presence of our troops had produced some effect and his adjutants had returned to the various territories, he would install himself in Saigon, making all the necessary contacts from there.

Meanwhile, I was developing a secret plan which might prove effective. This was to provide the former Emperor Duy Tan means to reappear if his successor and relative Bao Dai proved, as seemed to be the case, a victim of the turn of events. Duy Tan, dethroned in

1916 by the French authority, retitled Prince Vin Sanh and transferred to Réunion, had nevertheless insisted during the second
World War on serving in our army, in which he received the rank of
commander. The man possessed a strong character, and some thirty
years of exile had not obliterated this sovereign's image from the soul
of the Annamite people. On December 14th, I received him in order
to discuss with him, as one man to another, what we might accomplish together. But whoever the persons my Government was obliged
to deal with, I intended to go to Indochina myself to settle matters in
due form when the time came.

But it was still far away. At present, our problem was primarily a
military one. On September 12th, the first French troops, and on the
thirteenth a British unit, arrived in Saigon. Riots broke out in the
city on the twenty-third, and several Europeans and Americans were
killed by fanatics. Nevertheless, Allied forces, including a regiment
of French soldiers and officers who had recently been prisoners of
war, finally gained the upper hand. Jean Cédile negotiated a truce
and on October 5th General Leclerc entered the capital, acclaimed
by 10,000 Frenchmen who had been exposed to many threats and
insults for seven months. As the forces of our Expeditionary Corps
landed, matters improved in Cochin China, where swift operations
re-established law and order, and in Cambodia, where the ministers
installed by the Japanese were replaced by appropriate officials.
Moreover, the Japanese troops were gradually leaving the country,
and Admiral Mountbatten was withdrawing the British forces as
well. On October 31st, the French High Commissioner was installed
in the Norodom Palace.

In Indochina, France was now reappearing with suitable dignity.
The problems, certainly, remained thorny ones, in a territory strewn
with obstacles and beneath a sky heavy with storm clouds. But
already there had been a complete change in regard to the terrible
indigence that had damaged our prestige. Yesterday, we had apparently been definitely expelled from Hanoi, Pnompenh and
Luangprabang. Today, no one doubted any longer that what had
to be done could be done only with our co-operation.

In Europe, in Africa, in Asia, where France had suffered an
unprecedented humiliation, an astonishing recovery and an extraordinary combination of circumstances already offered her the
opportunity of playing a role in accordance with her genius. Were

these the first rays of a new dawn or the last rays of the setting sun?
The will of the French people themselves would decide that. For, if
we were weakened, on the other hand the fall of our enemies, the
losses suffered by our former competitors, the rivalry which opposed
the two greatest states in the world to each other, and the universal
desire to see France fulfil her mission, left us, for a time, a clear field.

As for myself, only too well aware of my limitations and my failings,
certain that no man can substitute himself for a people, how I longed
to implant in every Frenchman the same convictions that inspired
me! The goals I proclaimed were difficult, but worthy of us. The
road I pointed to was rough, but rose to the summits. Having made
my appeal, I listened for the answering echoes. The murmurs of the
multitude remained enthusiastic but confused. Perhaps the voices
that were making themselves heard in the forum, from the tribunal
of assemblies, the pulpit and in faculties and academies would support my own? In that case, there could be no doubt that the people
were in agreement with the spirit of their elite. I listened, but only to
hear the scuffles of their circumspection. Yet what were these
peremptory and conflicting cries that now resounded so noisily
throughout the nation? Alas, nothing but the clamour of partisans.

VI. DISUNION

THE ROAD TO greatness lay open before us, but France was in a pitiful
condition to follow it! While the reactions from every part of the
globe, the conversations with statesmen, the ovations of foreign
crowds conveyed the world's appeal to France, the graphs and
statistics laid on my desk, the reports made by our services, the
scenes of devastation offered by our territory, the councils where I
heard our ministers describing the extent of our misery and the
penury of our means gave me the measure of our debilitation. No
power now contested our right to play a major role in the world's
destiny. But at home, France's condition was expressed by a balance-
sheet of ruins.

One third of the nation's wealth had been annihilated. In all
forms and in all regions, devastation covered our territory. Naturally
the destruction of buildings was the most spectacular. As a result of
the battles of 1940, later the Allied bombings and finally the Liberation itself, 500,000 buildings had been completely destroyed and
1,500,000 seriously damaged. It was the factories which had chiefly
suffered and were causing an additional delay in economic recovery.
We also lacked housing for six million Frenchmen. And what of
ruined railway terminals, cut lines, blown-up bridges, blocked canals
and choked harbours? The engineers whom I asked for an estimate
of the time needed to restore buildings and communications replied,
'It will take twenty years!' A million hectares of land had been
reduced to non-productivity, spoiled by explosions, strewn with
mines, pitted with entrenchments; fifteen million more yielded
scarcely anything, since the farmers had been unable to cultivate them
properly for five years. Everywhere there was a shortage of tools,
fertilizers, plants and seeds. The livestock was reduced by half.

Though less apparent, the damage caused by theft was heavier still. We had been pillaged systematically. In the text of the 'armistice', the Germans had specified that the 'expenses of the occupation troops will be met by the French Government'. Under this rubric the enemy had laid hold of exorbitant sums, thanks to which he not only supported his armies, but also purchased (with our money) and shipped to Germany huge quantities of machinery and consumer goods. Further, a so-called 'compensation agreement' had imposed on the French treasury the settlement of the differences between the value of the exports 'freely made' to Germany and the cost of imports of coal and raw materials the Reich sent to France to supply the factories it was maintaining in operation to its own advantage. Since there were virtually no such exports and imports continued to be considerable, the 'agreement' had laid a terrible burden on us. In addition, all kinds of German purchases on the black market, partial requisitions, local fines and qualified thefts had completed the spoliation of France. And how evaluate the millions of days of labour imposed on French workmen to the enemy's profit and diverted from our production, the lowering of physical health inflicted on people by undernourishment, the fact that during five years everything in France had deteriorated without our being able to maintain, repair or renew? All in all, the occupation cost us more than 2,000 billion 1938 francs, that is, 80,000 billion today. Peace found the economy deprived of a large part of its means of production, our finances crushed beneath a colossal public debt, our budget condemned to bear the enormous expenses of reconstruction for a long time.

This disappearance of resources and the tools of labour was all the more ruinous in that it followed close upon the ravages of the first World War. The interval of twenty years between the end of the first and the start of the second war had not been long enough for us to recoup our lost wealth. In particular, the accumulated capital the French possessed in France and abroad before 1914 had evaporated, while the 500 million shells we fired from the Somme to the Vosges exploded over a period of fifty-one months. To reconstruct, afterwards, all that had been destroyed, to pension off the wounded, widows and orphans, to pay the war's innumerable expenses, we had been forced to borrow continually, to devalue our currency and to abandon renovation and modernization projects. In 1939, it was a poverty-stricken, outmoded France that entered the conflict; and in

the course of the latest ordeal, a large share of what remained had
been engulfed. To bind up her wounds and repair her ruins once
again, she had only minimum reserves at her disposal and a cruelly
reduced credit. How manage if we were reduced to our own poor
means? How maintain independence if we had recourse to others?

In this as in all domains, what we lacked could be compensated
for, up to a point, by human effort. But our losses were heavy here
too. More than 635,000 Frenchmen had died as a result of enemy
action, 250,000 in combat, 160,000 in bombardments or executed by
the occupiers, 150,000 victims of maltreatment in concentration
camps, 75,000 as prisoners of war or forced labourers. A further
585,000 men had become invalids. In relation to the total population,
the percentage of French losses had not reached that of the Germans
or the Russians. But it was higher than that of the British, the Italians or the Americans. Most important, the losses suffered by the
nation were relatively higher than the figures indicated. For it was
among our scarce youth that death had reaped this harvest. Again,
during the first World War, twice the number of victims had fallen
—that is, the highest proportion among all the belligerents—and at
a period when our birthrate was the lowest in the world. In short,
the French people, their average age the highest among nations and
their death rate the only one to exceed the birth rate since the beginning of the century, not yet having made good the losses of the
preceding hecatomb, had just suffered an extremely critical amputation of its rare active elements. Indeed the men it had lost were the
most enterprising, the most generous, the finest of its members.

In addition, the diminution of substance and consequently of
power inflicted upon France during two world wars had only accen-
tuated the abasement she had suffered in the space of two human
lifetimes. At the beginning of the last century—quite recently, in
historical terms—our country was the most populous in Europe, the
strongest and richest in the world, and her influence was unequalled.
Disastrous causes had combined to drive her from this dominant
position and to start her down a slope where each generation saw her
stumble lower. Mutilated of the territories nature intended her to
have, grotesquely costumed in artificial frontiers, separated from a
third of the population springing from her stock, France had been
living for a hundred and thirty years in a chronic state of infirmity,
insecurity and acrimony. When the economic capacity of the great

nations depended chiefly on coal, France had virtually none. Subsequently, when petrol controlled everything else, France had had no supply of her own. During the same period population doubled in England, tripled in Germany and in Italy, quadrupled in Russia, decupled in America; in France it remained stationary.

This physical decline went hand in hand with spiritual depression. The disasters which put an end to Napoleon Bonaparte's attempt at hegemony and later the defeat inflicted upon the nation by the might of Prussia and her German satellites had submerged the French beneath such waves of humiliation that henceforth they were to doubt themselves. Certainly the 1918 victory revived their faith, for a moment. But it cost so much and bore such bitter fruits that such hopes died at once under the shock of 1940. The soul of France died a little more. Thanks to the wakening of the resistance and to the miracle of our victory, it still survived, but lame and, so to speak, sclerotic. So many disasters had inflicted terrible wounds on national unity. Fifteen regimes had succeeded each other since 1789, each in turn installed by revolution or *coup d'état*, none succeeding in ensuring equilibrium, all swept away by catastrophes and leaving ineffaceable divisions behind them.

Today I was at the head of a ruined, decimated, lacerated nation and surrounded by ill will. Hearing my voice, France had been able to unite and march to her Liberation. She had subsequently accepted orders until the war was over. Meanwhile, the nation had gladly received the reforms which spared it social strife and allowed of its recovery. Lastly, it had allowed me to carry out a foreign policy which assured the recovery of its status. This was a great step, in relation to the disasters that had almost engulfed us. But it was a minute one in comparison to all that we must achieve before recovering our power, without which we would ultimately lose even our reason for existence.

I had conceived a plan which was nothing more than common sense. First, we must procure what we had so long lacked in sources of energy. Union with the Saar, now virtually accomplished, and the annual fifty million tons of coal we were about to obtain from the Ruhr would afford us twice what our own mines produced. There was every likelihood that the research group we had just established would discover reserves of petrol in the immense French possessions, since we had territories in each of the world's major geographical groups. As for the nascent atomic energy production, the resources of uranium which seemed abundant in our territories, as well as our scientific and industrial capacities, offered us an opportunity of reaching an exceptionally high level. The High Commission created to deal with this was to get the project under way. Further, and whatever our actual penury, a careful policy of modernization and equipment would replace our outmoded machinery. The High Commission on Planning took charge of this task. But of all our projects, those tending to increase the population were the most necessary; the measures already taken—assistance to families, allowances—would henceforth produce their effects. Finally, the social harmony to be established by the association of capital, labour and technology, the national independence maintained in any event, could cause a climate favourable to pride and effort to prevail in France.

Our country was in a position to achieve these goals if it remained united and the state led it forward. For how could it advance if it were divided against itself, if it were not guided in its progress by an authentic Government? Yet as France became free again, I realized with chagrin that political forces were making great efforts to divide her and that on various levels everything was tending to sever the nation from me.

I had every apparent justification for prolonging the sort of monarchy which I had recently assumed and which general consent had subsequently ratified. But the French people was itself, and not any other: if it did not want such a regime nothing could impose it. I would condemn France to upheavals by claiming to impose my absolute authority officially and for an unlimited period, once the danger which had put it into my hands had vanished. During the conflict, my declarations had deliberately left no doubt as to my resolution to restore its power to the French people once events allowed of elections. If my power had been increasingly recognized, it was to a large extent because of this commitment. To refuse to fulfil it now would stamp my mission with a fraudulent seal. But it would also gradually turn against me the nation which would no longer distinguish the reasons for this despotic action; the Communists, then at the peak of their energy and influence, would gain control of the opposition and simultaneously designate themselves as my necessary successors.

Opposition would be all the more certain since, save in periods of public danger, there can be no such thing as a lasting dictatorship, unless a single faction, resolved to overpower the rest, supports it against all comers. As the champion of France rather than of any class or party, I incited hatred against no one and had no supporters who favoured me in order to be favoured in return. Even the men of the resistance, if they remained emotionally loyal to the ideal that once united them, had already, to a large degree, abandoned me politically and split into various factions. Only the Army could give me the means of controlling the country by constraining the recalcitrant elements. But this military omnipotence, established by force in peacetime, would soon appear unjustifiable to adherents of every tendency.

Fundamentally, what was, what could be, dictatorship's resource if not great national ambition or the fear of a people imperilled by foreign powers? France had had two empires. She supported the first when she felt capable of dominating Europe and when she was exhausted by disorder and confusion. She consented to the second in her desire to efface the humiliation of treaties which had sealed her defeat and in the agony recent social upheavals had forced upon her. Yet each of these Caesarean regimes had ended badly. Today, no conquest, no revenge tempted our citizens; the mass of the people feared neither invasion nor revolution. Public safety was now a *fait accompli*, and I had no desire to maintain the momentary dictatorship which I had exercised in the course of the storm and which I would not fail to prolong or resume if the nation were in danger. Therefore, as I had promised, I would let the people make their own choice in a general election.

Even as I dismissed the idea of myself becoming a despot, I was still convinced that the nation needed a regime whose power was strong and continuous. The parties were obviously unqualified to provide such power. Apart from the Communists, who intended to dominate by any means whatever, whose Government would ultimately be infiltrated by an alien organization, who would find in France the resolute support of a portion of the population and of the Soviets abroad, but who would bring France to servitude, I saw that no political formation was in a position to assure the leadership of the nation and of the state. Although some among them could obtain the votes of an important fraction of the citizens, not a single one was thought of as representing public interest as a whole. Each would gather only the voices of a minority, and many electors would vote not so much for one party as against the others. In short, no organization commanded either the power or the credit which would allow it to lay claim to national authority.

To the parties' fractional character, which infected them with weakness, was added their own decadence. The latter was still concealed beneath rhetoric, but the doctrinal passion which was once their inspiration, their attraction and their greatness could not be maintained in a period of materialism so indifferent to ideals. No longer inspired by principles, no longer ambitious to proselytize since they found no audiences on these grounds, they were inevitably tending to degradation, shrinking until each became nothing more than the representative of a category of interests. If the Government fell into their hands again, it was certain that their leaders, their delegates and their militant members would turn into professionals making a career out of politics. The conquest of public functions, of influential positions, of administrative sinecures would henceforth absorb the parties and limit their activities to what they called tactics, which was nothing more than the practice of compromise and denial. Since all were minority representatives, they would have to share the positions of command with their rivals in order to accede to them at all. As a result they would proceed by giving themselves the lie in relation to the electorate. While the constant juxtaposition, within the Government, of conflicting groups and men could result only in impotence.

Considering France's immediate political realities and the extent and difficulty of the state's task, I had decided what the ideal institutions would be; to realize them, I had naturally taken into account the lessons of our recent disaster, still so painful, as well as my experience of men and affairs, and lastly the role which events enabled me to play in the establishment of the Fourth Republic.

As I saw it, the state must have a head, that is, a leader in whom the nation could see beyond its own fluctuations, a man in charge of essential matters and the guarantor of its fate. It was also necessary that this executive, destined to serve only the national community, must not originate in parliament which united the delegates of particular interests. These conditions implied that the chief of state should not belong to a party, that he be designated by the people, that he be empowered to appoint the Cabinet, that he possess the right to consult the nation, either by referendum or by the election of assemblies, that he receive, finally, the mandate of ensuring the integrity and independence of France in case of danger. Beyond those circumstances when it would be the President's duty to intervene publicly, Government and Parliament would collaborate, the latter controlling the former and authorized to cause its fall, but the national magistrate exercising his arbitration and having recourse to that of the people.

I could not overlook the fact that my project contradicted the claims of every party. None among them, whether by conviction or precaution, had as yet dared to oppose de Gaulle. Some who already expressed criticism and admonishment still refrained from challenging him outright. The Communists themselves, while brandishing trumpets and drums, were careful not to cross swords with me. But it was clear that in the crucial debate that was approaching, discord was inevitable. With various qualifications, all the parties intended the future constitution to re-create a regime whose power would depend directly and exclusively on themselves and in which de Gaulle would have no place, unless he were willing to be merely a figurehead. In this regard, the lessons of the past, the realities of the present, the threats of the future had absolutely no effect on their demands.

That the Third Republic had constantly failed to achieve equilibrium, finally collapsing in an abyss of capitulation, gave each party reasons for attacking the others on its own behalf, but not the necessity of renouncing the same weaknesses. That France could not re-establish herself without the cohesion of her people, the abnegation of factions, and the leadership of a recognized and continuous authority was a principle altogether alien to their universe. For them, on the contrary, it was a matter of opposing all competitors, of provoking those passions and claims by which they could support themselves, of seizing power not so much to serve the whole nation as to fasten their own particular programme to it. De Gaulle had succeeded in uniting the nation and leading it to salvation but that he should now be kept at its head was not what they envisaged for the future, though they were careful to lavish their praise on him now. Tomorrow, they agreed, his withdrawal would have to take place after certain transitions. They even attempted to create some sort of decorative position to which he could be relegated. Yet none of them supposed that leadership could long remain in the hands of a person whose mere presence was evidently incompatible with their regime.

Nonetheless, though I did not expect the spontaneous support of the parties, it seemed conceivable to me that the nation's instinct and the confidence it had hitherto accorded me were sufficiently obvious to oblige the 'politicians' to swim with the tide. It was my task to sound out French opinion as to whether the state should be constructed as I proposed. If they responded affirmatively, the parties would adapt themselves to it, and the new Republic would have my participation. If not, I would draw my own conclusions.

I had always intended that the people should ultimately make the decision but nevertheless I felt doubt and anxiety as to the result. The people, beneath the moving proofs of affection it lavished on me which nevertheless expressed their distress as much as their affection, was exhausted, discouraged and divided. These enormous enterprises, this vigorous action, these strong institutions which I proposed, perhaps exceeded their means and their desires. Had I the capacity, the skill, the eloquence necessary to galvanize them, when everything was sinking into mediocrity? Yet whatever the nation's eventual answer to the question which would be put to it, it was my duty, while I waited, to govern with all the authority that had been given to me.

Actually, during the first days after the German surrender, it was possible to believe in a renewal of political unity around me. For the moment, the press was loud in its praise. On May 15th the Consultative Assembly enthusiastically cheered my speech on the lessons the war had taught us. Prominent personalities outdid themselves in demonstrative gestures on my behalf. This was particularly the case among the former presidents of the Council of State whom the Germans had held as hostages and who now returned to their country. The first action of M. Paul Reynaud, M. Daladier and M. Sarraut was to assure me of their devoted support. The moment Léon Blum was free, he declared: 'France revives, thanks to General de Gaulle! We have had the luck to have a General de Gaulle. Deep in my prison, I always hoped my party could support him. All of France had every confidence in him. His presence is an irreplaceable guarantee of our nation's unity.'

Édouard Herriot, liberated by the Russians and passing through Moscow, broadcast a similar message: 'My conviction is that the nation is concentrated around Charles de Gaulle, under whose orders I place myself without reserve.' But these gestures and these words were without consequences.

As a matter of fact, it was now partisan and electoral concerns which dominated French public life. The renewal of the munici-palities gave them a first taste of this, for in its effort to set the democratic machinery in motion again, the Government had de-cided to begin with the communes. The municipal councils, elected in 1937, had been subject to Vichy's arbitrary interventions and to the upheavals of the Liberation. They now returned to their source, the suffrage of the citizens. Although many local contingencies influenced the votes of April 29th and May 13th, the dominant tendencies were nevertheless evident. Those members of the strongly hierarchized parties claiming to be the 'movement'—Communists, Socialists, Popular Republicans—won many votes and seats to the detriment of the various moderate and radical groups. The two categories of Marxists united for voting. Lastly, all tendencies played up those candidates who had played an active part in the struggle against the enemy, and the electorate enthusiastically confirmed this preference.

The conflict had therefore modified the distribution of votes, without, however, changing the nature of any French party or insti-gating a truly new current. In general, public opinion tended increasingly to fragmentation according to particular claims and disputes rather than to unite for a great national undertaking. In this atmosphere of rivalry, it was of course the Communists who set the tone and gained the ascendancy. Further, the electoral campaign had shown that as far as the nation's future institutions were con-cerned, only two ideas interested the 'politicians'. Radicals and moderates advocated the return to the constitution of 1875. The others proclaimed their desire to obtain 'a single and sovereign Assembly'. But over and above these divergencies, all demanded that the parties control the state as before, without any restrictions. There was no observer who did not therefore conclude that such would be tomorrow's results, if necessary without de Gaulle's presence. If, as Clemenceau remarks, 'the soul's worst agony is cold', it was evident that the atmosphere in which I was to function, during the months that followed, would be more painful for me every day.

The municipal elections were not yet over when the prisoners of war, the deported citizens and the forced-labour groups began to return. A great national event, charged with emotions, with joys, but also with tears! In a few weeks, the nation, its families and its cities recovered two and a half million of their sons, who were all the dearer for being the most wretched. This '*grand retour*' posed many grave problems for the Government. It was not easy to transport to France, then to restore to their homes such a great number of men, presenting themselves in impatient waves. It was perplexing to find means to feed and dress them decently, when the country was cruelly short of supplies and clothing. It was difficult to reintegrate them immediately and simultaneously into the national life while it still functioned at a retarded rate. It was not easy to hospitalize, nurse and re-educate all those who were sick, wounded or handicapped. Yet since the Reich's defeat immediately liberated all the Frenchmen held in Germany, questions concerning them had to be settled at once.

This tremendous operation had been foreseen and prepared for. The Ministry of Prisoners, Deportees and Refugees, created in Algiers in 1943, had taken steps long in advance in order to direct it as well as possible. The men had to be regrouped in Germany and their transport organized. This was relatively easy in the French Army zone. It was less so in those of the British and American armies. It was complicated in the Russian zone, for the Russians were distant and suspicious, and insisted on the observance of every formality, for they were in the process of moving the inhabitants of whole provinces. Nevertheless, an agreement immediately drawn up in Leipzig had provided for the co-operation of the various military commands. There were serious disappointments only in regard to the young Alsatians and Lorrainers forcibly incorporated into the Wehrmacht, captured by the Russians, and now classified as Germans in every prison camp in Russia. Our Ambassador General Catroux and his military mission in Moscow had difficulty in making contact with these men, establishing their identity and obtaining their repatriation. Some were not found until much later. Some did not return at all.

However, by June 1st, that is, three weeks after the movements had begun, the first million of our liberated men reached the French border. A month later, the majority of the captives had returned to their country. Received as well as possible in the hospital centres, supplied with a sum of money and demobilized, they resumed their place in a country lacking in everything but whose sons had never been needed so much.

Despite these steps, the return of a group this size and in such a short time could not be accomplished without mishap. Moreover, it was occasionally disappointment and disillusion which awaited those returning after an absence of such length. Then too, life was hard, though in the miseries of captivity it had been dreamed of differently. Lastly, some of those who behind barbed wire had imagined a renewed France were saddened by the moral mediocrity and the national apathy in which too many Frenchmen were steeped. To offset this acrimony was an obligation in the nation's highest interest, but partisan rivalry sought to exploit it. In this competition, the Communists naturally emerged victorious.

Utilizing calculation and rancour alike, they had taken under their influence the 'National Movement of Prisoners', which opened its battle against the Minister of Prisoners, Henri Frenay. In addition to the insulting motions the 'Movement' published in the papers and the speeches its orators delivered, it attempted to organize demonstrations in public places and in the hospital centres. The ceremonies inspired by the return of the prisoners, particularly the men deported for resistance activities, were so many opportunities for the 'Movement' to call out its noisy gangs. In Paris itself, parades were formed, filing down the boulevards and through the Avenue Foch under the windows of the Ministry of Prisoners, marching to cries of 'Down with Frenay!' In their ranks marched the men who had donned for the occasion the striped clothes of the concentration camp martyrs. Certainly the huge majority of the repatriated men took no part in such scandalous incidents. But the instigators hoped that the Government would turn the police against the demonstrators and excite popular indignation, or else yield to the threat and sacrifice the vilified minister. As for the other political factions, they observed this display of demagogy without giving the Government the slightest support.

Nevertheless, the matter was soon settled. I summoned the leaders of the 'Movement' to my office. 'What is happening,' I told them, 'is intolerable. I demand that it come to an end, and it is you who must see that it does.'

'These events,' they assured me, 'are an explosion of the prisoners' justified outrage. We ourselves cannot prevent them.'

I declared, 'Public order must be maintained. Either you are impotent to deal with your own men, and in that case you must indicate the fact to me in writing at once and announce your resignation; or you are really the leaders, in which case you will give me your formal promise that all agitation will stop from today. If, before you leave this building, I have not received either the letter of resignation or the promise, you will be arrested as you leave my room. I can give you only three minutes in which to decide.'

The leaders conferred in the window niche and returned at once. 'We will do as you say. We guarantee that the demonstrations will cease.' Which proved to be the case from that very day.

This affair proved that authority remained strong so long as it was not divided, but also that 'politicians' were not inclined to support it. I made a similar discovery in regard to financial and economic questions. These arose again, and sharply, during the summer following the victory. Since it was impossible to avoid this problem, and since, too, the measures to be taken concerned the interests of the electors so closely, I expected that the parties would allow my Government to do what was necessary, taking whatever advantage of the situation they could; which was, in effect, what happened.

We were faced with the simultaneous tasks of procuring exceptional resources for the treasury, opposing inflation and restraining the rise of prices. This was indeed a perpetual problem in a period when public expenditure inevitably increased, when the cessation of hostilities provoked a general tendency among the people to consume more, and when production was still far from reaching a satisfactory level. The arrangements made during the aftermath of the Liberation had allowed us to avoid the worst. Now we must make a new effort. In any case, there would be discomfort for all and heavy sacrifices for some. Given the imminence of the general elections, I might have postponed decisions for several weeks, so that the responsibility would be shared by the future National Assembly. Expedients would have sufficed, but they would have been costly. I decided not to wait, and to take the steps leading to recovery on my Government's responsibility alone.

The first of these was the exchange of bank notes. The operation's chief purpose was to reveal the wealth of each Frenchman. Already the administration knew the value of holdings in real estate, income, stocks and bonds. It remained to discover the distribution of the mass of bonds payable to bearer—bank notes and short-term bonds. The owners had to present and thereby declare their holdings. These were replaced, franc for franc, by new notes. The currency not exchanged, particularly that which the Germans had taken with them and that which its possessors preferred to lose rather than to admit *in toto*, immediately became null and void. Further, the owners of immense sums in bank notes frequently chose to convert them into bonds, since the aggregate of their fortune would henceforth be known.

All proceeded extremely smoothly, from June 4th to 15th, under Pleven's direction. Nothing, in French economic life, offered an analogy to the severe shock which a similar operation, though one involving the blocking of credits, had produced in Belgium. The bank note circulation, which rose to 580 billion francs at the end of May, reached only 444 billion by July. But this 'photography' of taxable matter was also to allow the Government to establish the extraordinary contribution it intended to levy on a firm basis.

Until it did so, it would have to keep prices from rising to excess. Though it had not adopted the extremely rigorous plan proposed by Mendès-France, though it had not officially suppressed three quarters of the currency and definitively frozen wages and prices—in short, though it had not attempted to achieve immediate and decisive results at the risk of breaking the nation's incentive to activity, the Government was no less resolved to construct dikes against the rising flood. In any case, stabilization could not be realized before the supply of products corresponded to the demand, which would not be the case for a long time. But we had the means of preventing brutal shocks and of punishing abuses. The two decrees of June 30th codified what was necessary; one established the procedure by which the authorities fixed or modified prices, the other controlled the way infractions were dealt with. These decrees, immediately applied, are still in effect today.

Whatever my Government's concern to spare the scarcely convalescent nation and to effect changes gradually, we had to establish the 1945 budget and provide means of maintaining that of 1946. Since it was impossible to renew the 'liberation loan' and dangerous to increase our short-term debt, we decided to have recourse to a special levy. The decree of August 15th instituted the 'solidarity tax', intended to meet the exceptional expenses involved in the return of the prisoners, the demobilization and repatriation of the troops, the transport of the Expeditionary Corps to Indochina, and the initial reconstruction costs. We had set at 80 billion francs—900 billion today—the resources to be obtained, and determined that they would be furnished by those who possessed capital. Who else could do so? Were they not, moreover, those chiefly interested in the equilibrium of the nation's finances, as they had been in the re-establishment of law and order and the maintenance of social peace? Quite simply, the decree prescribed a levy on inheritance, a tax on war profits, a contribution from corporate funds, the whole constituting an 'exceptional tax for national solidarity'.

The Consultative Assembly was to give its opinion of the project. The parties, during the discussion which took place on July 15th, spared us no criticisms; those of the Left, in speeches by Philip, Moch, Duclos and Ramette, proclaiming that the Government was not going far enough in the direction of the amputation of private capital; those of the Right, whose grievances were expressed by Laniel and Denais, insisting that the projected levy would do incalculable damage to normal business. Nevertheless, when the matter was put to a vote, the text was approved almost unanimously. This was to be the last time the Assembly moved to follow the Government. Soon the discussions relative to the constitution would set it openly and entirely in opposition.

Meanwhile, I had insisted that the painful affair of Pétain, Laval and Darnand be settled, for it occupied everyone's mind and continued to inspire antagonism and anxiety. Without actually intervening in the High Court's handling of the case, the Government had informed that body of its desire to see the proceedings concluded as soon as possible. The trials were therefore opened, beginning with that of the Marshal. There had been predictions on all sides that the result would provoke profound upheavals. No such thing occurred. Certainly the men who took part in the melancholy sessions, whether as magistrates, jurors, witnesses or lawyers, could not always contain their emotion or their excitement. But the disturbances never went beyond the walls of the Palais de Justice. The public followed the sessions with tense interest, as they were reported, in abbreviated form, in the newspapers, but there was no mass demonstration of any sort whatever. The nation, in fact, considered it necessary that justice give a decision, and for the immense majority the result was inevitable.

I shared this point of view, yet what seemed to me essential in the arraignment was not regarded as such in the eyes of many. For me, the capital error of Pétain and his Government had been to conclude with the enemy, in the name of France, the so-called 'armistice'. Certainly, at the time this was signed, the battle in Metropolitan France had been indisputably lost. To cease fire between the Atlantic and the Alps, to bring the debacle to an end would have been entirely justified as a military and local action. The command of the forces concerned was responsible to the Government until its leadership had changed. That Government might have reached Algiers, taking with it the treasure of French sovereignty which for fourteen centuries had never been surrendered, continuing the battle, keeping its word to the Allies, and asking for their help in return. But to have retired from the war with the Empire intact, the fleet untouched, the air force largely undamaged; to have withdrawn our African and Levant States troops without a single soldier lost; to have abandoned all those forces which, in France herself, could be transported elsewhere; to have broken our alliances; above all, to have submitted the state to the Reich's discretion—this is what had to be condemned in order to clear France of the stigma. All the faults Vichy had been led to commit subsequently—collaboration with the invaders; hostilities in Dakar, Gabon, Syria, Madagascar, Algeria, Morocco and Tunisia against the Free French or the Allies; fights against the resistance in direct liaison with German troops and police; the surrender to Hitler of French political prisoners, Jews and aliens seeking refuge in France; assistance, in the form of forced labour, raw material and propaganda, to the enemy's war machine—all flowed inevitably from this poisoned spring.

Consequently I was irritated to see the High Court, parliamentary circles and the newspapers abstain to a large degree from excoriating the 'armistice' and instead concentrate in detail and at length on facts which were accessory to it. Further, they emphasized those facts which related to the political struggle rather than to that of the nation against the enemy at its gates. Too often, the discussions assumed the nature of a partisan trial, even, on occasion, of a settling of accounts, whereas the matter should have been treated only from the point of view of national defence and independence. The old conspiracies of the Cagoulards, the dispersion of parliament after its abdication, the detention of its members, the Riom trial, the oath demanded of magistrates and officials, the labour charter, the anti-Semitic decrees, the persecution of Communists, the mistreatment of parties and trade unions, the campaigns led by Maurras, Henriot, Luchaire, Déat, Doriot, etc. before and during the war—all this took up more place and time, during the discussions and commentaries, than the regime's capitulation, its betrayal of our Allies, and its collaboration with the invader.

Philippe Pétain, during his trial, shrouded himself in silence. In view of his age, his exhaustion and the fact that what he had shielded was indefensible, his attitude seemed to me one of discretion. By remaining silent, he gave a kind of last consideration to the military dignity in which his former great services had cloaked him. The facts cited, the testimonies given, the prosecution's summary and address made it clear that his had been the drama of senility lacking the strength necessary to lead men and control events. Beneath the appearance of firmness, behind the screen of subterfuge, the Marshal was only a victim served up to servile or threatening intrigues. The court pronounced a sentence of capital punishment but at the same time expressed the hope that there be no execution. I was, moreover, determined to sign a reprieve whatever the result. Furthermore, I had taken the necessary steps to withdraw the Marshal from the insults which threatened to assail him. Scarcely was the judgment pronounced, on August 15th, than he was flown to Portalet. Later he was confined on the Île d'Yeu. My intention was that after two years' detention in fortified captivity, he should finish his days in retirement in his home near Antibes.

Pierre Laval appeared next before his judges. At the time of the Reich's capitulation, a German plane had taken him to Spain, where he hoped to find a refuge. But General Franco had had him arrested and flown back to German territory. Perhaps the fugitive hoped for some appeal from the United States? In vain! The American Army handed him over to the French authorities, and in October the head of the Vichy Government appeared before the High Court.

At first Laval attempted to account for his behaviour not as deliberate collaboration with the Reich, but as a stratagem by a statesman compromising with the worst in order to limit its depredations. Since the jurors were yesterday's or tomorrow's parliamentarians, the accused hoped the discussion would turn into a political debate, opposing various professional theories, and resulting in a state of contention which would ultimately get him off with 'extenuating circumstances.' His tactics, however, had no effect on the tribunal. Realizing this, Laval played all or nothing, adopted a provocative attitude with regard to his judges, and manipulated them into several unfortunate namecalling sessions. Immediately taking this irregular behaviour as his pretext, he refused to appear again before the Court. Thus he attempted to surround his trial with an aura of irregularity so that justice would either have recourse to some new trial or commute the sentence of capital punishment which Laval guessed was inevitable and which was, in fact, pronounced. However, he obtained neither revision nor reprieve. In a supreme attempt to avoid execution, the condemned man took poison, but was revived. Then, all avenues of escape barred, Pierre Laval stood up, walked straight to the scaffold and died bravely.

A few days before, Joseph Darnand had suffered the same sentence and had been put to death without showing any more weakness than Laval. His trial was brief. The accused bore the responsibility of a large number of crimes committed by Vichy in the name of order. The former 'secretary general' invoked in his defence only the service of the Marshal. The doctrinal aspects of National Socialism had certainly attracted Darnand's intellect, exasperated by low motives and the ideological flabbiness of his milieu. But above all, this man of energy and resolution had regarded collaboration as a thrilling adventure which justified every audacity and every means. Had the occasion presented itself, he would have accepted other inducements in the opposite direction, as was proved by his exploits at the war's beginning, at the head of his guerrilla group, and also by the fact that even wearing the uniform of a German officer and covered with the blood of resistance fighters, he had sent me a request to join Free France. Nothing revealed more dramatically than the behaviour of this great adventurer the failure of a regime which had alienated from the nation men born to serve it.

The condemnation of Vichy in the person of its leader detached France from a policy which had been one of national renunciation. It was still essential that the nation deliberately adopt the opposite course. During the years of oppression, it was faith and hope in

France which had gradually led the French towards resistance and liberation. The same motives had later operated to prevent subversion and make recovery possible. Today, no others would have any effect, from the moment we hoped to advance towards power and greatness. If this state of mind prevailed in the masses, the future National Assembly would certainly be influenced by it. Until the date of the elections, I was consequently to do everything possible in order to inspire the country with enthusiasm for its efforts and confidence in its destiny.

On May 9th, immediately after the victory, I went to Notre Dame for the ceremonial *Te Deum*. Cardinal Suhard received me beneath the portal. The whole body of officials was there, while a huge throng filled the building and overflowed around it. While the hymn of victory echoed through the vaults, and a kind of vibration rising from those present swept towards the portico, the quays and the streets of Paris, I stood in my traditional place in the choir and was stirred by the same feelings which had exalted our fathers each time glory crowned our nation. Unable to forget the tragedies that offset our triumphs, or the obstacles that rose in the nation's path this very day, there was, in this perenniality, substance to support our courage. Four days later, the feast day of Joan of Arc provided a similar occasion for patriotic fervour. This was the first time for five years that we were able to celebrate it according to the traditional ceremonies.

Yet on May 24th I broadcast an austere address to the French people couched in severe terms. I spoke of our losses, our duties, the sacrifices it would cost 'to become what we desire to be—that is, prosperous, powerful and fraternal'. I indicated how difficult a task it would be to re-establish France 'in her place in a universe which is not easily influenced'. I declared that 'our capacity to work and to produce and the scene of order that we must present in the political, social and moral spheres are the conditions of our independence and, even more, of our influence. There is no influence to be had in confusion, nor progress in chaos.' They must, therefore, expect the Government to control prices, wages and salaries, whatever the inconvenience of such steps and the opposition to them. This rigour would be accompanied, moreover, by various reforms. I announced that before the year's end the state 'would appropriate the production of coal, electricity, and the distribution of credit, levers of command which will allow it to direct the whole of the nation's activity'. Further, new measures concerning the nation's population would be applied with the same goal in view—to re-establish France's power. I compared the French to Christopher Columbus' sailors who sighted land on the horizon when they were at the worst moment of their fear and their fatigue. And I exclaimed, 'Only look up! Beyond the sacrifices and the mists of the present, a magnificent future is ours!'

With the same intention of charging the atmosphere with electricity, I visited the departments of the Manche and the Orne, which with Calvados were the most ravaged of all, on June 10th. Accompanied by Dautry, I visited St-Lô, Coutances, Villedieu-les-Poêles, Mortain, Flers, Argentan and Alençon, as well as many smaller towns. A flood of joyous recognition broke over the ruins. On June 18th, all Paris was on its feet to greet the troops from Germany which paraded down the Champs Elysées with Leclerc and Béthouart at their head. Among the delighted soldiers, the people weeping for joy, and de Gaulle standing at the centre of the ceremony passed that magical current activated by great and mutual emotion. On June 30th and July 1st I travelled through the Auvergne, which in its sober cities of Clermont-Ferrand, Riom and Aurillac, as in its scattered villages, proved as enthusiastic as the capital had been.

National elections were approaching, having been planned for the month of October. Consequently I hastened the demonstrations. The one in Paris on July 14th was suitably marked by an impressive military parade. But this time, the triumphal march took place from east to west. General de Lattre presented to me, in the Cours de Vincennes, detachments furnished by all the major units of his victorious army. Then the general and the combatants of the 'Rhine and Danube' paraded beneath a storm of cheers and a riot of flags through the Avenue du Trône, la Nation, and the Faubourg St-Antoine to march before me in the Place de la Bastille.

The following week I went to Brittany, accompanied by Pleven and Tanguy-Prigent. But it was at Brest, Lorient and St-Nazaire, all in ruins, that popular enthusiasm was the most affecting. I then proceeded to La Rochelle, liberated without excessive damage and already functioning as a port.

Picardy and Flanders next showed me that their faith in the future was of a kind to surmount all obstacles. At Beauvais, then in

Amiens, where I was received on August 11th, accompanied by Dautry, Lacoste, Laurent and Mayer, every voice was raised in a concert of enthusiasm. Through Doullens, St-Pol and Bruay I reached Béthune where 50,000 miners awaited me before the *hôtel de ville*. From the balcony I addressed them and the nation:

'We have been,' I said, 'among the most afflicted because we were the most exposed. But we are in the process of effecting an extra-ordinary recovery, and I declare with great French pride, that we are swiftly marching towards the moment when it will be said of us, "They came through!" ' Then I cited figures. In regard to coal, during the month following the liberation of the pits, the miners of France had produced a million and a half tons, yet in the course of the last four weeks, they had mined double that amount. In electricity, we had advanced from 400 to 1,350 million kilowatts a month —that is, to the 1938 level. In the same period, we had tripled our production of cast iron, steel and aluminium, and decupled the amount of iron ore mined. Immediately after the Liberation, we were producing 23,000 tons of cement a month; during the last month, the figure had risen to 120,000 tons. We had taken 40,000 tons of lime from our kilns in thirty days; now, we were producing 125,000 tons. We had filled 160,000 railway cars a month; now, we were loading 470,000. 'Having my eye necessarily fixed on the dial marking the degree of our advance, my official duty is to remark that not a day has passed without some progress over the one before.'

But in speaking of the future, I avoided demagoguery. 'Whether it is a question of the reform of prices, of wages or of elections, we know that no decision will satisfy everyone. Yet we continue on our way. We shall postpone the accounting of our grievances, our disappointments and our disillusions. We realize that the important thing is to survive—that is, to advance. We are doing so, and we *shall* do so by effort, unity and discipline, not by internal divisions. We are doing so and we *shall* do so by gradually and logically rebuilding, not by returning to old formulas or by taking mad risks ... To work!'

The next day, after visiting Bergues, I went to Dunkirk. Seeing the harbours, the locks and the quays which were nothing but rubble and wreckage, and the houses mostly ruined, it seemed unlikely that the great port could ever revive. But the huge crowd that had

gathered in the Place Jean-Bart allayed my doubts. To the words I
addressed them, the people replied with such cheers that after hearing them I had no further doubts and no half-heartedness. All
together, before the great sailor's statue, still miraculously standing,
we sang the 'Marseillaise', and then 'Jean Bart! Jean Bart!' which
dispelled all our misery. Next Calais gave me a similar reception.
The St-Pierre district was relatively undamaged but the port was in
ruins. Nothing remained of the old town except the Watch Tower
and the walls of the Église de Notre Dame. But the people, crowded
before the *hôtel de ville* where I was received by the mayor, my
brother-in-law Jacques Vendroux, made it clear by thunderous
cheers that the future was in their hands. At Boulogne, in the lower
town all was ruin and desolation which did not keep the population
from expressing their ringing confidence. This was particularly the
case among the sailors, fishermen, dock workers and stevedores
whose spokesman declared, 'Here we are! There is the sea! The two
of us must come to terms!' Amid the general ardour, the crowds of
workingmen were, as always, the most vibrant and spontaneous. My
visit to Portel, reduced to a heap of rubble but determined to revive,
concluded the final trip.

But while the people's cheers showed that they were ready to rise
above all divisions, to follow de Gaulle on the road to national
recovery, and to approve his intention of instituting a strong state,
political activity took the opposite direction. All my Government's
decisions and attitudes were now received with criticism or resentment on the part of the various parties. The 'politicians' showed
mounting caution toward me.

During the month of June, the parties raised their banners. It
should be said that on the third I myself had told a press conference
how I saw the problem of the Constituent Assembly. 'Three solutions,' I remarked, 'are conceivable. Either return to yesterday's
ways and weaknesses, separately elect a Chamber of Deputies and a
Senate, and then unite them at Versailles in a National Assembly
which either will or will not modify the 1875 Constitution. Or else
regard this constitution as extinct and proceed to elections for a
Constituent Assembly which will do what it thinks best. Or finally,
consult the country on the terms which would serve as a basis for
determining its wishes and to which its representatives would have
to conform.' I did not specify which was my own choice, but it could

be guessed from the very fact that I invoked the hypothesis of a referendum. This was enough to provoke formal opposition or at least strong reservations on all sides.

My referendum project had a triple end in view. Since the 1875 system had been swept away by 1940's disaster, it seemed to me that it would be arbitrary either to re-establish it myself or to forbid its return. After all, the sovereign nation was there to decide the matter. Although I had no doubt as to its response, I would ask the people if it desired to return to the Third Republic or to create another. Further, when the people's vote had obliterated the old constitution, the new one would have to be elaborated by the Assembly which would emerge from the elections. But must this Assembly be omnipotent, determining the national institutions exclusively and finally, possessing all rights without exception, restraint or appeal? No! Thanks to the referendum, a balance could be set up between its powers and the Government's, so that the constitution subsequently elaborated would be subject to approval by universal suffrage. The referendum, then instituted as the first and the last act of the constitutional undertaking, would provide me with an opportunity of speaking directly to every Frenchman and would give the latter the occasion to approve or disapprove of my attitude on a subject affecting the nation's destiny for generations. My intention, once it was realized, provoked stubborn opposition from every party. On June 14th the Politburo of the Communist party let it be known that it had determined to pursue its 'campaign for the election of a sovereign Constituent Assembly'; that it opposed 'any plebiscite, avowed or not, in the form of a referendum'; that it rejected 'any consideration of a presidential character'. The Confédération Générale de Travail (CGT) immediately adopted a similar resolution. On June 21st, the Socialists, in their turn, formally announced, by the organ of the executive committee, their desire to obtain 'a Constituent and Legislative Assembly' which nothing must hamper. They further declared themselves 'resolutely opposed to the method, contrary to democratic traditions, which would consist in asking the electorate to express its wishes by means of a referendum on a constitutional draft prepared by restricted commissions'. The committee for Socialist-Communist understanding meeting on June 22nd; the executive committee of the Popular Republican Movement (MRP) in a communiqué on June 24th; the Democratic and Socialist Union

of the Resistance declared at its inception on June 25th; the National
Council of the Resistance meeting on June 29th; the central committee of the League of the Rights of Man in a motion on July 1st—
all demanded the renowned single and sovereign Assembly and
expressed the disapproval of the nation of a referendum.

Those who had held office under the prewar system expressed
resentment that a referendum should even be discussed. Since 1940,
whether they had sided with Vichy or with the resistance, they had
applied their efforts to the restoration of what had been. To their
minds, de Gaulle need only ask the electorate to indicate deputies,
and the formally qualified colleges to appoint senators, in order that
parliament might reappear in its old form. That the nation evidently
condemned the Third Republic's vacillations was in their eyes a
further reason for not allowing the former to judge the latter. The
various moderate groups therefore came out in favour of the election
of a Chamber and a Senate, according to yesterday's procedures.
On June 18th, the executive committee of the Radical-Socialist
party demanded the 're-establishment of republican institutions' as
they had been before the conflict, and declared itself 'opposed to any
plebiscite and any referendum'.

Thus the political factions, divided as they were between the
creation of an omnipotent Assembly and the return to the old system,
were unanimous in rejecting my own conceptions. The prospect of a
direct appeal to the nation seemed scandalous to all of them. Nothing
showed more clearly to what distortions of the meaning of democracy
the spirit of faction led. According to the parties, the Republic was
their property, the nation being sovereign only to delegate its rights
and even its free will to the men they selected for it. Further, my
concern to assure the Government's authority and effectiveness con-
flicted with their fundamental nature. They instinctively believed
the state should be weak so they could manipulate it more readily
and win from it not so much the means of action as office and
influence.

Thoroughly aware that party tendencies might lead us to adopt a
disastrous constitution, I clung to my intention of submitting the
result to the nation's approval. But before crossing swords with the
parties, I attempted to obtain the assistance and co-operation of
qualified men variously situated in the political sphere and
whom I regarded as likely to influence public opinion. I called on

President Léon Blum, Édouard Herriot and Louis Marin, upon whom the years and the events they had lived through had perhaps conferred serenity.

Léon Blum, as a matter of fact, had just emerged from the long imprisonment which first Vichy and then the Third Reich had inflicted upon him. He was, as I knew, more attached to socialism than ever. But I also knew that during his ordeal, certain scruples had troubled him as to the convictions professed and the policies lately advocated by his party. He had re-examined them in the light of that lucidity which prison affords a noble soul. The question of political power in particular had appeared to him in a new aspect. In his prison meditations, which he published under the title *On the Human Scale*, he remarked that 'parliamentary government is not the only nor even the purest form of democracy'. He indicated that the presidential system was, in his eyes, the best. 'Personally,' he wrote, 'I incline toward a system of the American type, based on the separation and the balance of powers.' No sooner had his freedom been restored, than Léon Blum publicly expressed his confidence in me. To help me in my first project of renovating the Republic, I meant to rely on his support first of all.

I was soon obliged to abandon this hope. As a matter of fact, Léon Blum was quickly caught up again in the habitual inclinations of the Socialist group. At our first meeting, he refused to enter the Provisional Government as Minister of State, giving his poor health as an excuse and also his desire to devote himself entirely to his party. On May 20th, that is, ten days after his return to France, he declared at a meeting of Socialist Federation leaders, 'No man has the right to power. But *we* have the right to show ingratitude.' In the daily articles he wrote for *Le Populaire*, influential because of the quality of their writing as well as because of their subject matter, Blum substantially supported the idea of the single and sovereign Assembly. He did not reject the principle of the referendum, provided that it determined only whether the prewar regime was to be re-established. But for Léon Blum the question was less one of making the state stronger and more effective than of preventing the reappearance of the Senate of recent years, against which he nursed stubborn personal grievances. Nothing, according to Blum, should offset the Assembly's powers. It was from the same viewpoint that he considered what he called 'the de Gaulle case'. He lavished praise on me personally, but

in proportion to his kind words in this regard, he raised his guard
against my authority and bitterly opposed any attempt to designate
the chief of state by enlarged suffrage. In short, he too had adopted
the fundamental principle of the French parliamentary regime again:
'Let no head show above the trenches of democracy!'

Shortly before the elections, I asked for a meeting with Blum,
during which I said, 'My task of national defence and public safety
is reaching its conclusion. The nation is free, victorious and in order.
It will speak with complete sovereignty. For me to reach a new stage
at its head, its elected representatives must support me, for in the
realm of politics, no one can govern against all the rest. Yet the party
spirit leads me to doubt whether I will be able to conduct the affairs
of tomorrow's France as I believe proper. I therefore plan to withdraw. In that case, I believe you are the man to assume the burden
of leadership because of your merits, your experience and the fact
that your party will be one of the largest in the Assembly which is
about to be elected as well as situated in the centre of the prepon-
derant wing. You can be sure that I will make it easy for you at that
time.'

Léon Blum made no objection to my eventual withdrawal, which
gave me to understand that he welcomed the idea. But he declared
in response to my plans regarding himself, 'No, I can't accept that,
for I have been so long excoriated and criticized by a section of
public opinion which I loathe, that now I cannot honestly entertain
the idea of holding power. Then, too, I cannot accept because the
functions of the chief of state are terribly demanding and my
strength will not allow me to support the burden.' I then asked him,
'If, after my retirement, you were to decline, who do you think could
continue in my place?' 'Gouin is the only one!' Blum told me. And
referring to Churchill's replacement by the Labour leader, he added,
'Gouin is the man most like Attlee.' Evidently Blum considered the
great national problem we were discussing only from the Socialist
viewpoint. I must admit that in view of the experiences the country
had just survived and of which Blum himself had been a victim, I
felt considerably discouraged.

I had still less success with Édouard Herriot. Despite the shifting
attitude he had shown toward Laval and Abetz when, on the eve of
the liberation of Paris, the latter proposed that he reconvene the
1940 'National Assembly' and form a Government which would not

be mine, I had made every effort to receive this parliamentary veteran cordially. The rites and the honours of the Third Republic clung to this still-affecting bard of the contradictory impulses between which yesterday's regime had vacillated, this patriot in whom the sorrows of France had wakened despair rather than resolution, had nonetheless courageously endured the ordeals inflicted upon him by Vichy and by Hitler. When Herriot returned by way of Russia and the Middle East from his detention in Germany, I sent my own plane to Beirut for him. On the first visit he paid me, I restored his cross of the Legion of Honour which he had returned to Pétain during the occupation. I invited him, in his turn, to participate in my Government. If he consented to do so, he would be Minister of State in charge of United Nations affairs. I expected to find him cordial beneath the frankness of his good will, but he proved, on the contrary, full of grievances and malevolence.

Herriot was most annoyed by the reversal in the general attitude towards himself. He spoke acrimoniously of the rather indifferent reception he had been given at Moscow, so different from the treatment he had enjoyed there on other occasions. He did not conceal his vexation at the meagre enthusiasm the city of Lyons had just shown on his behalf. When he asked me to let him return to the presidential palace of the Chamber of Deputies, his former residence, and when I made the impossibility of such a step clear to him, he expressed his dissatisfaction in the strongest terms. Finally and above all, the relative and moreover rather unjustified collapse of the Radical party with which he identified himself caused him great distress. As for institutions, Édouard Herriot insisted upon a return to those he was used to; he therefore advocated the immediate election of a Chamber of Deputies and a Senate which would appoint their presidents, send a policy without character to the Élysée and furnish a series of cabinets composed of interchangeable parliamentarians! He regarded all that had happened and particularly the collapse of the regime so dear to him as a horrible episode, but learnt no lesson from it. Édouard Herriot declined my invitation to join the Government. I asked him to help in the reconstruction of France; he declared that he would devote himself to rebuilding the Radical party.

Louis Marin also showed that his principal concern was to revive a political grouping in accordance with the ideas he had served throughout his career. He was using his influence and his activity to unite the Moderates before the forthcoming elections. As long as it was a question of driving the Germans from national soil, this old Lorrainer had given me his unreserved loyalty and adherence. Now he insisted on his autonomy in relation to me. A parliamentarian of wide experience, moreover, deeply attached to the life of Assemblies, relishing the acrimonious and heady ferments; in fact he hoped for nothing better than to see them reappear as he had practised them. My intention of limiting their powers was of little interest to him. Like Blum and Herriot, he refused to enter the Provisional Government. However he strongly assured me that in regard to my policy of national security, he would support me with all the means in his power.

Without having these three personalities in my camp who could have helped stamp the accession of the Fourth Republic with the sign of unity and publicity, I approached the constitutional discussion surrounded by the Government I had reconstituted during the aftermath of the liberation of Paris. However, so that the same men need not constantly serve as targets, at the end of May I replaced Paul Ramadier as Minister of Supply by Christian Pineau, recently returned from Buchenwald, and appointed Pierre-Henri Teitgen to the Ministry of Justice, while François de Menthon represented France on the Nuremberg tribunal. Teitgen relinquished the Ministry of Information to Jacques Soustelle. Shortly afterward, Augustin Laurent left the Ministry of Postal Services for reasons of health, and I entrusted this post to Eugène Thomas, recently returned from deportation. On July 9th I informed the Council of the projected statute which I had established with the devoted collaboration of Jules Jeanneney.

The discussion was calm and searching. Since the majority of the ministers belonged to parties and since the latter had all expressed their disapproval, I let it be known that I accepted in advance the resignations which would be offered. None, however, was sent in. The Council adopted the text unchanged and unanimously.

The election of an Assembly was set for the month of October. The nation was to decide by referendum whether the Assembly would be a Constituent Assembly. The reply, yes or no, to this question would mean either the accession of the Fourth Republic or a return to the Third. If the Assembly was to be Constituent, its powers would be determined by the second question on the referendum; either the nation would adopt the Government's plan (limiting the duration of the Assembly's mandate to seven months, restricting its legislative powers to voting on budgets, structural reforms and international treaties, according it no initiative in the matter of expenditure but granting it power to elect the President of the Government, who would remain in office as long as the deputies, and lastly—and most important—subordinating the adoption of the constitution to its ratification by universal suffrage); or, if the nation refused the Government's proposal, the Assembly would be omnipotent in all matters and for as long as it chose to exist. The reply, yes or no, would establish, or not establish, the balance of the executive and legislative powers for the 'preconstitutional period'.

During the same session, the Council further decided that the cantonal elections would take place in two ballots on September 23rd and 30th. In this way, general councils would be constituted before the referendum. If, contrary to every expectation, the referendum favoured the re-establishment of former institutions, the Senate could then be elected by limited suffrage, as had previously been the case.

On July 12th, I made a nationwide broadcast, discussing the points on which the people were to be consulted and told them what I thought they ought to do. After reading the text of the questions the referendum would ask, I declared, 'As for my opinion, I shall express it in this way: I hope and trust that the French people will answer Yes to both questions.'

Then it was the Consultative Assembly's turn. I foresaw an animated discussion, as acrimonious as it was inconclusive, which proved to be the case. The delegates expressed their virtually unanimous opposition to the Government's text, but could frame no constructive proposal of their own.

In the name of the Radicals and certain Moderates, Plaisant, Connevay, Labrousse, Bastid and Astier passionately demanded the restoration of the old constitution and, first of all, the election of a Senate at the same time as that of a Chamber of Deputies. To strengthen their position, these delegates did not abstain from likening General de Gaulle's referendum to Bonaparte's and the Prince-President's plebiscite. The Communists and those members of the Assembly who had taken their stand with them, represented by Cogniot, Duclos, Cot and Copeau, pointed at the same bogeys, but unlike the centre speakers concluded that the Constituent Assembly must be allowed to decide of its own free will on all matters, particularly the nation's institutions. The Socialists, Popular Republicans, and representatives of the new Democratic Union of the Resistance, as well as some Moderates, probably calculating that there would be an electoral advantage in not breaking with me, adopted a middle course. These factions now accepted the principle of a referendum, but nonetheless proclaimed their desire to achieve a single and sovereign Assembly and their opposition to the restriction of the latter's powers.

Thus the Consultative Assembly split among three tendencies, none of which was in a position to achieve a majority. But without being able to agree on tomorrow's institutions, or on the means of doing so, they were unanimous in demanding the absolute primacy of the parties. Further, none made any concession or even allusion to the crucial necessities of separation of powers or the effectiveness of the state's powers.

Yet it was these very conditions that I particularly stressed when I mounted the tribunal at the end of the discussion. In my opinion, it was in order to fulfil them that the nation must assign limits to the Constituent Assembly's duration, impose restrictions upon its powers, and attach regulations to its relations with the executive power. It was the responsibility of the Provisional Government to propose these limits, restrictions and regulations to universal suffrage. But I urged the delegates to join with the Government in order to do so. I characterized as spurious all comparisons between my referendum and the Napoleonic plebiscite. Pretending to fear I would stifle the Republic when I was releasing it from its tomb was simply ridiculous. When the parties and parliament had betrayed and denied the Republic in 1940, I had 'taken up its arms, its laws and even its name'. Now I was doing what was needed to bring to these elections an Assembly to which I would hand over my powers, hardly the procedure employed on December 2nd or the 18th Brumaire. But tomorrow the Republic must have a true government, and must not revert to yesterday's deplorable practices.

Insisting on this point, which for me was a crucial one, I declared:

'This perpetual threat hanging over the men who had the task of governing, this almost chronic state of crisis, these bargainings with foreign powers, their intrigues within the Council, all consequences of such a situation—what this cost the nation is probably incalculable.' I reminded my audience that 'from 1875 to 1940, we had had one hundred and two Governments, while Great Britain's numbered twenty and America's fourteen'. What, consequently, could be the authority, at home and abroad, of the cabinets formed under such conditions in comparison to that of the ministries functioning in other countries? I indicated what Franklin Roosevelt had told me: 'Even I, the President of the United States, sometimes found myself incapable of remembering the name of the current head of the French Government.'

'Tomorrow, still more than yesterday', I declared, 'the state can take no effective action and—I say it categorically—French democracy can have no future if we return to a system of this kind.' And I added: 'In the disaster of 1940, the abdication of the Republic and the accession of Vichy, how much was directly accountable to the nation's disgust with this absurd game it had watched for so long and which conducted its affairs so badly.'

But these considerations were not those which preoccupied the parties. The Consultative Assembly listened to me deferentially; then it indicated that my concerns were not its own. By a vote of 210 to 19 it rejected the Government's whole proposal. An enormous majority subsequently rejected an amendment providing for the election of a Senate and thereby a return to pre-war institutions. When, to conclude, Vincent Auriol and Claude Bourbet defended a compromise proposal accepting a referendum but greatly reducing the Government's draft, their text was defeated by a vote of 108 to 101. The session therefore ended without the Consultative Assembly's having managed to formulate any positive opinion.

Once again, I had to intervene decisively. On August 17th, the Council of Ministers adopted the final terms of the statute relative to the referendum and the elections. In relation to the original text, the only modifications were specifications intended to avert possible ministerial crisis for the duration of the Constituent Assembly's mandate. The latter could, as a matter of fact, overthrow the Government only by a special vote and an absolute majority and after a delay of at least forty-eight hours. No change

I*

was made in the two essential points. The French people were to
settle the final destiny of the Third Republic. The sovereignty of
the people, formally established despite the Consultative Assembly's
opposition, would ultimately determine the nation's institutions.

The August 17th statute, at the same time as formulating the
text of the referendum's two questions, determined the means of
balloting. On this last point too, the decisions reached also gave
rise to vehement protests.

Two opposing and, in my opinion, equally distressing conceptions divided the political factions. The partisans of prewar institutions advocated a return to the former electoral regime as well,
that is, to voting for only one candidate in each arrondissement.
All principles aside, Radicals and Moderates inclined to think that
the prominent men they had formerly put up for office would again
find approval from the electors in the old constituencies. On the
other hand, Communists, Socialists and Popular Republicans, who
expected to obtain votes thanks to the attraction of their programmes
rather than by the personal fame of their candidates, insisted on
'integral' proportional representation. According to these doctri-
naires, equity could be arithmetically and morally satisfied only if
each party, proposing a single list of all candidates to all of France,
was granted a number of seats exactly proportional to the total of
votes received throughout the nation. Should this 'perfect' system
fail and if, more modestly, proportional representation functioned
in multiple constituencies (such as the departments), they insisted
that the votes not comprising part of the local quotients be added
on the national scale. Thanks to these returns, which would obtain
additional seats, each party would be sure of bringing in some of
its leaders who would have been defeated in the provinces or not
even have stood for election anywhere. In short, a representation
by arrondissement that was too narrow and a proportional representation that was too wide were advocated and argued over by
impassioned and partisan apostles. I did not favour or even discuss
the arguments of either camp.

Yesterday's means of balloting did not appeal to me. First of
all, I considered it somewhat unfair, given the great differences in
population among the arrondissements. In the past, Briançon with
7,138 electors, Florac with 7,343, and a part of the Sixth Arrondissement of Paris with 7,731 elected a deputy, just as did Dunkirk,

Pontoise or Noisy-le-Sec, which included respectively 33,840, 35,199 and 37,180 electors. To introduce more equity into this system, we would have to institute throughout the national territory a hasty remodelling of the constituencies, amid innumerable and fierce discussions. But what now particularly discouraged me about balloting by arrondissement was the prospect of the effect it would have on the nation's future by assuring the primacy of the Communist party.

If the election was determined by a single ballot, as many advocated, by analogy with the British practice, there was no doubt that a Communist would be returned in most constituencies. The 'party's' candidate in each arrondissement would be faced by at least one Socialist, one Radical, one Popular Republican, one Moderate, and one exemplary resistance fighter, not to mention several dissidents and various theoreticians. Given the number of votes which the Third International would garner throughout the country and which gave a good indication of the imminent results of the municipal and cantonal elections, it was the Communist candidate who would most frequently be elected. If there were two ballots, Communists and Socialists, provisionally united by their contractual understanding and by their basic tendencies, would combine their votes in all ballots, which would get the greatest number of seats for their coalition and also yoke together, by common electoral interest, both sorts of Marxist. In any case, balloting by arrondissement would bring to the Palais Bourbon a majority that would vote as the Communists wished. This result doubtless escaped the adherents of the old formula. But being responsible for the destiny of France, I could not run such a risk.

The concept of 'integral' proportional representation was no more to my liking. To propose to some 25 million electors an unlimited number of lists, each consisting of 600 names, would characterize almost all the mandataries by anonymity and eliminate all human contact between those voting and those elected. And by common sense, by tradition and by public interest, the various regions of the nation should be represented as such within the Assemblies, and should be represented by men who would maintain contacts with the local voters. Moreover, only the chief of state should be elected by the nation as a whole. If, however, each party used the remaining votes it obtained in the constituencies on the national level, this would mean instituting two kinds of deputy—those elected by departments, and those put into office by a mythical collection of votes, though the citizens had not actually voted for them. I was flatly opposed to this procedure.

The Provisional Government therefore adopted balloting by list and proportional representation on a departmental basis. Further, the most densely populated departments were also subdivided. No constituency would have more than nine deputies. None would include less than two. All in all, the assembly would include 522 elected representatives from Metropolitan France and 64 from the French Union. The electoral system instituted by my decree subsequently remained in effect. The parties made only one—hardly suitable—modification to it later on: that of party alliances.

At the moment, a violent outcry was raised on all sides against the decision taken. Since the Consultative Assembly had disbanded on August 3rd, a 'Delegation of the Left' was constituted, intended to organize the ensemble of protests. On the initiative of the Confédération Générale de Travail (CGT), totalling some four million adherents under the leadership of its Secretary General Léon Jouhaux, the mandataries of the Communist, Socialist and Radical parties, and of the League of the Rights of Man united; although the members of this delegation were not in agreement among themselves as to the means of balloting, they unanimously disapproved of the solution adopted by the Government and agreed to take spectacular action with regard to General de Gaulle in order to indicate their opposition. On September 1st, Jouhaux asked me to receive him along with several other delegates.

I felt a great deal of cordial respect for Léon Jouhaux. This eminent trade unionist had devoted his life to the service of the working class, applying his great intelligence and skill to clearing a path for labour's well-being and dignity. Under the occupation, he had immediately adopted an attitude of marked opposition to the 'national revolution' and had shown that he regarded the enemy as the enemy. Imprisoned by Vichy, then deported to Germany, he had now resumed the leadership of the Confederation, in so far as the growing influence of the Communists allowed him to do so. I had frequently discussed social problems with him. But on this occasion, my duty to the state prevented me from receiving him. According to law, the Confederation's exclusive object was 'the study and the defence of economic interests'. I had no intention, now less than ever, of admitting the trade union's qualifications to interfere in political and electoral questions. I replied to Jouhaux's letter that I could not accede to his request for an audience. Then, despite the indignation which every faction and every newspaper chose to express, I refused to modify my position, and as a result each group decided to adapt itself to it as well as possible. On the bases established by the statute, the parties prepared themselves to confront universal suffrage.

The electoral campaign was extremely animated, not so much as a consequence of the opposing candidate lists as because of the passions provoked by the referendum questions de Gaulle had insisted upon. Actually, the nation's response to the first was known in advance. It was only a matter of discovering how large a proportion of Frenchmen would ask for something better than the Third Republic. But the second question began a passionate debate throughout the nation.

The Communists, imitated in many areas by Socialist elements and indirectly helped by the Radicals and some Moderates, made great efforts to obtain a negative majority in order to put me in check. Thus the French section of the Third International openly showed whom it regarded as the chief adversary. As a consequence the Popular Republican Movement (MRP), the Democratic Union of the Resistance and several rightist groups championed a positive reply to the referendum. As for the Socialist Party, it had finally and officially subscribed to my cause. But rather than fight on behalf of a cause that was not of its own making and that divided its own militants, it left the 'questions' in obscurity and applied itself to publicizing its own programme, which was not receiving much attention from the public. All in all, the electoral battle, waged with a great many posters, tracts, and slogans painted on walls, had at stake the 'Yes' asked for by de Gaulle and the 'No' insisted on by the Communist party. While refraining from appearing at meetings or ceremonies during the three weeks the campaign lasted, I insisted on reminding the French, on October 17th, of how much depended on this ballot and what my own opinion was.

On October 21st, the voting offices received the ballots in two urns, one for the referendum, the other for the election of deputies. Out of 25 million registered voters, there were about 20 million votes cast. Of the five million abstainers, the majority were women avoiding unfamiliar formalities. Once the results were counted for both Metropolitan France and North Africa and a certain number of obscure ballot papers were cleared up, it was found that the Communists had 160 elected representatives, the Socialists 142, the Democratic Union of the Resistance 30, the Popular Republicans 152, the Radicals 29, the Moderates 66.

Thus the Communist party, although it had obtained a quarter of all the votes cast, did not carry the great mass of the nation's seats. However, the events from which France had just emerged had provided it with exceptional opportunities for victory. The disaster of 1940, the national failure of many former leaders, the resistance in which it had played a leading role, the long misery of the people during the occupation, the political, economic, social and moral upheavals the country had endured, the victory of Soviet Russia, the abuses committed towards us by the western democracies—all were favourable conditions for its success. If, indeed, the 'party' had not been able to seize its opportunity, it was because I had been there to incarnate France as a whole. Conversely, by associating the Communist party with the liberation of the country and subsequently with its recovery, I had given it the means to integrate itself in the community. Now the people accorded it a considerable hearing, but not the right to domination. Would it choose to be a functioning element of French democracy or merely a separate group manipulated by foreign masters? The answer would in part depend on the nature of the Republic itself. Strong, proud and fraternal, it would perhaps offset such dissidence. Impotent and motionless, it would surely incline this power to become centrifugal once again.

But would the other political factions be willing to unite around me to reconstruct the state? The referendum proved that this was the nation's profound desire. By more than 96 per cent of the votes, the people had answered 'Yes' to the first question, testifying that they condemned, almost unanimously, the regime without a leader and consequently without direction or authority which had collapsed in the disaster. Further, they expressed their confidence in me personally by a more than 66 per cent vote approving my

proposal reducing party omnipotence. This evidence was confirmed
by the electoral results among the various political formations,
depending on the attitude they had adopted towards me. The
hostility the Communists showed me certainly cost them a degree
of popular suffrage. The Radicals were crushed as much because
their leaders opposed Charles de Gaulle as because they symbolized
and advocated the old system. For lack of having adopted a favourable position towards me the Moderates lost almost two-thirds of the
seats that had once been theirs. If the Socialists, surprised and
disappointed as they were by the results, did not come in first, the
growing reserve which they showed me, though so many of their
men had remained so close to me for so long, sufficed to explain
the fact. On the other hand, the Popular Republican Movement
(MRP), scarcely out of its cradle but declaring for the moment, a
'resolute Gaullism', came in ahead of all the other groups, except the
Communists, in regard to votes and seats.

Certainly the referendum had not revealed a great national
renewal, yet it gave me the impression that the country as a whole
wanted me to lead it, at least until it had ratified its new institutions. It seemed to me essential, moreover, both historically and
politically, that this ratification be carried out with my approval
and agreement, considering what it was that events had led me to
represent.

But I had to admit that at this point in my journey, the support
the nation offered me was growing slight and uncertain. Now the
rudimentary powers which it had lately given me for battle were
fading; the dispersion of the resistance forces was a *fait accompli*.
Further, the current of popular enthusiasm which had been poured
so generously on me was now channelled in various directions. As
for the voices which traditionally expressed the nation's conscience,
I received little encouragement from them. As a matter of fact,
the nation no longer delegated anything but parties around me.
And the latter, after the elections, whether they were pleased or
disappointed by the results, were less concerned than ever to follow
me. Particularly since, though the distant horizon was still dark with
clouds, there were no immediate threats discernible. France had
recovered her integrity, her status, her equilibrium and her overseas territories. Here was substance to nourish for a while the
strategies of party politicians, their desire to control the state,

their opinion that the 'man of the storm' had now played his part
and must step aside.

For myself, having summed up the possibilities, I had decided on
my conduct. It was my task to be and to remain the champion of an
orderly and vigorous Republic, and the adversary of the confusion which had brought France to the abyss and risked casting
her into it once again tomorrow. As for my Government's power, I
should in any case be able to withdraw from events before they
withdrew from me.

VII. DEPARTURE

Now it was November. The war had been over for two months, the nation's attention was flagging and great actions no longer held the stage. Everything pointed to the reappearance of yesterday's regime, less adapted than ever to the nation's needs. I was still in power but it could only be provisionally. To France and the French, I owed something further—to leave as a man morally intact.

The Constituent Assembly met on November 6th. Cuttoli, a Radical deputy and the senior member, presided. Although this first session was a purely formal one, I insisted on being present. Some may have felt that the transmission of public powers from de Gaulle to the national representation should be made with some formality. But the notion that my visit to the Palais Bourbon might involve a degree of ceremony antagonized the provisional committee and even the protocol experts. So everything was accomplished without a show of state and, on the whole, in a mediocre way.

Cuttoli made a speech paying homage to Charles de Gaulle but lavishing criticisms on his policy. The praises found few echoes among those present but the disparagements received strong applause from the Left, while the Right abstained from any demonstration whatever. Then the presiding officer read aloud my letter announcing that the Government would resign once the Constituent Assembly had elected its committee. There was no particular reaction. As for myself, sitting in a lower row in the arena, I sensed converging upon me the ponderous stares of six hundred parliamentarians and felt, almost physically, the weight of general uneasiness.

After the Assembly had elected Félix Gouin as its president, its next task was to elect the President of the Government. Naturally I abstained from submitting my candidacy or making any reference

to my eventual policy. They would take me as I was or not take me
at all. For a whole week, there were many trying conferences among
the various groups. Meanwhile, on November 11th, I presided over
the ceremony in the Place de l'Étoile. Fifteen coffins, brought
from every battlefield, were arranged around the Tomb of the
Unknown Soldier, as if the combatants had come to pay the final
homage of their own sacrifice before being transferred to a case-
mate of the Mont Valérien military cemetary. Speaking a few
words at the foot of the Arc de Triomphe, I appealed for unity
and fraternity in order to cure wounded France. 'Let us walk
together', I said, 'on the same road, at the same pace, singing the
same song! Let us look towards the future with the eyes of a great
united people!' Around the circumference of the Place de l'Étoile,
the crowd was as enthusiastic as ever; but at my side the official
faces indicated that the Government was about to change its nature.

Nevertheless, two days later, the National Assembly unanimously
elected me President of the Government of the French Republic and
proclaimed that 'Charles de Gaulle had deserved well of his
country'. Although this demonstration only took place after eight
days of disagreeable palavers, it might be interpreted as expressing
a conscious intention of rallying round me in order to support my
policy. This was what Mr Winston Churchill, for example, seemed
to believe. After passing through Paris on November 13th, dining
with me and subsequently hearing the election results, Churchill
expressed his enthusiasm in a generous letter. Recalling Plutarch's
remark, 'Ingratitude towards men is the sign of a strong people',
which had recently been taken as an epigraph for a celebrated
book, he wrote, in his turn, 'Plutarch lied!' But I knew that the vote
was a form of homage addressed to my past actions, not a promise
for the future.

This was immediately brought home to me. On November 15th,
undertaking to form the Government, I was to step in one wasp's
nest of intrigue after another. The leftist groups, who formed a
considerable majority in the Assembly, raised many objections. The
Radicals informed me that they would not participate in any
Government of mine. If any of their members accepted a portfolio nevertheless, it would be against the explicit will of the party.
The Socialists, suspicious and anxious, made inquiries as to my
platform, multiplied their conditions and declared that in any case

they would grant their votes only to a Cabinet that had the support and the participation of the Communists. The latter were playing for high stakes; for them Maurice Thorez asked for at least one of the three ministries they regarded as most important: National Defence, Interior or Foreign Affairs. This was indeed the crucial question. If I yielded to their demands, the Communists would hold one of the state's essential powers and thereby have means of taking control in a moment of confusion. If I refused, I ran the risk of finding myself powerless to form a Government. But then the 'party', having demonstrated that it was stronger than de Gaulle, would become the master of the situation.

I decided to take a decisive step: I would oblige the Communists either to enter government on my conditions or to leave it altogether. I informed Thorez that neither the Ministry of Foreign Affairs, nor that of War, nor that of the Interior would be assigned to any member of his party. To the latter I offered only 'economic' ministries. As a result of this move, the Communists published furious diatribes, declaring that by refusing to give them what they asked 'I was insulting the memory of the war dead', and invoking their '75,000 assassinated men', an entirely arbitrary figure, moreover, for happily the total number of their adherents who had fallen before the firing squads did not amount to a fifth of this number, and furthermore those Frenchmen who had sacrificed their lives had done so—Communists included—for France, not for a party.

Thereupon I was flooded by the alarmed reproofs of various men of the Left who urged me to yield in order to avoid a fatal crisis, while the other factions remained silent and withdrawn. But my resolution was firm. I intended to oblige the National Assembly to support me against the Marxist Left, and on November 17th, I therefore wrote to the President of the Constituent Assembly that since I was unable to create a unified Government, I was restoring the mandate it had entrusted to me to the national representations. The following day, speaking on the radio, I called the people to witness the abusive demands which partisan groups claimed to impose upon me. I announced that for obvious national and international reasons, I refused to put the Communists in a position to dominate our policy by surrendering to them 'the diplomacy which expresses it, the Army which sustains it, or the police which pro-

K

tects it'. This being so, I would form a Government with the support
of those who chose to follow me. Otherwise, I would resign from
office immediately and without bitterness.

Moreover, however threatening the atmosphere, every intangible
factor, the expression of every apprehension, led me to believe that
I would succeed in my design. And indeed, after a debate I did not
attend, the Assembly re-elected me President of the Government
by every vote save those of the Communists. It is true that André
Philip, spokesman for the Socialists, had tried to explain his party's
reluctant adherence by proclaiming that the Chamber was con-
veying to me the 'imperative charge' of setting up a Ministry in
which the extreme left would be represented. This formula deceived
no one. It was clear that the Communists had not been able to
impose their will. Not a single deputy, outside their own group, had
supported them, and in the decisive vote, they were isolated against
all others, without exception. Thus was broken, from the start, a
spell which had threatened to become calamitous.

The Communists drew the appropriate conclusions at once. The
next day, their delegation called to inform me they were willing to
enter my Government without stipulating conditions, and asserting
that I would find no firmer support than theirs. Without deluding
myself as to the sincerity of this sudden reversal, I accepted their
support, considering that for a while at least their rallying to my
cause could further the social harmony of which the nation stood in
such need!

On November 21st, the Government was formed. Four portfolios
went to Communist deputies—Billoux, Croizat, Paul and Tillon;
four to Socialists—Moch, Tanguy-Prigent, Thomas and Tixier;
four to Popular Republicans—Bidault, Michelet, Prigent and
Teitgen; two to resistance leaders of the Democratic Union—
Pleven and Soustelle; one to Giacobbi, a Radical; one to Dautry
and one to Malraux, neither of whom was a parliamentarian or
had any party affiliation whatsoever; the whole structure was surmounted by four Ministers of State—a Socialist, Auriol; a Popular
Republican, Gay; a Moderate, Jacquinot; a Communist, Thorez.
As expected and announced, the Marxist Left received only
economic ministries—National Economy, Labour, Production and
Armament Manufacture.

On November 23rd, I made a speech before the Assembly in

which I emphasized the gravity of the nation's present circumstances, the necessity of adopting as soon as possible institutions assuring 'the responsibility, the stability, the authority of the executive power', and lastly the duty of the French and their representatives to unite in order to re-create France. Once again, the national representation supported me unanimously. In the crisis which had been prolonged for seventeen days without any valid reason, only the political parties had found their sustenance and their satisfaction.

Despite the unity achieved, I could not doubt that my power hung by a thread. Nevertheless, during the month of December I had the Government adopt and the Assembly pass a law nationalizing the Bank of France and four credit establishments, and instituted a National Credit Council serving under the Minister of Finance. Shortly after, another law settled the terms of transferring the production and distribution of gas and electricity to the state. In both these issues all demogogic amendments had been successfully discarded. Furthermore, on December 15th I had the satisfaction of inaugurating the National Administrative School, an important institution which would co-ordinate and standardize the recruiting and training of the principal public servants who had hitherto come to office from various training establishments. The school, springing full-fledged from the brain and the labours of my adviser, Michel Debré, saw the light of day, it was true, in an atmosphere of scepicism on the part of the major bodies of public service and the parliamentary milieus. Yet it was to see their prejudices dissolve as it gradually became, from the point of view of administrative training, attitude and action, the foundation of the new state. Nevertheless, and by a sort of ironic coincidence, at the very moment when this nursery of the future servants of the Republic was being created, the threat of a general strike of civil servants sorely tried the cohesion of the Government and my own authority.

It was only too true, of course, that the standard of living of these public servants had suffered greatly from the inflation. Their wage increases were not sufficient to meet the rise of prices. But what the trade unions asked for for them could not be granted without unbalancing the budget and depleting the treasury. Although this was acknowledged by the Council of Ministers, although I indicated my determination not to allocate more than the reasonable

increase proposed by René Pleven and my resolve to forbid the
strike under threat of penalties to be imposed on the offenders, I
noticed violent agitation rising within the Government itself. Several
Socialist members, following their party's instructions, gave me to
understand that they would retire rather than send a refusal to the
trade union and penalize the officials and employees who abstained
from work. At the same time, the civil servants were convened by
their federations on December 15th at the Vélodrome d'Hiver in
order to stigmatize 'the absurd inadequacy of the measures contemplated by the Government' and to call for a general strike.

By a curious complication, at the moment when a major crisis
seemed inevitable, it was Communist support that permitted me to
avert it. Within the Council, which was holding another session,
Maurice Thorez suddenly declared that there must be no yielding
to such intolerable pressures; provided a few minor modifications
were made, the arrangements proposed by the Finance Minister
and approved by the President should be applied. Immediately the
possibility of a Cabinet checkmate vanished from sight. That afternoon, at the Vélodrome d'Hiver, when the speakers mandated by
the trade unions and in conjunction with the Socialist party had
requested the audience to stop work and take action against the
Government, the Communist representative, to the general astonishment, violently opposed the agitators. 'If the civil servants go on
strike,' he declared, 'they will be committing a crime against their
country!' Then, taking advantage of the confusion produced by this
unexpected outburst from the 'workers' party', he caused the decision to strike to be postponed. Thereafter, in order to settle the
question, there remained only the parliamentary procedures to be
executed.

On December 18th, at the end of the debate the National
Assembly had opened on the subject, I made it clear that the
Government could not go beyond the measures it had adopted,
whatever its regret at being unable to do more for the state workers.
'We have come,' I said, 'to the moment when, economically and
financially speaking, we may lose everything or save nothing.' I
added, 'We must know if the present Government, confronting a
serious difficulty and offering its solution, has or has not your
confidence. We must know too if the National Assembly will or
will not be able to devote itself to the nation's general interest

beyond party concerns.' The order of the day ultimately voted was as confused and ineffectual as I could wish.

But this success was a temporary one. A few days later, I was shown still more clearly how precarious General de Gaulle's power had become in relation to the parties and to the Assembly.

The 1946 budget was under discussion. For form's sake the Government insisted that the final vote be taken on January 1st. But on that day, as the discussion seemed to draw to a close, the Socialists suddenly demanded a 20 per cent reduction of the credits assigned to National Defence. It was obvious that so sudden and summary a proposition, directed against an order of expenditure which evidently could not be reduced to such proportions from one day to the next, was inspired by both electoral demagogy and hostility towards me.

Since I was detained in the Rue St-Dominique on New Year's Day by the visits of the diplomatic corps and the authorities, the Palais Bourbon debate dragged on without reaching an outcome. Though Minister of Finance Pleven, Minister of the Armies Michelet, Minister of Armament Tillon, and Minister of State Auriol followed my instructions and declared that the Government rejected the proposal, the Left—Socialists, Communists and the majority of the Radicals—who together comprised the majority, was prepared to vote it through. However, and as if to prove that the real issue was de Gaulle, the Assembly postponed the vote until I came in person to take part in the discussion.

I did so during the afternoon. In my presence, M. Philip and M. Gazier led the attack with passion, supported by the applause of their Socialist colleagues, the Radicals counting the blows. Actually, the challengers protested that their intention was not to destroy the Government; they were taking action, they said, only to oblige it to yield before the parliamentary will. The Popular Republicans made it clear that they did not approve the aggression launched against me on such grounds, while the Right voiced its anxiety, but these fractions of the Assembly were careful not to condemn the opposition in explicit terms. As for the Communists, hesitating between the immediate imperative of demagogy and their tactics of the moment, they informed me that the assault had not been made with their agreement, but that if the Socialists were to bring the matter to vote, they themselves would be obliged to deny me their support.

That evening, probing hearts and hopes, I realized that the matter was already decided, that it would be vain and even unworthy to presume to govern when the parties, their power restored, had resumed their old tricks; in short, that I must now prepare my own departure from the scene.

In two brief interventions, I indicated to the Assembly the absurdity of the constraint they hoped to impose upon me and the frivolity with which the representatives of the people were preparing to cut into national defence in order to give themselves the advantage of a partisan manoeuvre. Then, proceeding to the heart of the matter, I declared that this debate raised the whole problem of tomorrow's institutions. Once the Government, acting in full knowledge of the facts, had assumed responsibility in so serious a matter, was it acceptable that the parliament should wish to oblige it to contradict and humiliate itself? Were we imitating the regime of the Assembly? For my part, I refused to do so. If the credits requested were not voted that same evening, the Government would not remain in office another hour. 'I should like to add a word,' I said, 'which is not for the present, but even now, for the future. The point that divides us is a general conception of government and its relations with the national representatives. We have begun to reconstruct the Republic. After me, you will continue to do so. I must tell you in all conscience—and no doubt this is the last time I shall be speaking to you from this place—that if you do not take into account the absolute necessities of Governmental authority, dignity and responsibility, you will find yourselves in a situation which I predict will cause you bitter regret for having taken the way you have chosen.'

As if the opposition wished to emphasize the fact that its attitude had been nothing but ruse and palinode, it suddenly fell silent. The order of the day, adopted virtually unanimously by the Assembly, imposed no conditions upon me. After which, the budget was passed without difficulty. But although my defeat had not been accomplished, the mere fact that it had appeared possible produced a profound effect. My Government had been breached by the majority during a threat-crammed debate. Henceforth, perhaps, the same effect could be accomplished apropos of virtually any issue. It was apparent that if de Gaulle tolerated this situation in order to remain in office, his prestige would decline, until one day

DEPARTURE 275

the parties would either no longer tolerate him or else relegate him to some harmless and decorative function. I had neither the right nor the inclination to lend myself to such calculations. As I left the Palais Bourbon on the evening of January 1st, I had determined upon my departure from office. All that remained was to select the date, without making any concessions whatever.

Certainly it would be before the end of the month. For the constitutional debate would then begin, and I was convinced that by remaining in the nascent regime I would not have the possibility of imposing my views nor even of supporting them. The draft which the committee created by the Constituent Assembly had prepared was precisely the opposite of what I considered necessary, instituting as it did the absolute government of a single and sovereign Assembly; the executive having no other role than to apply what was prescribed; the President of the Council being elected by the parliament and permitted to form his Cabinet only after passing a thorough examination as to his tendencies and policy and assuming commitments which would severely bind him beforehand. As for the President of the Republic, it was agreed, after many hesitations, that there might be one, though he must be deprived of any political role and not have the slightest effect on the machinery of state— in other words, be the prisoner of his insipid symbolic function. This was probably the position intended for General de Gaulle by those who were calling the tune. Moreover, the committeemen, as well as the parties, were careful not to have any communication with me on the subject. Once, when I summoned the chairman, M. François de Menthon, to inquire as to the progress made, I was told that the Assembly and its committee considered that I was not to participate in the debate, since I was not a member myself. Under such conditions, to attempt to pursue my goals in this crucial area as in all other respects, would be to invite impotence and insult.

The imminent dismemberment of Charles de Gaulle's Government did not, of course, escape the notice of various foreign offices. As a result, the state of relations with them, which had at first improved, now declined once more. At the beginning of December, Paris learned through the news agencies that a meeting of the British, American and Soviet foreign ministers would take place on the fifteenth, in Moscow, 'in order to discuss certain questions of particular interest to all three countries'. This looked like a return

to the systematic exclusion of France—which the London Conference, the installation of quadripartite Governments in Germany and
Austria, the fact that we occupied a permanent chair on the Security
Council of the United Nations, our participation in the Japanese
armistice, etc., had seemed to bring to an end.

It was true that the purpose of the 'Big Three' meeting was to
prepare the peace treaties with Bulgaria, Rumania, Hungary and
Finland, and that London, Moscow and Washington alleged, in
order to justify our exclusion, that since the opening of hostilities
against the Reich's satellites had occurred during the Vichy regime,
France had not been officially in a state of war with Sofia, Bucharest,
Budapest and Helsinki. But for the participants of the Yalta and
Potsdam Conferences, it was actually a question of applying their
recent decisions, without consulting us, to these unfortunate states—
that is, of handing them over to the discretion of the Soviets. To the
notification we received from our allies on December 26th as to
the conclusion of their conference, we replied on January 3rd that
they did not commit us, the less so since France had, in these
various parts of Europe, primary interests which had not been
taken into account. But the dilatory reception accorded our note
made it clear that all three powers were waiting for an imminent
change in the French Government in order to get what they wanted.

The same was true of the final settlement of the complex situation
in the Levant. Since the crisis of the preceding May, Franco-
British relations had remained in the refrigerator, as I had recom-
mended. In Syria and Lebanon, the weak forces we maintained and
the major units the British had sent remained at their positions;
political agitation continued to provoke incidents; the Damascus
and Beirut Governments multiplied their notes and communiqués
insisting on the departure of all foreign troops; finally, the neighbouring Arab states—Egypt, Iraq, Transjordan, Palestine—joined
in the chorus with their 'oppressed brothers', all accommodating
themselves, nevertheless, to British protection and occupation.

This is how matters stood when, at the beginning of December, I
was informed of a projected agreement which had just been established between the British Government and our embassy in London.
The text appeared to call for French and British forces to evacuate
Syrian territory simultaneously, the French regrouping in Lebanon
though it was not specified that the British would do the same. This

would not greatly modify the situation, for the majority of our units were already stationed on Lebanese soil. But for the British, such an agreement appeared to involve considerable concessions: first of all, the end of their military presence in Syria along with ours; further, their departure from the Lebanon where we should remain; and lastly the recognition of our right to maintain a military establishment in the Lebanon until the United Nations Organization was in a position to relieve us of the responsibilities of the mandate. Aware on the one hand of the British Foreign Office's skill and on the other of our own diplomacy's horror of a vacuum when our relations with England were at stake, I doubted, at first sight, that matters were as they seemed to be. But when the Quai d'Orsay in Paris and our embassy in London assured me that this was indeed the significance of the draft, I gave my consent. On December 13th, Mr Bevin and M. Massigli signed two agreements in Whitehall, one relative to the regrouping of troops; the other providing for consultations between the two Governments to avoid the recurrence of incidents in the Middle East.

However, it soon appeared that our diplomats' interpretation of the agreement was not shared by the British. General de Larminat, sent to Beirut to settle the details of the military measures to be taken by either side with General Pilleau, commander of the British Ninth Army, discovered at the first contact that there existed a profound divergence between the instructions he had received and those sent to his colleague. The British were perfectly content to have everyone leave Syria. But they then expected that their forces, like our own, would regroup in the Lebanon—in other words, about 7,000 of our men and more than 35,000 of theirs. After which they would leave that country only if we ourselves left too. In other words, the 'agreement' would come down to this: the French would retire from the Middle East altogether—for our troops, embarking at Beirut, could go nowhere but to Algiers, Bizerta or Marseilles—while the British alone, remaining in force in Cairo, Baghdad, Amman and Jerusalem, would dominate that part of the world.

I immediately cancelled my orders and recalled de Larminat. But regarding the steps to be taken on diplomatic grounds, either to correct this strange misunderstanding or else to cancel the 'agreement', I discovered our own men had all kinds of reservations.

The British, on their side, refused all the more obstinately to reconsider what they regarded as a *fait accompli*, since they realized
that a little patience would enable them—once I had left the
Government—to realize their goal. I must say that in such a serious
matter and one which was close to my heart, this proof that I no
longer held the reins of command would have made the cup run
over if, for many other reasons, it were not leaking on all sides
already.

Before taking the decisive steps, I felt it would be wise to withdraw. Antibes offered me the refuge of Eden-Roc, and for the first
time for more than seven years, I took a few days' rest. Thus I
assured myself and could assure others that my departure was not
to be the effect of thoughtless resentment or of depression caused by
fatigue. As I meditated by the sea, I decided on how I would withdraw from public life—leaving the tribunal in silence, without
attacking anyone, either in public or in private; without accepting
any further function, either honorary or emeritus; lastly, without
giving any indication of what I intended to do afterwards. More
than ever, I would hold myself above contingencies.

After eight days in the south, I returned to Paris on January
14th, a Monday. My resignation was to be made the following
Sunday. I spent the week promulgating the laws and decrees whose
texts, accumulated in my absence and needing to be put into
immediate effect, required my signature. To several of my ministers,
particularly those of the Interior, Justice and War, I announced my
imminent retirement; I also informed the Commissioners of the
Republic whom I had sent for for this purpose. Thus those who,
either in the Government or locally, were responsible for public
order would not be surprised by the event.

Before my withdrawal, I had one further opportunity to discover
the parliamentary state of mind toward me. M. Herriot, who was a
past master at such things, considered that the moment had come
to take me to task personally. He did so on January 16th. A few
days before the regularization of certain citations made in 1943 by
General Giraud to soldiers, sailors and aviators killed or wounded
during the unfortunate North African engagements that Darlan had
ordered against the Americans had been published. I had not
wanted to efface these poor tributes, but the president of the
Radical party, brandishing the list published in the *Journal Officiel*,

invoked 'my own justice' to condemn a measure in which he claimed to see an insult to our allies and the glorification of a battle disastrous to France. Applause and jeers, spreading over several rows, supported this intervention.

Such an attack, on such a subject, was naturally disagreeable to me. But the reception given it, in my presence, by an Assembly the majority of whose members had but lately answered my call to honour filled me, I must admit, with sadness and disgust. I answered Édouard Herriot that there was no question of snatching from the coffins of the lamented dead and from the breasts of the wretched wounded the crosses which had been awarded them three years before for having obeyed the orders of their leaders, though those orders were wrongly given. Then, speaking directly to this challenger who, on the eve of the liberation of Paris, had had the weakness to negotiate and to dine with Laval and Abetz, I added that I was the better judge of those citations since 'I have never had dealings with Vichy or with the enemy save by gunfire'. The quarrel Herriot had sought with me fell flat, but I had seen how indelibly prejudice and political resentment tainted men's souls.

On January 19th, I asked the ministers to meet the next day in the Rue St-Dominique. With the exception of Auriol and Bidault, in London at the time, and Soustelle, on tour in the Gabon, all met on the morning of Sunday, January 20th, in the 'hall of arms'. I came in, shook hands all around and before anyone sat down, spoke these words: 'The exclusive regime of parties has reappeared. I disapprove of it. But aside from establishing by force a dictatorship, which I do not desire and which would certainly end in disaster, I have no means of preventing this experiment. I must therefore withdraw. Today, in fact, I shall send the President of the National Assembly a letter informing him of the Government's resignation. I sincerely thank each of you for the support you have given me and urge you to remain at your posts in order to assure the conduct of business until your successors are appointed.' The ministers impressed me as being more grieved than astonished. None of them uttered a word, either to ask me to reconsider my decision or even to say that it was regretted. After taking my leave of them, I returned to my residence.

I was informed that after my departure the ministers conferred together for several minutes. M. Thorez, apparently, remarked,

'A departure made with greatness!' M. Moch said, 'This retirement
is indeed a serious one, but good can come of evil. The General's
personality stifled the National Assembly. Now the latter can reveal
itself freely.' M. Pleven made the voice of bitterness and anxiety
heard, 'Now see what your factions have brought us to!' He reproached his colleagues, whose parties had raised obstacles to my
action. 'We are confronting,' declared M. Gay and M. Teitgen,
'the heavy responsibility of succeeding de Gaulle. Our movement
will try to be worthy of it.' 'Come now,' M. Thorez exclaimed,
'since you couldn't get anywhere with the General, how can you
do better without him?'

In the letter I wrote to the President of the Assembly, I made sure
there was not the trace of polemic. 'I remained,' I wrote, 'at the head
of the Government after November 13th 1945, in order to give it the
necessary continuity . . . Now the parties are in a position to assume
their responsibilities.' I abstained from pointing out in what state
the nation was when 'I assumed the burden of directing it towards its
liberation, its victory, and its sovereignty'. But I remarked, 'Today,
after terrible ordeals, France is no longer in a state of emergency.
Certainly many sufferings still weigh upon our people, and grave
problems remain. But the very life of the French people is, in all
essential respects, assured. Our economic activity is staging a recovery. Our territories are once again in our own hands. We have
re-established ourselves in Indochina. Public order is not threatened.
Abroad, despite the anxieties which persist, our independence is
firmly re-established. We are holding the Rhine. We are participating, in the first rank, in the new international organization, and
it is in Paris that the first peace conference is to be held this coming
spring.' Finally, I expressed the 'profoundly sincere hope that
tomorrow's Government may succeed in its task'. M. Felix Gouin's
reply was extremely gratifying.

But if my own soul was calm, this was not the case of the world of
politics. After being greatly disturbed by my presence, it was
equally shaken by my absence. There were even rumours that I was
plotting a coup d'état, as if the fact that I had resigned from power
of my own free will was not enough to stigmatize such alarms with
the absurdity they deserved. Without going so far as these suspicions,
others felt it was prudent to show their vigilance. Thus M. Vincent
Auriol, hurriedly returning from London on the supposition that

I was going to speak on the wireless to arouse popular indignation, wrote to me on the evening of January 20th to say that by so doing 'I would divide the country to the advantage and the satisfaction of democracys' enemies'. I calmed the Minister of State's fears. As a matter of fact, had I chosen to explain the reasons for my retirement, I would not have failed to do so, and this explanation, given to a sovereign people, would not have been contrary to democratic principles. But I considered that my silence would weigh more heavily than anything else, that thoughtful minds would understand why I had left, and that the rest would sooner or later be informed by events themselves.

Where was I to go? Contemplating the prospect of my resignation from office, I had resolved to live in Colombey-les-deux-Eglises, and had begun repairing my war-damaged house with this in mind. But these arrangements would take several months. At first I thought of travelling to some distant region where I could wait in peace. But the tide of insult and invective launched against me by political headquarters and the majority of newspapers determined me to remain in Metropolitan France so that no one could suppose that such attacks upset me. I therefore rented the Pavillon de Marly from the Service des Beaux-Arts, and lived there until May.

Nevertheless, while the regime's personnel gave itself up to the euphoria of old habits regained, the mass of the French people, on the contrary, sank back into distress. Gone was that atmosphere of exaltation, that hope of success, that ambition for France which supported the national soul. Every Frenchman, whatever his tendencies, had the troubling suspicion that with the General had vanished something primordial, permanent and necessary which he incarnated in history and which the regime of parties could not represent. In the sidetracked leader, men persisted in seeing a kind of capital of sovereignty, a last resort selected in advance. They supposed such legitimacy could remain latent in a period without anxiety. But they knew it could be invoked by common consent as soon as a new laceration threatened the nation.

My attitude, through the years, would be dictated by this mission which France continued to assign me, even when, in the immediate circumstances, many tendencies did not follow me. Whatever I said or was made to say, my words, real or supposed, would pass into the public domain. All those I dealt with reacted as if, invested with the supreme authority, I had received them in the national palaces. Wherever I happened to make an appearance, those present would burst into enthusiastic cheers.

It was this atmosphere which enveloped me during the course of the first public action I took once I had abandoned my official status: I made a speech in Bayeux, describing what our institutions should be. I spoke on many subsequent occasions, condemning the constitution wrung from the country's lassitude; appealing to the French people to unite in order to change the bad regime; launching ideas to deal with the future from many platforms; appearing before crowds in every French and Algerian department, at least twice in each and more in some, in order to keep the spark alight and to make contact with many touchingly loyal friends. It was these same tributes which were lavished upon me after 1952, when I determined to withdraw from the situation as it stood, the disease being too advanced for any remedy to affect it before the inevitable upheaval; when I occasionally presided at some ceremony; when I visited our territories in Africa and the Indian Ocean, travelling around the world from one French territory to the next, watching the oil gushers being brought in in the Sahara. At the moment of finishing this book, I feel the same countless hearts turning towards my simple house.

This is my home. In the tumult of men and events, solitude was my temptation; now it is my friend. What other satisfaction can be sought once you have confronted history? Moreover, this section of Champagne is imbued with calm—wide, mournful horizons; melancholy woods and meadows; the frieze of resigned old mountains; tranquil, unpretentious villages where nothing has changed its spirit or its place for thousands of years. All this can be seen from my village. Situated high on the plateau, near a wooded hill, it weathers the centuries among the fields cultivated by its inhabitants. The latter, though I am careful not to force myself upon them, surround me with discreet friendship. I know their families, I respect and love them.

Silence fills my house. From the corner room where I spend most of my daylight hours, I look out far into the west. There is nothing to obstruct my view for about fifteen kilometres. Above the plain and the woods, my eyes follow the long slopes descending towards the valley of the Aube, then the heights of the slope opposite. From a rise in the garden, I look down on the wild depths where the forest envelops the tilled land like the sea beating on a promontory. I watch the night cover the landscape. Then, looking up at the stars, I steep myself in the insignificance of things.

Of course letters, the wireless and the newspapers bring news of the outside world into this hermitage. During brief visits to Paris, I receive visitors whose remarks reveal the course of men and events. In the holidays, our children and grandchildren surround us, with the exception of our daughter Anne, who left this world before us. But how many hours slip by in reading, writing, dreaming, when no illusion sweetens my bitter serenity.

Yet, on our little property—I have walked around it fifteen thousand times—the trees, stripped by the cold, rarely fail to turn green again, and the flowers my wife has planted bloom once more each spring. The village houses are decrepit, but suddenly laughing girls and boys come out of their doors. When I walk to one of the nearby woods—Les Dhuits, Clairvaux, Le Heu, Blinfeix, La Chapelle— their solemn depths fill me with nostalgia; but suddenly the song of a bird, the sun through the leaves, or the buds of a thicket remind me that ever since it has existed on earth, life fights a battle it has never lost. Then I feel a secret solace spreading through me. Since everything eternally begins anew, what I have done will sooner or later be a source of new ardour after I have gone.

As age triumphs, nature comes closer to me. Each year, in the four seasons which are like so many lessons, I find consolation in her wisdom. In spring she sings: 'Whatever has happened, I am in the beginning! All is bright, even the snow flurries; young, even the wizened trees; beautiful, even the stony fields. Love raises the sap within me and with it certainties so radiant and powerful that they will never end!'

In summer she proclaims: 'Consider the glory of my fruitfulness. Striving, everything that nourishes life comes from me. Each life depends on my warmth. These seeds, these fruits, these herds the sun now floods with light are a victory nothing can destroy. Henceforth, the future belongs to me!'

In autumn, she sighs: 'My task is near its term. I have given flowers, my harvest, my fruits. Now, I retire within myself. See how beautiful I am still in my robe of purple and gold, beneath the brilliant sun. Alas, the winds and the frosts will soon tear away my garments. But one day, upon my naked body, my youth will flower again!'

In winter, she moans: 'Here I lie, barren and frozen. How many plants, animals and birds have I created and loved, who die now on my breast that can no longer feed or warm them! Then is my destiny sealed? Is death's the victory for ever? No! Already, deep in my inert soil, a secret labour is being accomplished. Motionless in the heart of darkness, I can feel the marvellous return of light and life!'

Old Earth, worn by the ages, wracked by rain and storm, exhausted yet ever ready to produce what life must have to go on!

Old France, weighed down with history, prostrated by wars and revolutions, endlessly vacillating from greatness to decline, but revived, century after century, by the genius of renewal!

Old man, exhausted by ordeal, detached from human deeds, feeling the approach of the eternal cold, but always watching in the shadows for the gleam of hope!

INDEX

militias, 43–4; Consultative Assembly, 45, 58–61, 103, 105–7, 127, 194–5, 219, 237, 243, 257–9, 262; recognized by Allies, 48; diplomatic changes, 49; attitude to post-war Europe, 49–51, 58–61, 71–2, 89, 90, 178–9, 208–10, 213–19; excluded from Allied conferences, 51–2, 54, 83, 87–9, 199–200; invited to European Commission, 54, 86; British attitude towards, 54–7, 184–93; suggested pact with Britain, 54, 56, 72–3; pact with Russia, 66, 68, 71, 72, 79–82, 105; desires Polish independence, 68–70, 72–5, 76, 79–80; American attitude towards, 84–6, 89–92, 196, 205, 208–11, 223; social security measures, 98–100; Communists join, 101–3; criticisms of, 102–3, 106–7, 124–5, 250; institutes High Court, 110–13; encourages free Press, 114–15; 'military' ministers of, 123–4; functioning of, 125–8; co-operation in final offensives, 132–3, 151–77; problem of military command, 143–9, 166, 169–70; and participation in German campaign, 151–62, 166–77; and Indochina, 162–6, 222–7, 243; and German surrender, 175–6; and disputed Alpine frontier, 179–82; and Levant, 181, 183–96, 276–8; and United Nations, 196–9; settles zones of occupation, 202–3, 204; attitude to Africa and Asia, 209–10; and London Conference, 213–14; policy for Germany, 214–17; envisages Western European union, 218–19; and North Africa, 219–22; and industrial and scientific development, 232–3, 249; party strife in, 235, 236–7, 250–2; and municipal elections, 238–9; and return of war prisoners, 239–41, 243; and national elections, 248, 260–5, 267; and Constituent Assembly, 250–2, 256–7, 267, 269, 273, 275; search for new constitution, 250–75; de Gaulle's referendum project, 251–2, 256–60, 263, 264–5; changes in, 256. *See also* Fourth Republic
Freudenstadt, 167, 168

Frey, Mayor (Strasbourg), 141
Friedeburg, Admiral, 175
Front national, 115

Galicia, 60
Gambsheim, 149
Gander Airport, 213
Garbay, General, 135, 158, 161
Garreau, Roger, 58, 64, 68, 71, 78, 79, 80
Gascony, 129
Gasperi, Alcide de, 182
Gaulle, Madame de, 128
Gaulle, Anne de, 128, 283
Gaulle, Elisabeth de, 128
Gaulle, Philippe de, 128
Gay, F., 270, 280
Gazier, Albert, 273
Genèvre Pass, 160, 162, 182
Genoa, Gulf of, 134
Georges-Leygues (cruiser), 18, 134
Gérardmer, 136, 141
Gerardot, General, 40, 134
Gerbeviller, 39
Gerlier, Cardinal, 16
German Air Force, 112, 144
German Army: in France, 20–1, 22, 28 *et seq.*, 135, 136–9, 149–50, 153–4, 157–62; in Tunisia, 111; Ardennes offensive, 139, 142–4, 149; in German campaign, 167–71; surrender, 175–6
German Navy, 138
Germany: post-war policy for, 50–1, 52, 54, 58, 59–60, 71–2, 83, 208–9, 214–15; Russian attitude to, 65–6, 72, 80, 202, 204; Yalta decisions on, 87–8, 199; campaign in, 151–7, 166–71; capitulation, 171, 174–6; Potsdam decisions on, 199–201, 202; zones of occupation, 202–3, 204, 215–17, 239; Russo-American rivalry over, 202; France pillaged by, 230
Germersheim, 155
Gers, 18, 19
Giacobbi, Paul, 10, 125, 270
Giap, Vo Nguyen, 224
Gillon, M., 218
Giraud, General Henri, 25, 27, 278
Giromagny, 135, 143
Gironde, 20, 21, 133, 158–9
Givet, 144
Gloire (cruiser), 18, 134, 224